IMAGES
of America

FRANKLIN

On the cover: John Hahn and his family are shown boarding their carriage to attend church on Sunday around 1910. The Hahn farm was located on Oakwood Road. (Courtesy of Franklin Historical Society.)

IMAGES
of America

FRANKLIN

Doug Schmidt

ARCADIA
PUBLISHING

ISBN 978-0-7385-6048-9

Published by Arcadia Publishing
Charleston, South Carolina

Printed in the United States of America

Library of Congress Control Number: 2009921049

For all general information, please contact Arcadia Publishing:
Telephone 843-853-2070
Fax 843-853-0044
E-mail sales@arcadiapublishing.com
For customer service and orders:
Toll-Free 1-888-313-2665

Visit us on the Internet at www.arcadiapublishing.com

Dedicated to all my friends, neighbors, and fellow members of the Franklin Historical Society who take pride in preserving local history

Contents

Introduction		7
1.	Birth of St. Martins	9
2.	Life on the Farm	21
3.	Life outside the Farm	37
4.	Politics and Protection	49
5.	Sports and Leisure	59
6.	One Room, Eight Grades	71
7.	Franklin High School	87
8.	Franklin Historical Society	105
9.	The Building Boom	119

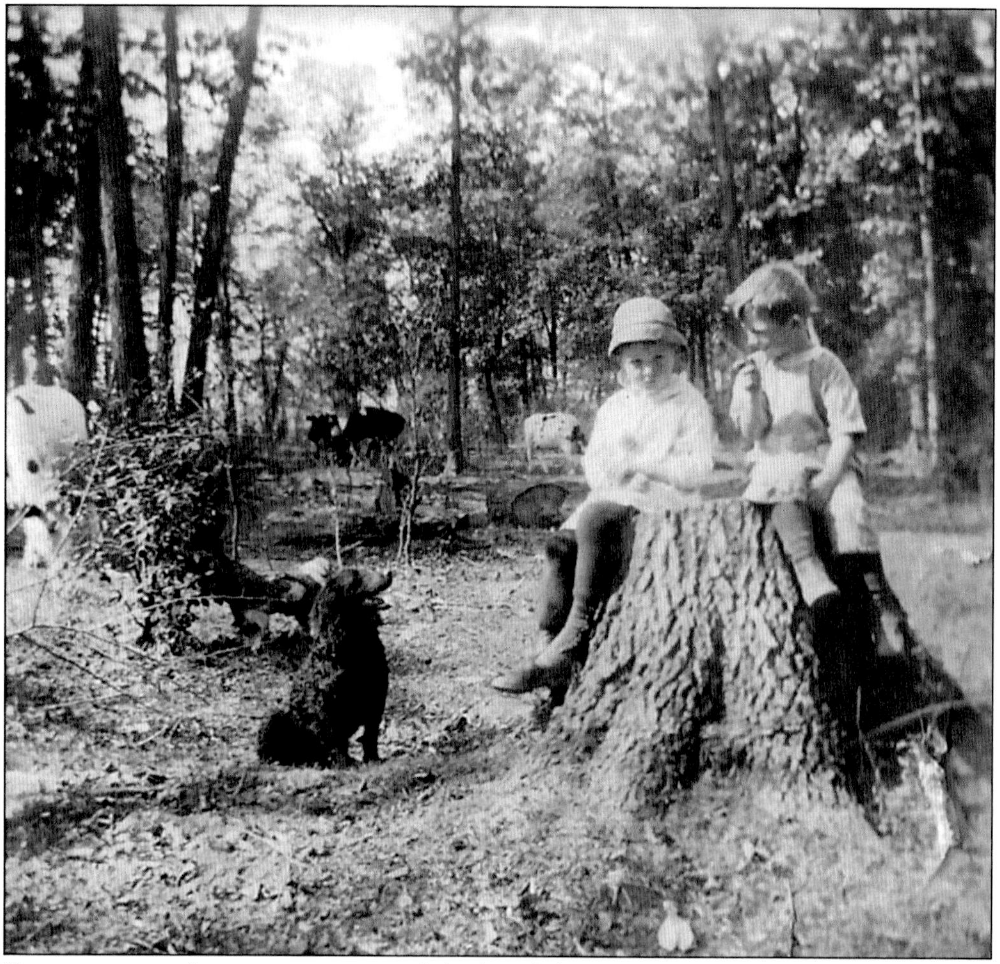

Two youngsters relax on a tree stump while their father's cows graze in a clearing on wooded Franklin farmland during the late 1800s. Most of the 80-acre plats that went up for sale in the township of Franklin in 1838 had to be cleared of walnut, oak, aspen, and hickory groves before the land could be tilled to plant crops. (Courtesy of Fred Ludwig.)

Introduction

Before the state of Wisconsin was established in 1848, there was a town of Franklin. This wooded territory formed the southwest quadrant of what became Milwaukee County during the 1830s.

By virtue of the Northwest Ordinance of 1785, the United States government established that land in the Wisconsin Territory be surveyed into townships and sold in 80-acre plats.

Land in Milwaukee County went up for sale in 1838 at a price of $1.25 per acre, and Franklin became designated as town 5 north, range 21 east on December 20, 1839. In 1842, the township adopted the name of statesman, author, and inventor Benjamin Franklin.

During the 1800s, Franklin consisted of wetlands and groves of hardwood trees such as walnut, oak, aspen, and hickory. It was dissected by the Root River, which began in Waukesha County and meandered southeast through Franklin into Racine County where it spilled into Lake Michigan. Early on, the Root River served as a water road through the heavily wooded area, and the abundance of wild game made the township a popular hunting ground for white settlers as well as Native Americans.

Significantly, Franklin covered 36 square miles and was sold in 80-acre tracts to German, Dutch, and Irish immigrants who cleared the land for crops of wheat, oats, and corn while stocking the farm with dairy cows, pigs, ducks, and chickens. By 1938, Franklin was the only town in Milwaukee County that still retained its 36-square-mile configuration. Later that year, however, 1.4 square miles along Loomis Road was annexed for the village of Greendale, thereby reducing Franklin to a still substantial 34.6 square miles.

As such, Franklinites were essentially self-sufficient, so there was little commercial development for over 100 years, as the rural landscape remained virtually unchanged. As late as the 1950s, Franklin businesses were primarily farm implement stores, grain mills, gas stations, and taverns.

The first real seeds of growth were planted in the 1950s when two low-cost housing developments called subdivisions emerged. One was Security Acres located west of Seventy-sixth Street, and the other was the Towne subdivision south of Rawson Avenue. These developments triggered Franklin's first wave of nonfarm families, forcing the community to begin dealing with a new set of economic, political, and educational issues. The era of the one-room schoolhouses ended in 1953, and by the 1960s, the need for a high school was apparent. Ground was broken for Franklin High School in 1961.

In danger of being annexed by the City of Milwaukee, Franklin pursued incorporation as a city in 1956. Franklin actually lacked the minimum 10,000 residents necessary to incorporate, but local politicians averted disappointment by listing prisoners incarcerated at the Milwaukee

County House of Correction on Sixty-eighth Street as residents, boosting the town's population to 10,006.

Franklin retained a semirural flavor through the 1970s, with the population totaling 16,871 in 1980. Since then, however, it has become one of the fastest-growing and most progressive communities in Wisconsin. By 2006, the population had surpassed 32,500 with a median household income of $78,470.

Unless otherwise noted, all images are courtesy of the Franklin Historical Society.

One

Birth of St. Martins

While portions of Franklin Township were platted and sold to immigrant farmers beginning in 1838, the first semblance of a community was the unincorporated village of St. Martins, which was platted by Fr. Martin Kundig in 1850. The Catholic Church had assigned Father Kundig to serve the ill and poverty stricken living in the Michigan Territory before he arrived in Franklin.

The new village consisted of 80 acres containing 104 lots. It was platted on land viewed as a potential location for a canal that would provide navigation between the Root River and Big Muskego Lake. However, the concept of a canal was never fulfilled because railroads fostered a new wave of transportation. Instead St. Martins became a stop along the interurban railway.

The first plat was sold to Margaret Sheehan on May 5, 1850, for the sum of $15. Michael and Patrick Sheehan had already built the first European-style log cabin in the township in the 10600 block of what became St. Martins Road. The original log cabin was moved to Franklin's historic Lions Legend Park in 1975 and restored in 2004.

Early businesses in the village featured a five-story windmill for grinding grain that was moved from Kenosha County to St. Martins in 1868 and a small brewery operated by a local farmer, Gottfried Gross. The brewery closed in 1896, but records indicate it was tied into the fledgling Miller Brewing Company after Fredrick Miller married a Gross daughter, Elisabetha, in St. Martins in 1906.

Other longtime businesses that sprouted up along St. Martins Road were John Herda's farm implement store and the R. A. Mayer Equipment Company, which became a major dealer in Allis-Chalmers tractors.

St. Martins was anchored by two Catholic churches. The first Holy Assumption Church built by Father Kundig in 1847 was destroyed by fire in 1866 and replaced with a new brick building that catered to Irish Catholics. German Catholics built Sacred Heart of Jesus and Mary Church in 1858 because they sought to worship in their own language. Eventually, however, the two congregations merged under a new name, St. Martin of Tours. Over 150 years later, both parishes are still thriving.

St. Martins Road became the site of a farmers' market the first Monday of each month and for decades has hosted a two-day Labor Day weekend festival that attracts nearly 100,000 fairgoers or more annually.

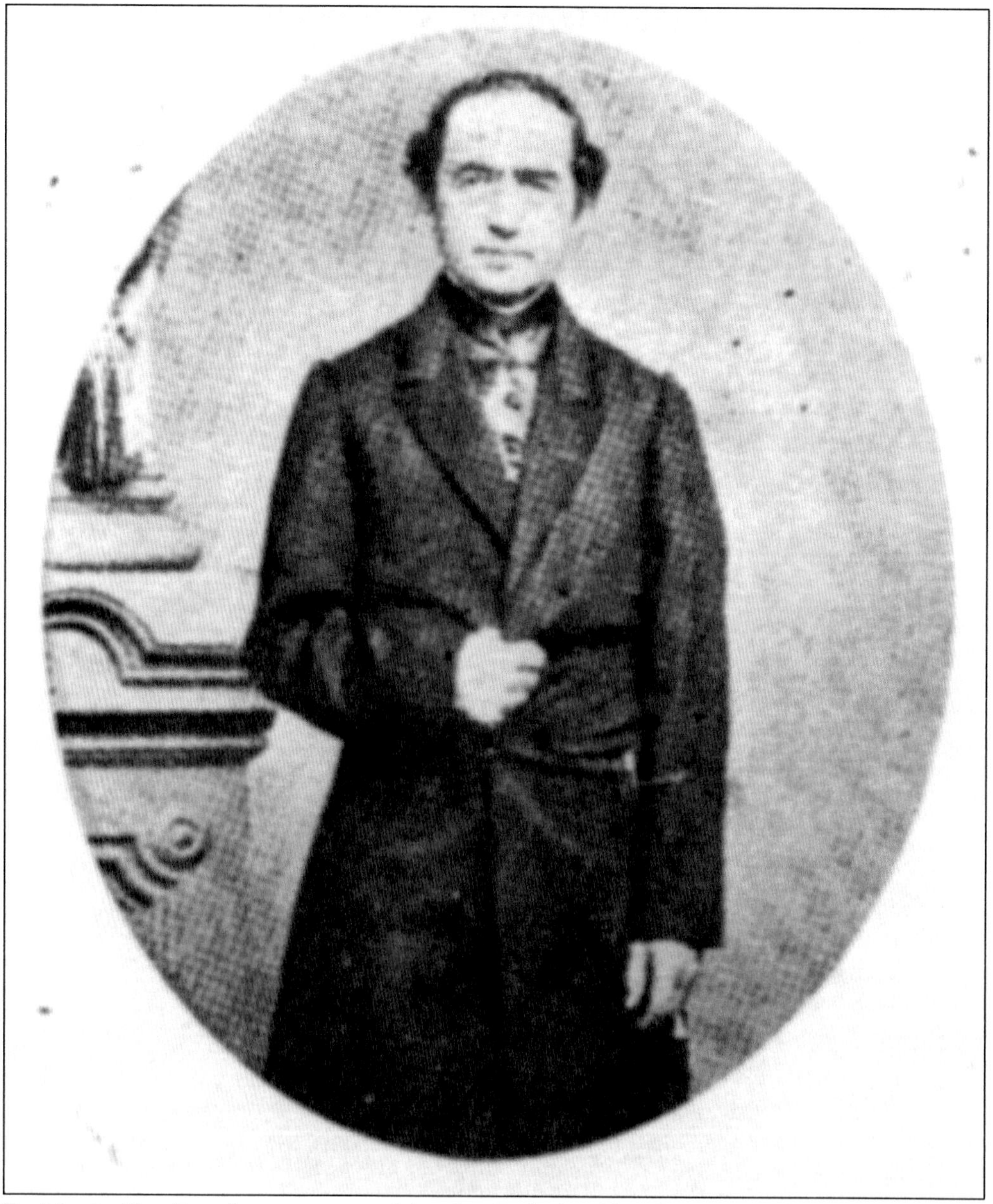

Fr. Martin Kundig, who was assigned by the Catholic Church to serve the ill and poverty stricken in the Michigan Territory, arrived in Franklin during the 1840s and established Holy Assumption Church in 1847. As a clergyman, Father Kundig is reported to have had an instrumental role in plotting and promoting the village of St. Martins. The village contained 80 acres. The establishment of Holy Assumption Church and St. Martins were closely tied.

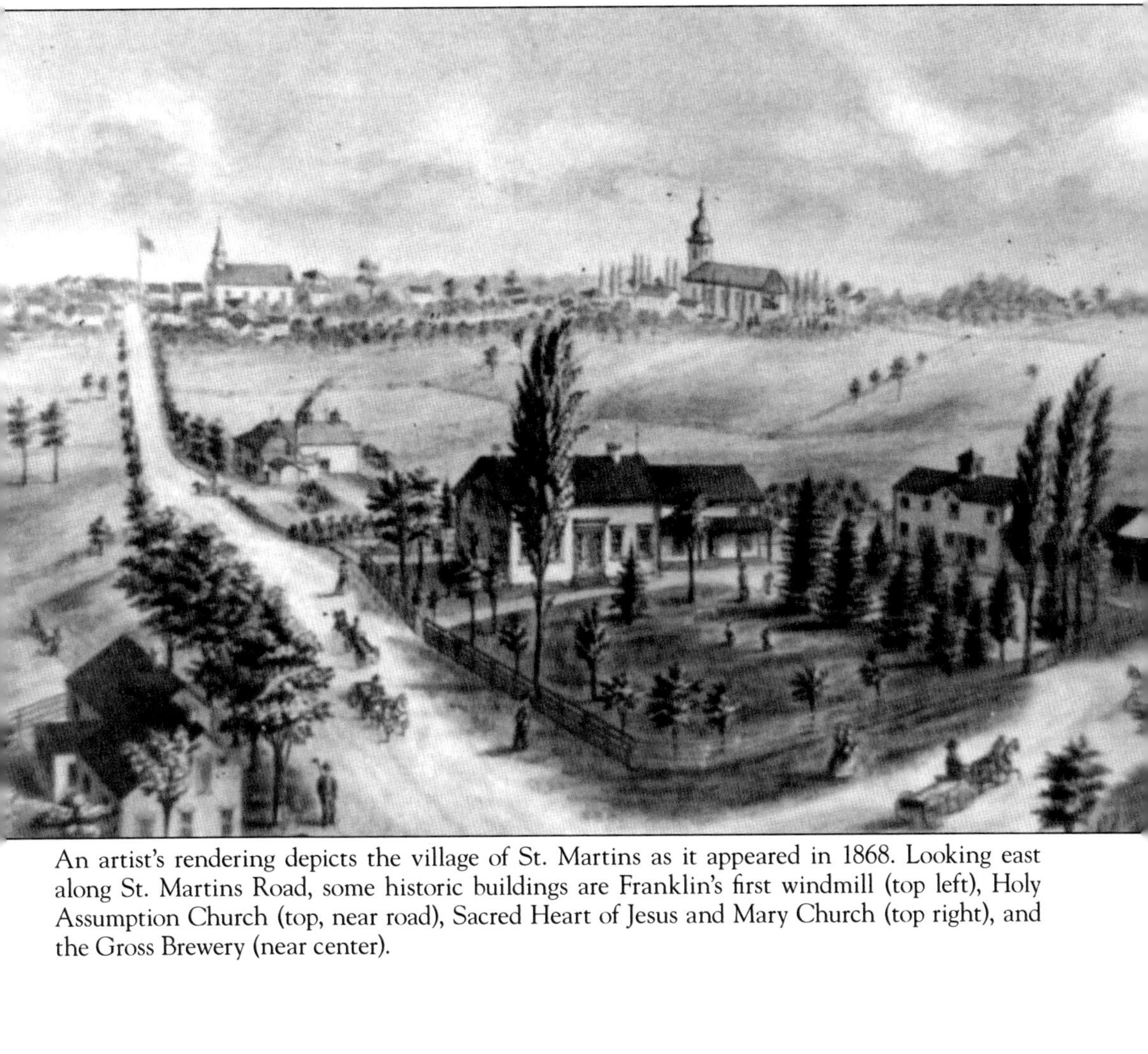

An artist's rendering depicts the village of St. Martins as it appeared in 1868. Looking east along St. Martins Road, some historic buildings are Franklin's first windmill (top left), Holy Assumption Church (top, near road), Sacred Heart of Jesus and Mary Church (top right), and the Gross Brewery (near center).

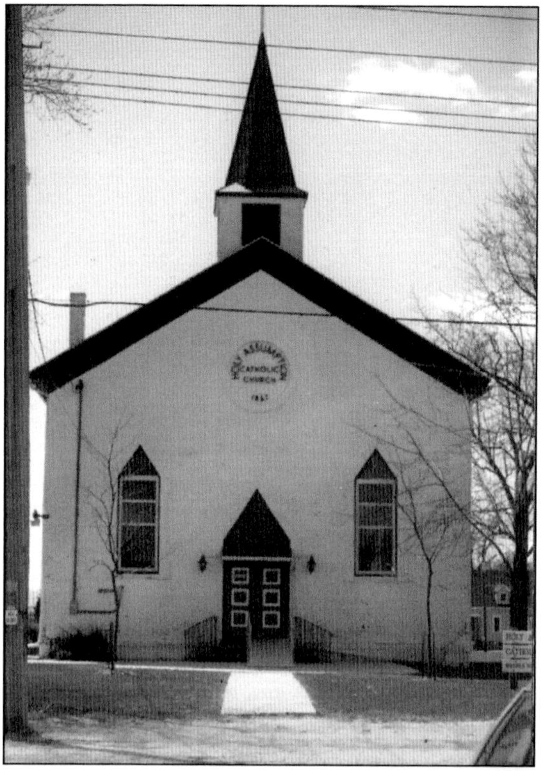

Holy Assumption Church was established by Fr. Martin Kundig as a log church and rectory on April 13, 1847. However, it was struck by lightning and burned down in 1866. The following year, a new Irish Catholic church was built of Cream City bricks purchased from Solomon Juneau. Holy Assumption merged with Sacred Heart of Jesus and Mary Church in 1998 , and the combined parishes became known as St. Martins of Tours. Holy Assumption officially closed on July 1, 1999.

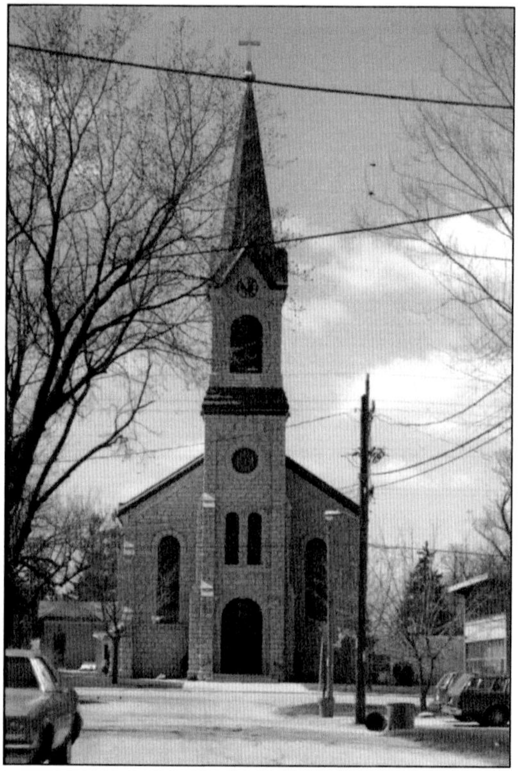

During the 1840s and 1850s, German immigrants joined Irish settlers in worship at Holy Assumption Church. However, the Germans had difficulty understanding Irish English preaching, and Fr. Fran Weinhart was instructed to build a new Catholic church where they could worship in their own language. Built on property a block behind Holy Assumption, Sacred Heart of Jesus and Mary Church was dedicated on June 5, 1858.

In 1868, Joseph Nelesen purchased a seven-story windmill and moved it from Kenosha County to St. Martins. He dismantled the mill and transported the top five stories to St. Martins in 33 horse-drawn wagons. It was placed on a foundation near St. Martins Road and Spring Street. Nelesen sold the mill in 1892 to John Mayer, and it remained in St. Martins until it was demolished in 1937.

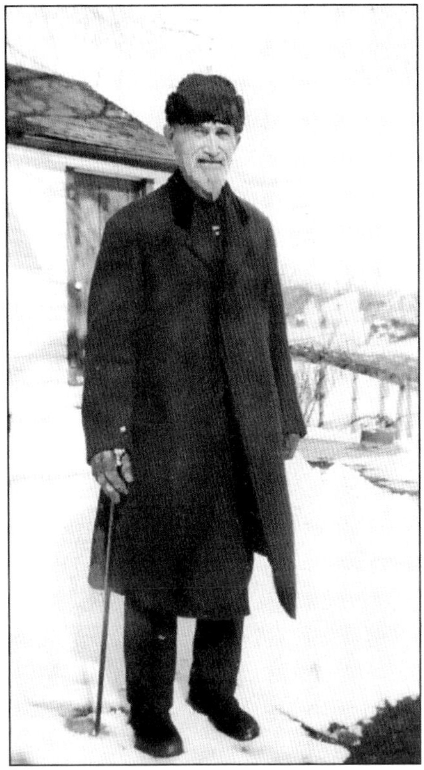

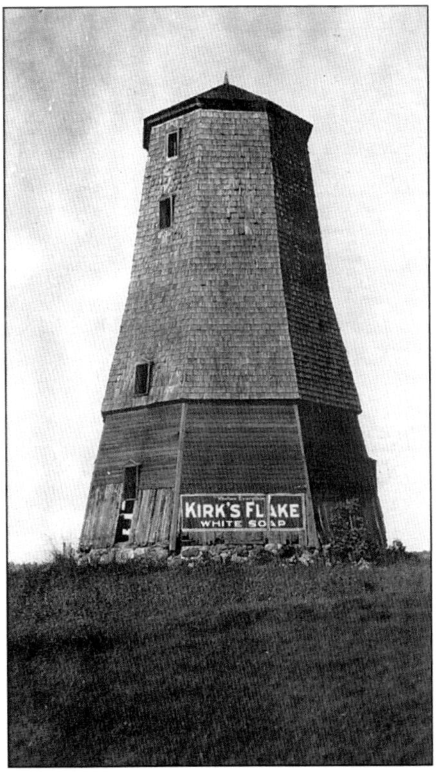

Joseph Nelesen's gristmill ground a variety of grains after it was reassembled in St. Martins. Power for grinding came from a large windmill made of wood and steel. Canvas sails on each arm could be unrolled to catch the wind and control the speed of the wheel. The mill was a Franklin landmark until it was torn down in 1937.

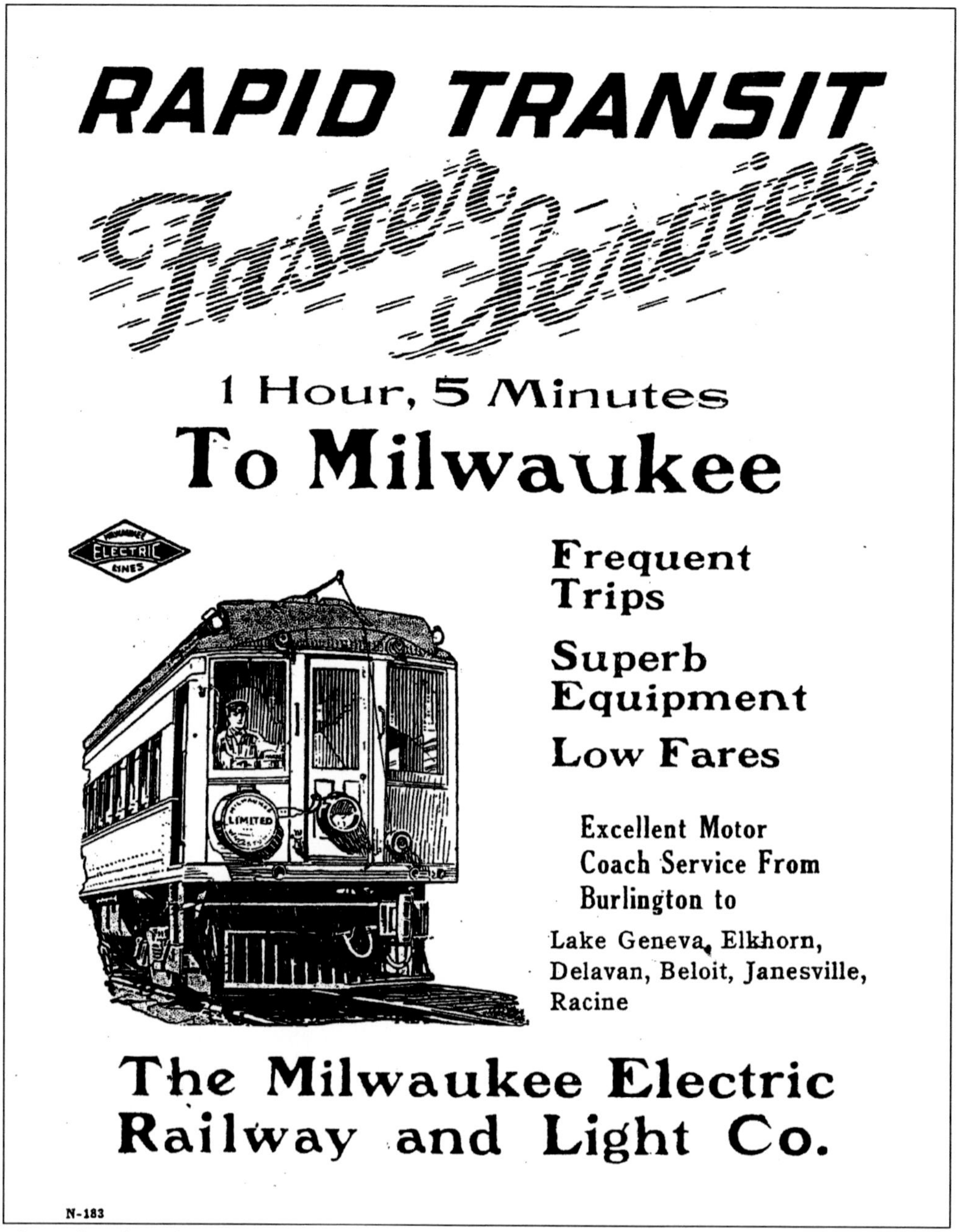

The Milwaukee Electric Railway and Light Company began advertising a new efficient means of transportation with rapid transit in the second decade of the 20th century. This advertisement boasts that a trip from Burlington to Milwaukee with stops in between would take only one hour and five minutes.

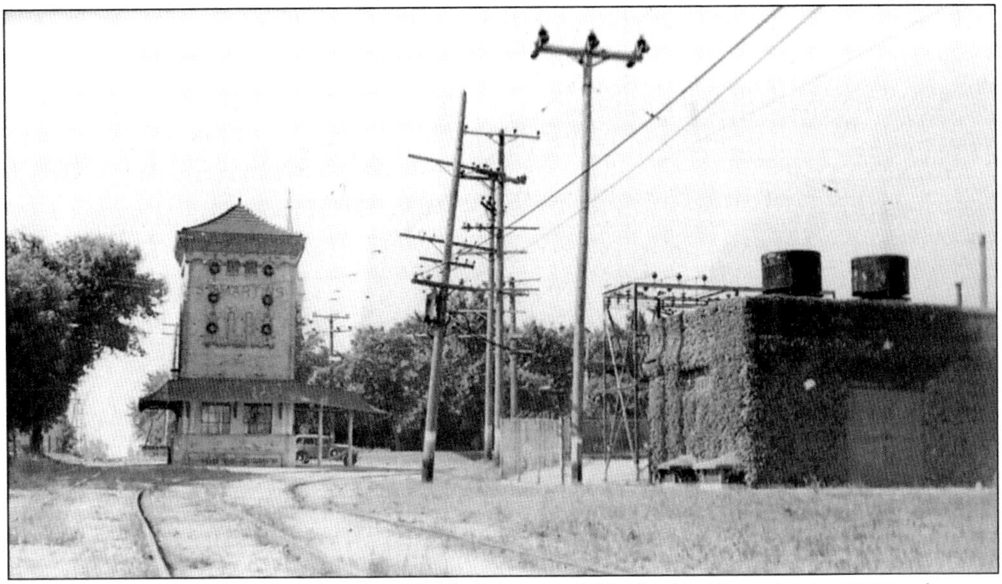

Electric rail service began connecting Milwaukee and Waukesha Counties in 1904, when an interurban depot was established in St. Martins at the intersection of 116th Street and Swiss Street. Mail was delivered to Franklin on the interurban from 1904 to 1939.

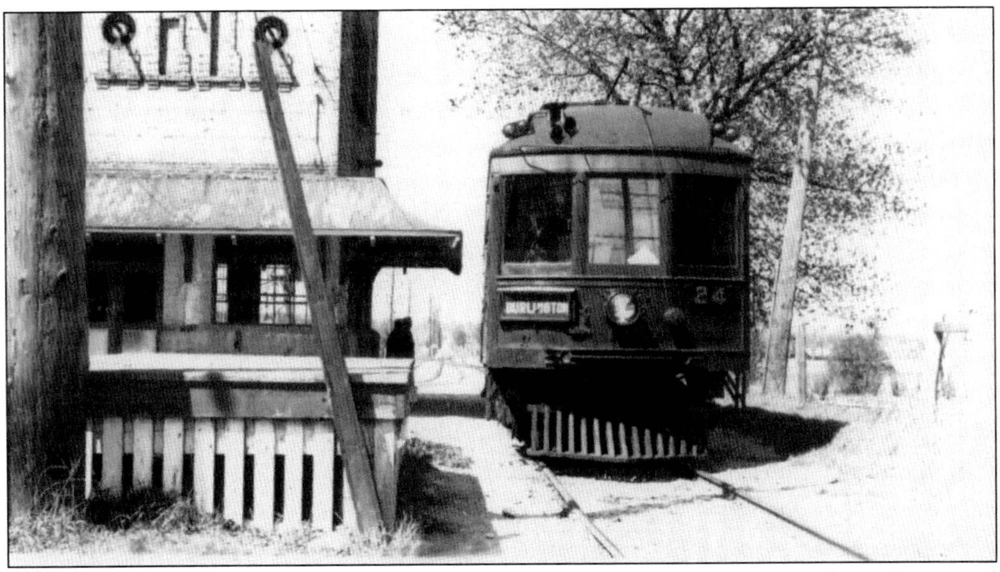

From 1904 to 1939, the St. Martins depot was a popular stop for the interurban electric rail between Milwaukee and Waukesha. From the St. Martins junction, the line branched in two directions. One tracked through Muskego and Big Bend to East Troy. The other wound its way through Wind Lake to Burlington.

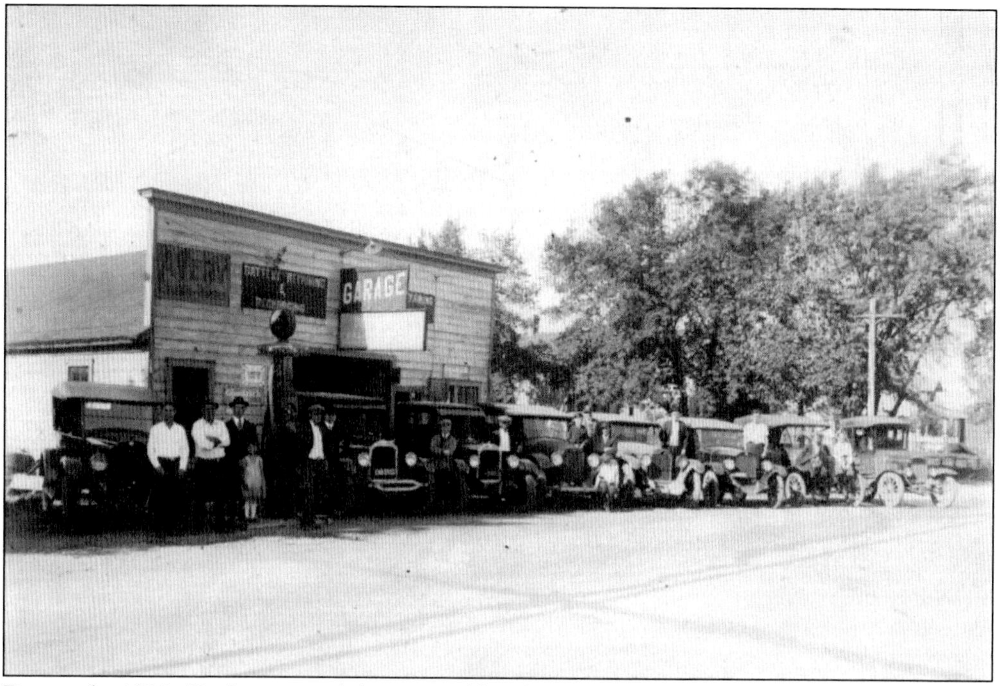

During the 1920s, Dodge automobiles were sold and serviced at the Mayer Garage on St. Martins Road. The business was started in 1917 by Robert Albert Mayer, a local entrepreneur born in St. Martins in 1888. The R. A. Mayer Equipment Company began selling steel-wheeled Allis-Chalmers tractors in 1928 and later branched into lawn and garden equipment. A new store was built at the same location in 1946. Mayer's three sons, Gordon, Robert and David, continued the business until their retirement in 1987.

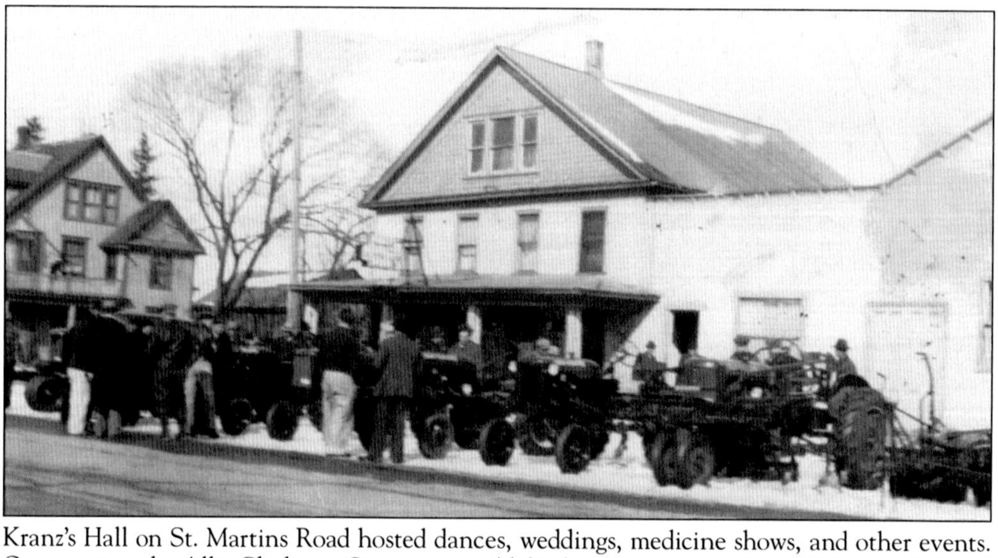

Kranz's Hall on St. Martins Road hosted dances, weddings, medicine shows, and other events. On occasion, the Allis-Chalmers Company would display its tractors in front of Kranz's Hall and show silent cowboy movies to attract customers.

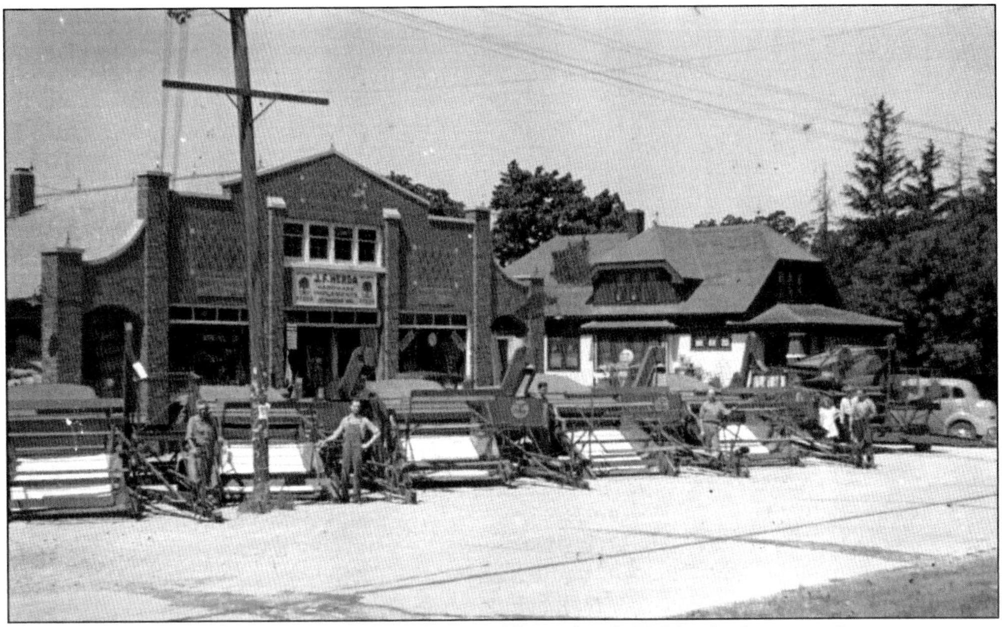

Combines were among the many products sold at the J. F. Herda farm implement store at 11133 West St. Martins Road through most of the 20th century. Founded by brothers John and Joseph Herda, the all-purpose store sold feed, tools, fences, horse bits, cattle leaders, dynamite, refrigerators, and stoves, as well as farm machinery and homemaker supplies. Herda's closed as a True Value hardware store in 2005.

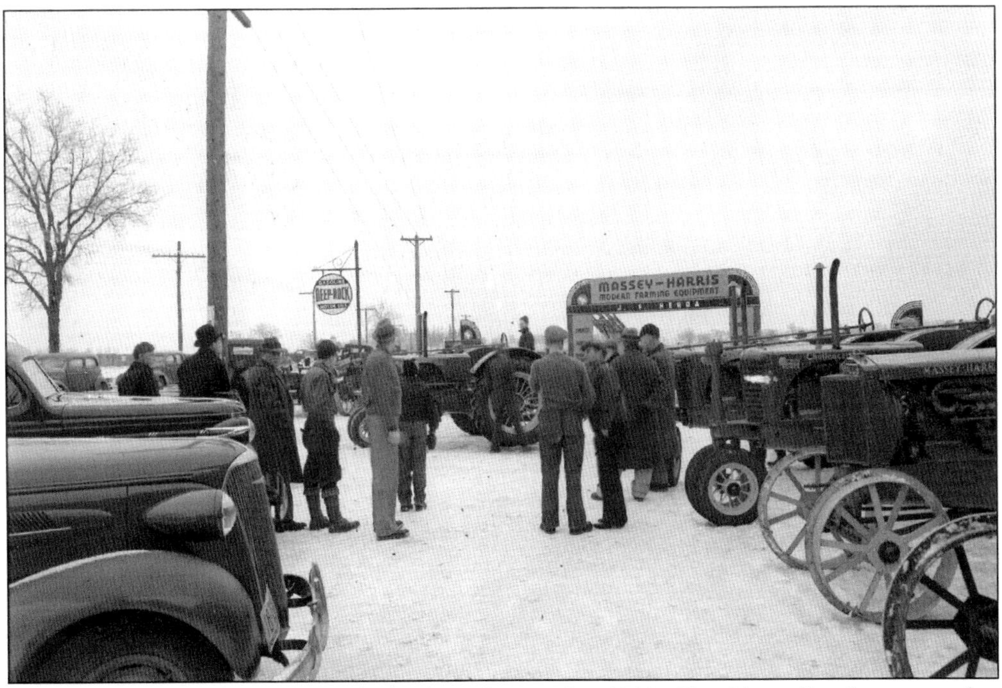

While some cities featured car dealerships during the 1940s, Franklin offered tractor sales. Farmers stop to view the latest inventory of Massey-Harris tractors on sale at the J. F. Herda property in 1941. Some of the older models still featured steel-rimmed wheels.

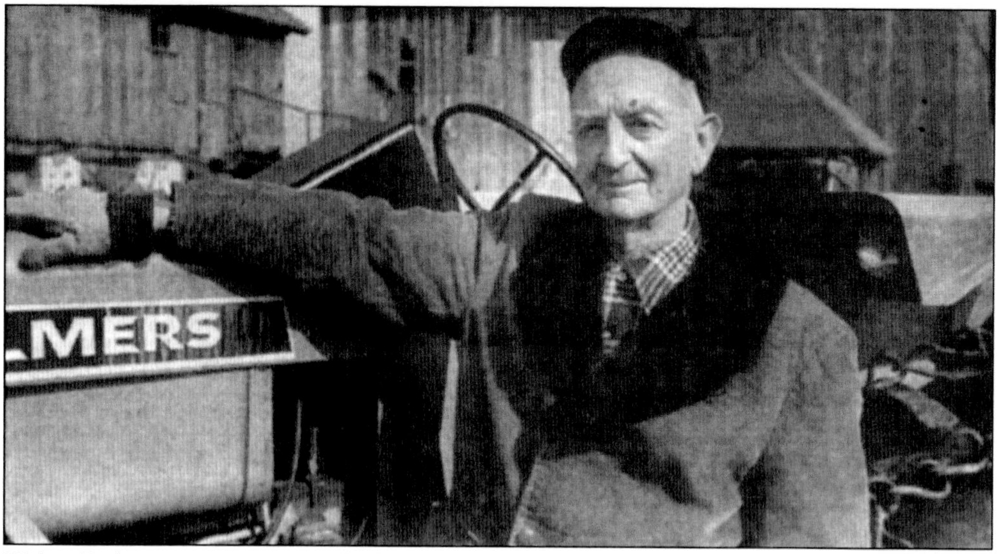

Walter Barbian was instrumental in bringing the farmers' market to St. Martins in 1958. The market began as a means for farmers to sell fresh produce and other wares at roadside stands along Highway 100 in Hales Corners in 1865. In addition to a once-a-month market, there was an annual event in Franklin known as the Labor Day fair. The event continues to draw over 100,000 fairgoers each Labor Day weekend. (Courtesy of Milwaukee Journal.)

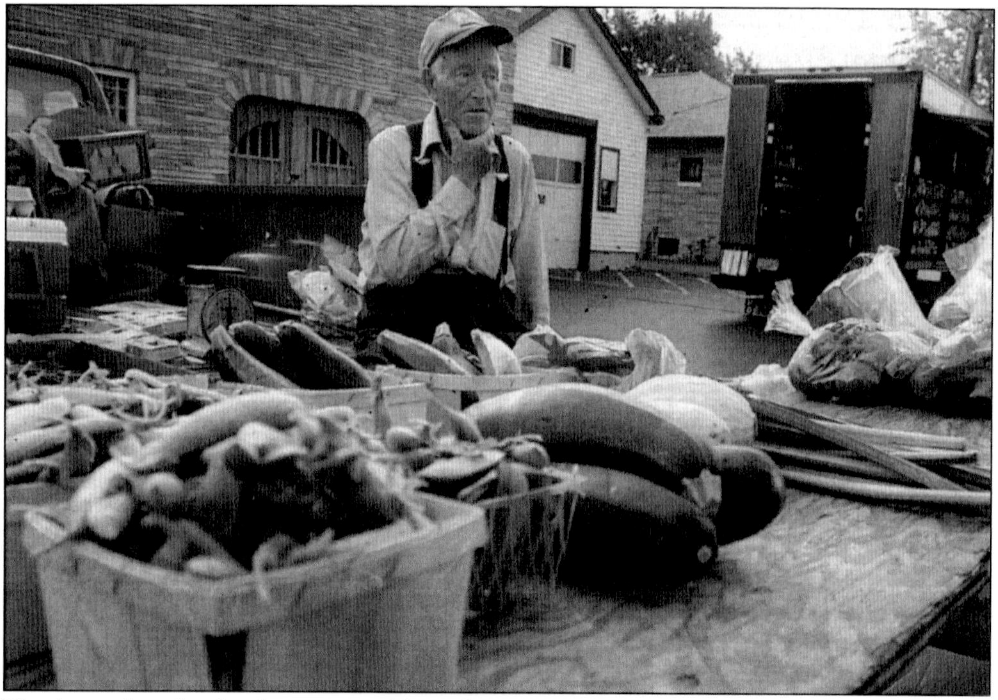

The farmers' market has been a monthly tradition in St. Martins for decades. The first Monday of each month local merchants sell fresh farm and garden products. For one weekend each September since 1958, the local market is replaced by the Labor Day festival, a two-day event that annually attracts over 100,000 visitors in search of bargains, music, and food along a one-mile stretch of St. Martins Road.

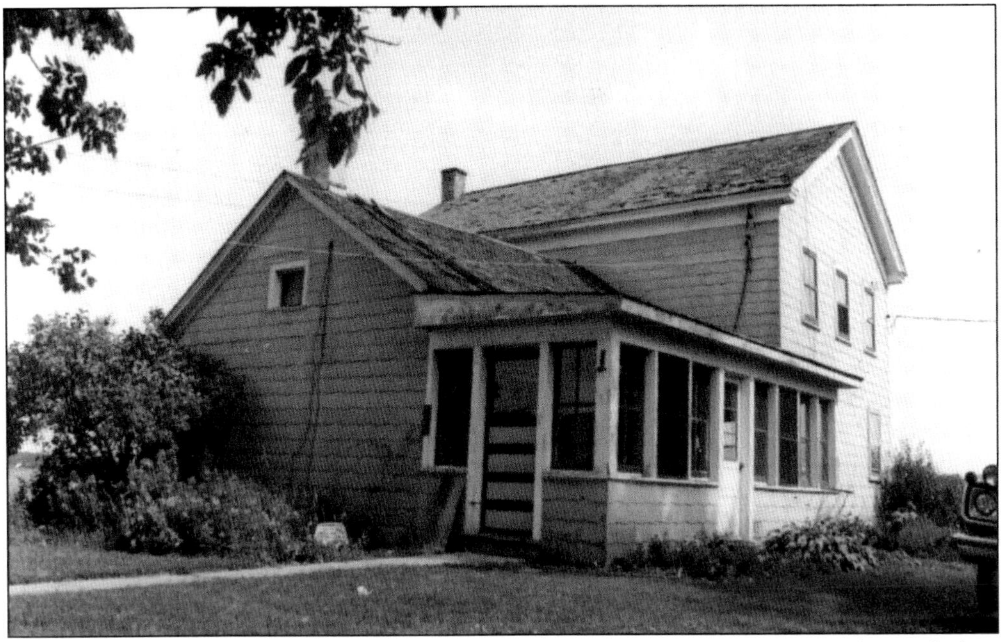

Franklin's first log cabin, built in 1836 by Michael and Patrick Sheehan, became obscured when a two-story addition was attached to the cabin during the 1850s. This farmhouse remained a Sheehan residence until the family sold the farm at 10600 St. Martins Road to Michael Godsell in 1911.

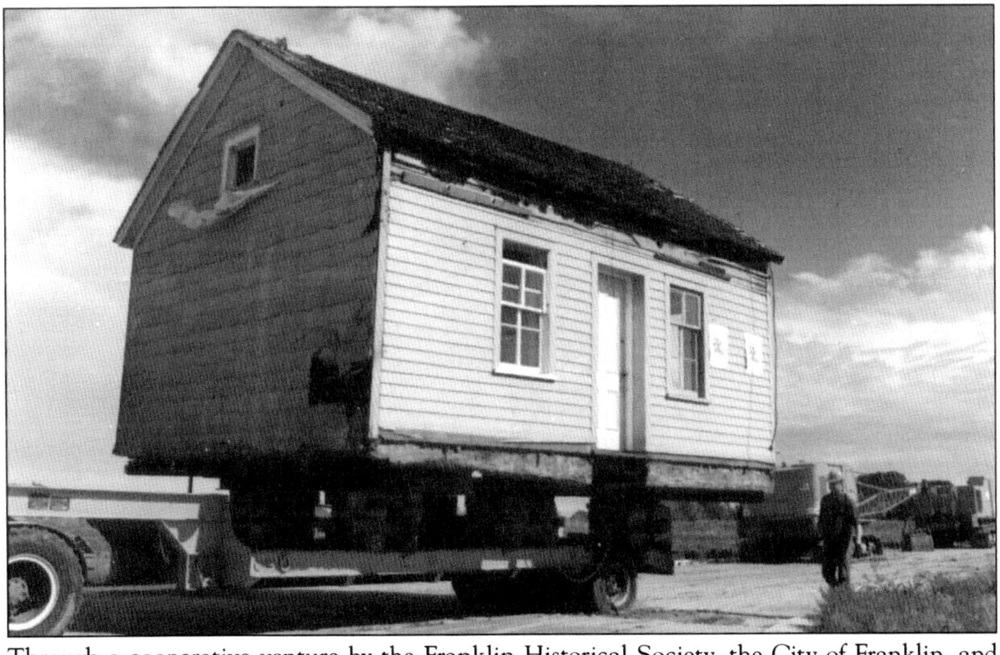

Through a cooperative venture by the Franklin Historical Society, the City of Franklin, and the Franklin Bicentennial Commission, the Sheehan-Godsell cabin was detached from the farmhouse in 1975 and towed to Lions Legend Park where it joined other historic Franklin buildings. With the cabin removed, the Godsell farm was developed into the Mission Hills subdivision.

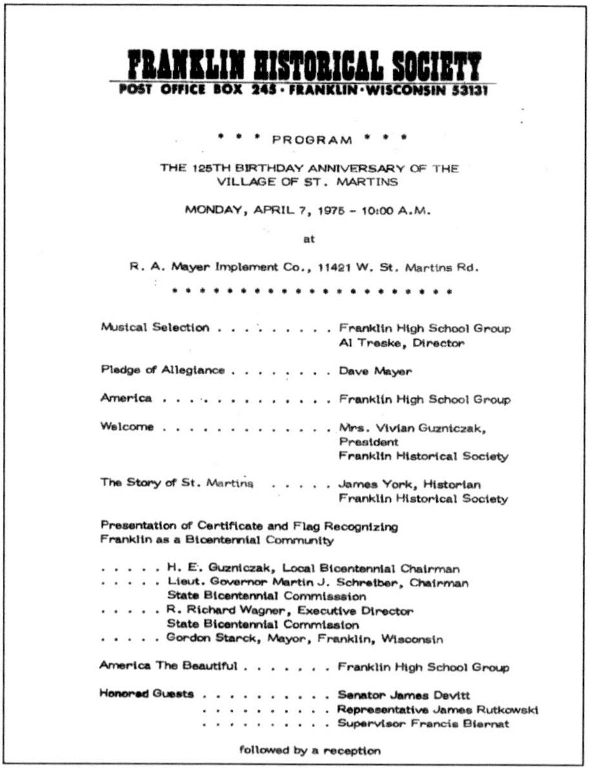

FRANKLIN HISTORICAL SOCIETY
POST OFFICE BOX 245 · FRANKLIN · WISCONSIN 53131

* * * PROGRAM * * *

THE 125TH BIRTHDAY ANNIVERSARY OF THE
VILLAGE OF ST. MARTINS

MONDAY, APRIL 7, 1975 – 10:00 A.M.

at

R. A. Mayer Implement Co., 11421 W. St. Martins Rd.

* *

Musical Selection . . . . Franklin High School Group
Al Treske, Director

Pledge of Allegiance . . . . Dave Mayer

America . . . . Franklin High School Group

Welcome . . . . Mrs. Vivian Guzniczak,
President
Franklin Historical Society

The Story of St. Martins . . . . . James York, Historian
Franklin Historical Society

Presentation of Certificate and Flag Recognizing
Franklin as a Bicentennial Community

. . . . . H. E. Guzniczak, Local Bicentennial Chairman
. . . . . Lieut. Governor Martin J. Schreiber, Chairman
State Bicentennial Commission
. . . . . R. Richard Wagner, Executive Director
State Bicentennial Commission
. . . . . Gordon Starck, Mayor, Franklin, Wisconsin

America The Beautiful . . . . Franklin High School Group

Honored Guests . . . . Senator James Devitt
. . . . Representative James Rutkowski
. . . . Supervisor Francis Biernat

followed by a reception

The Franklin Historical Society and Bicentennial Commission collaborated on a celebration of the village of St. Martins' 125th anniversary on April 7, 1975. Local and state dignitaries were invited to attend the program at the R. A. Mayer Equipment Company.

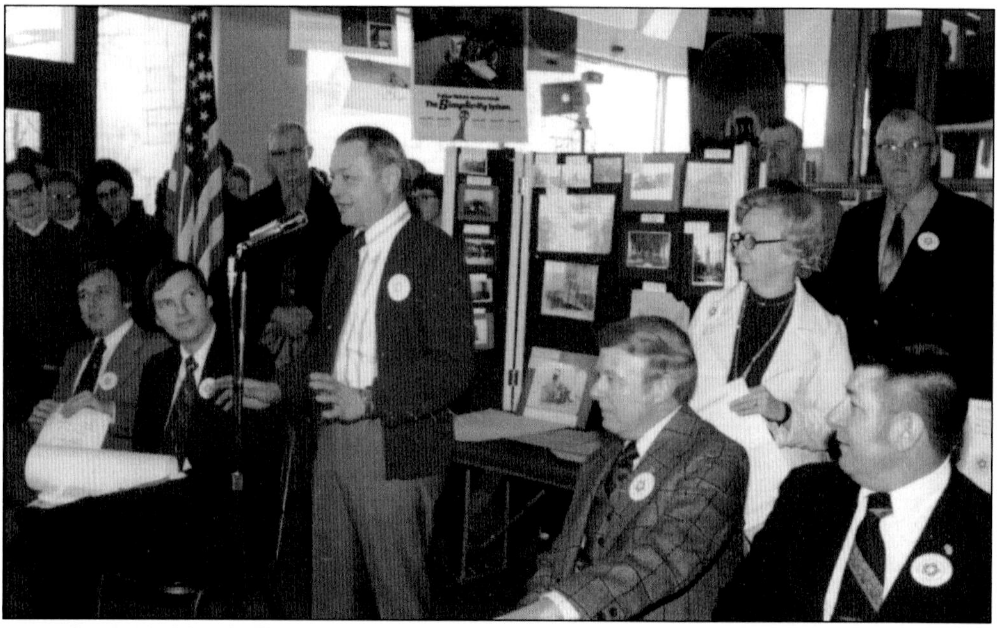

Several state and local officials participated in the 125th anniversary celebration of St. Martins in 1975 at the R. A. Mayer Equipment store. Among them are (seated, from left to right) Lt. Gov. Martin Schreiber, Milwaukee County supervisor Francis Biernat, state senator James Devitt, and Franklin mayor Gordon Starck. At the microphone is business owner David Mayer while historical society president Vivian Guzniczak and historian James York (top right) look on.

Two

Life on the Farm

The population of Wisconsin began to change during the 1850s as the migration of western Europeans extended beyond the coastlines of the United States to the Midwest. Whether they came alone or with families in tow, they were eager to pursue new opportunities in a country that had been the domain of Native Americans and trappers.

After the Milwaukee Patent Office opened in 1839, settlers scrambled to purchase 80-acre plats in the town of Franklin. Irish immigrants gravitated to the western edge, Dutch to the south of Ryan Road, and Germans to the central and eastern sections. The land was heavily wooded and had to be cleared for crops to be planted and livestock to graze. With the exception of St. Martins Road, the town had no semblance of a commercial district. The few businesses that did spring up related to the needs of farmers—a general store and farm equipment, hardware, and blacksmith shops.

Each farm had a somewhat unique layout, but the buildings were similar in purpose and function. They included a two-story house; a barn; a shed to store equipment; a milk house; a chicken coop; perhaps a summer kitchen, a smokehouse, or a blacksmith shop; and, of course, an outhouse.

Life on the farm was hard but self-sustaining. There was no time for vacations. Cows had to be milked; barns had to be cleaned; chickens, ducks, and pigs had to be fed; eggs had be collected; the soil had to be tilled; and crops had to be planted and harvested. If the farm included an orchard, apples had to be picked. Even in the dead of winter, animals had to be tended to and milk had to reach the dairy.

Sundays were a time for worship and relaxation. It was a time for picnics, fishing, and family gatherings. The pleasures were simple.

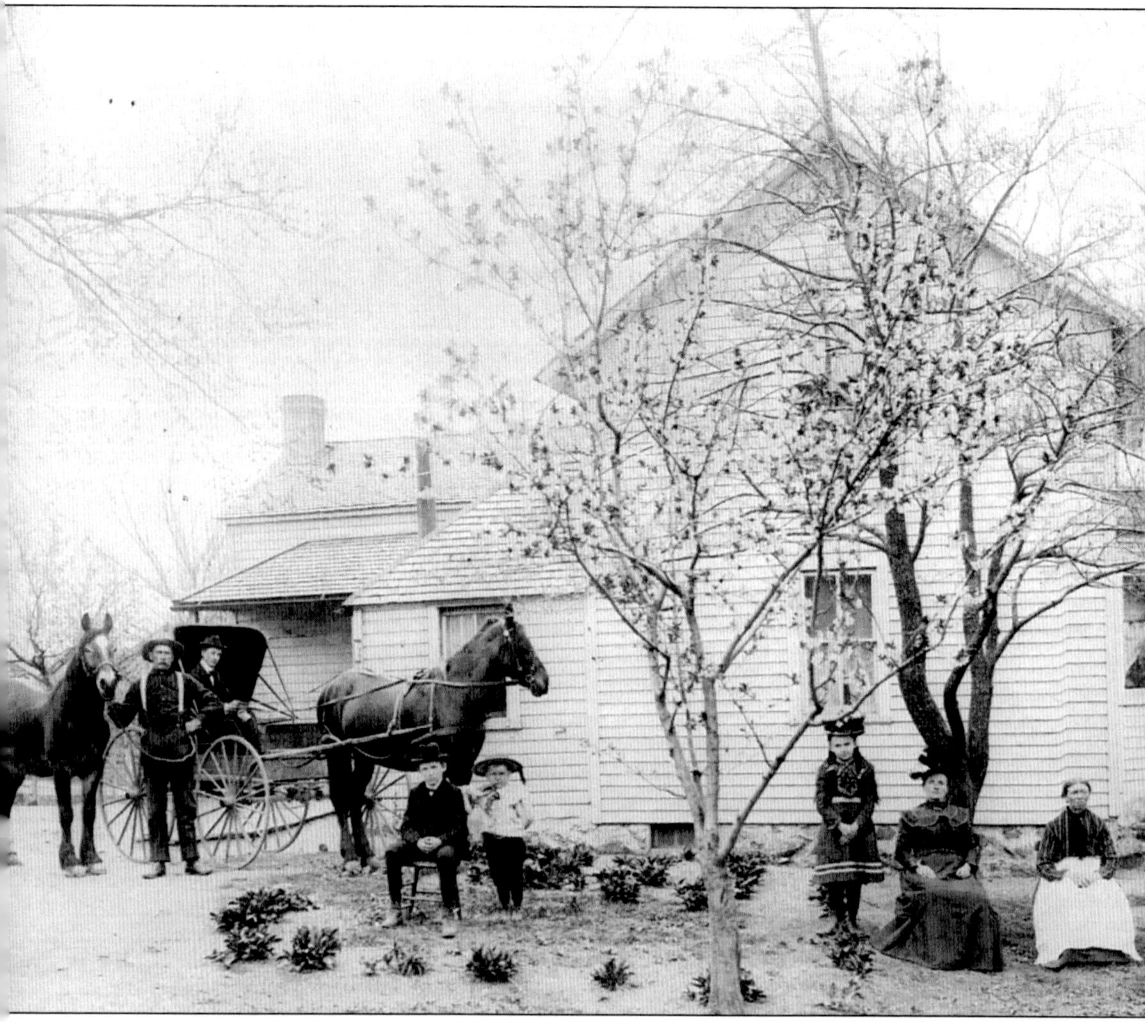

Samuel Giese, his wife Maria, and their son Jacob emigrated from Switzerland to Franklin in 1848 and bought an 80-acre farm on the corner of Fifty-first Street (Smith Road) and Ryan Road. This photograph, taken in 1910, features the family of Samuel's grandson Gottfried and his wife, Ottillia Steinhaus, who were married in 1887. Shown are (from left to right) Gottfried, Fred, John, Arthur, Agnes, Ottillia, and Gottfried's aunt Elizabeth Giese. Elizabeth's fiancé was killed in the Civil War, and she never married, living on the farm until her death in 1923. Gottfried also ran a blacksmith shop and turned over another farm he owned on Oakwood Road to his son John. Agnes left the farm to become a cook for the Uihleins, who owned the Schlitz brewery, and later moved to Beverly Hills, California, where she cooked for actress Joan Crawford.

Wilhelm Staatz immigrated to Franklin from Hamburg, Germany, in 1863, bringing with him his wife Caroline and four children. In the 1870s, he purchased the Peter and Michael Merkel farm located along Loomis Road, which today is the site of the Franklin Post Office, Brenwood Park, the Franklin Police Department, and the Evans Pond condominiums. Wilhelm died in 1910, and his son Julius took over the farm, later to become treasurer for the Town of Franklin.

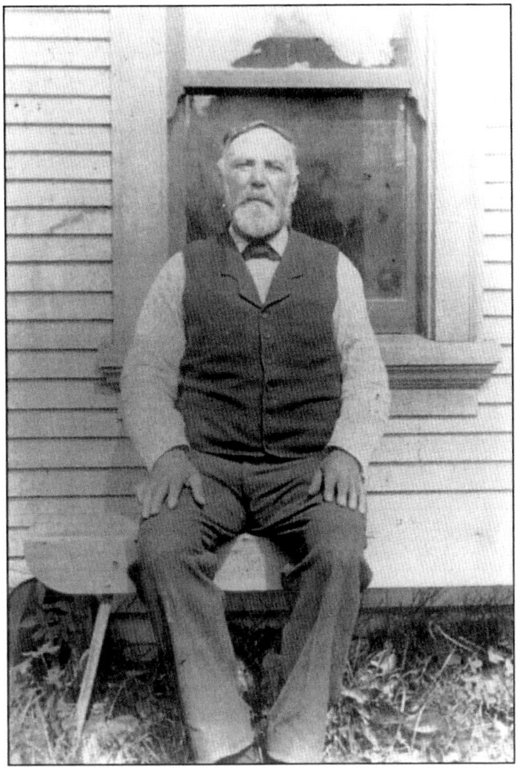

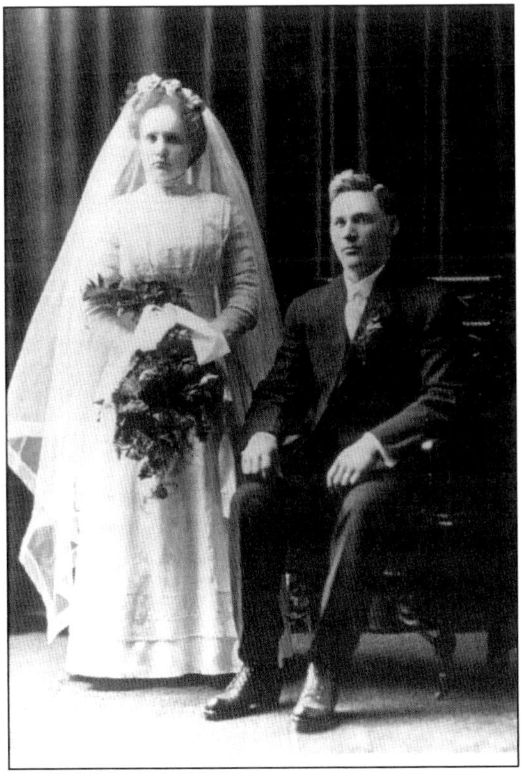

Louise Staatz, a daughter of Julius Staatz, was united with William Nitz in 1911. William and Louise purchased the Staatz farm in 1928 and eventually divided it among their six children, Wilmer, Edna, Norma, Clarence, Elroy, and Irene. Following in his grandfather's footsteps, Clarence Nitz served as treasurer for the City of Franklin from 1955 to 1965.

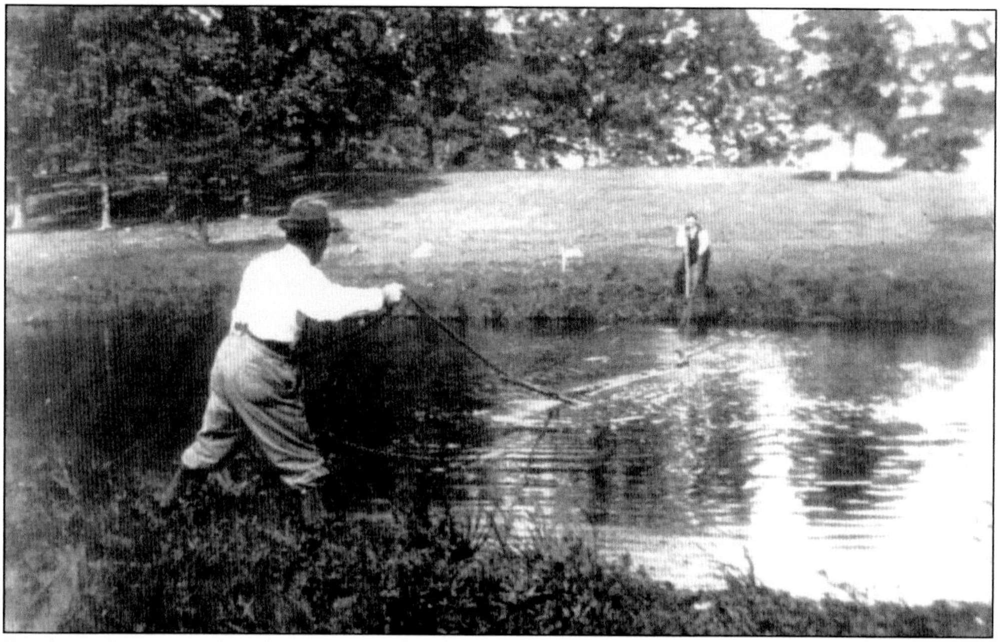

Dredging Evans Pond with a net to catch fish was one method employed by William Nitz and an unidentified relative to make farm life self-sustaining. Freshwater ponds and creeks often yielded panfish and crabs for Franklin farmers during the early part of the 20th century.

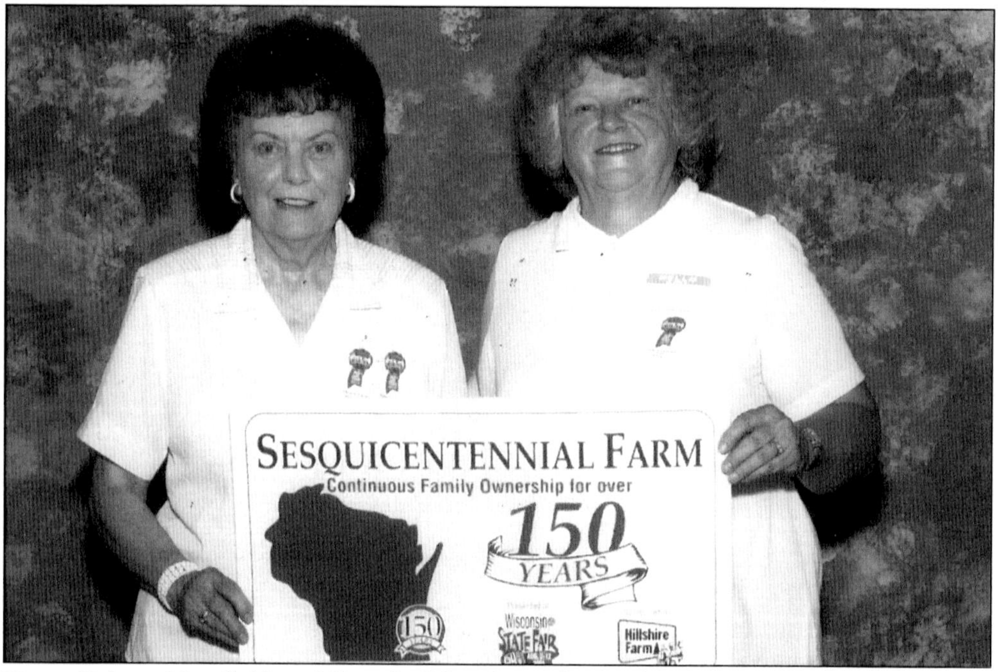

Sisters Delores Nitz (left) and Beverly Biba, descendants of Samuel Giese and daughters of Arthur and Hilda Giese, still own what remains of the Giese family farm. In 1998, they received a sesquicentennial award from the state for 150 years of continuous family ownership of the Franklin farm. Some of the land and buildings were lost in 2006 when the widening of Ryan Road began.

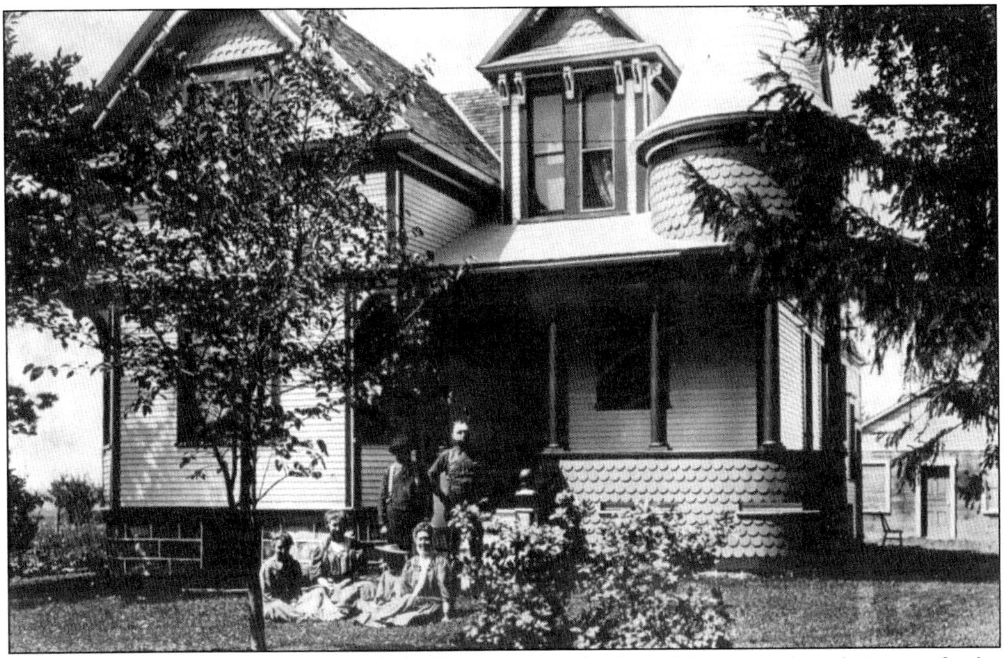

Early Franklin homes were generally built two stories high and functional in design to fit the needs of hardworking farm families. In contrast, however, was the home of Herman Ninneman on South Sixtieth Street, which featured an ornate fish scale exterior. Here the Ninneman family relaxes on the front lawn on a sunny Sunday afternoon.

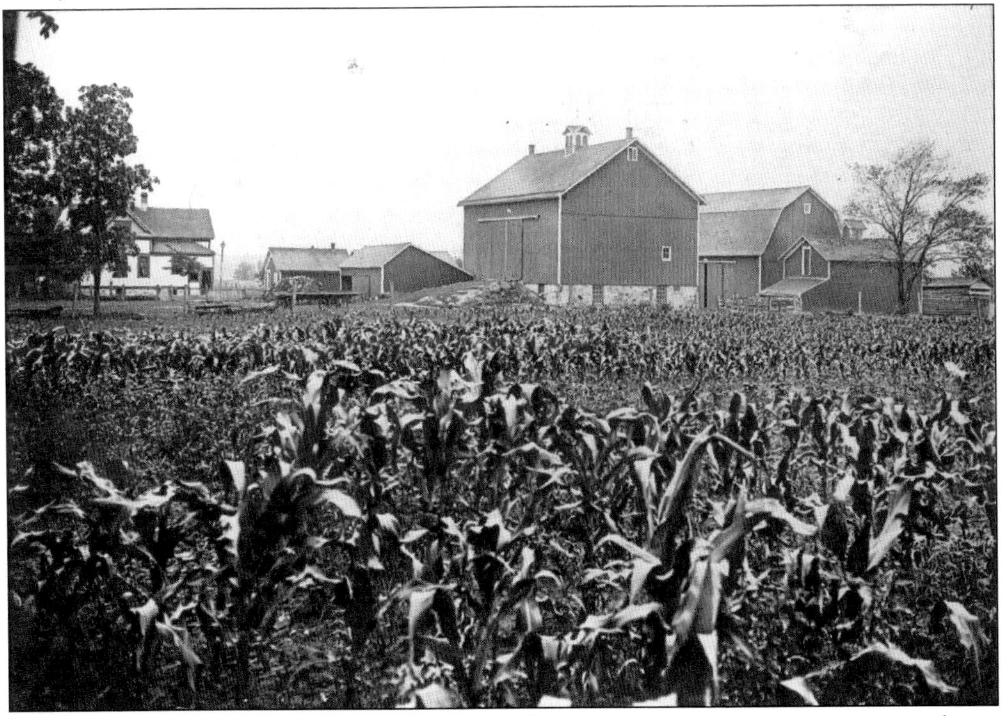

For close to 100 years, rows of corn waving in a July summer breeze were a common sight on 80-acre Franklin farms like Herman Ninneman's on Sixtieth Street.

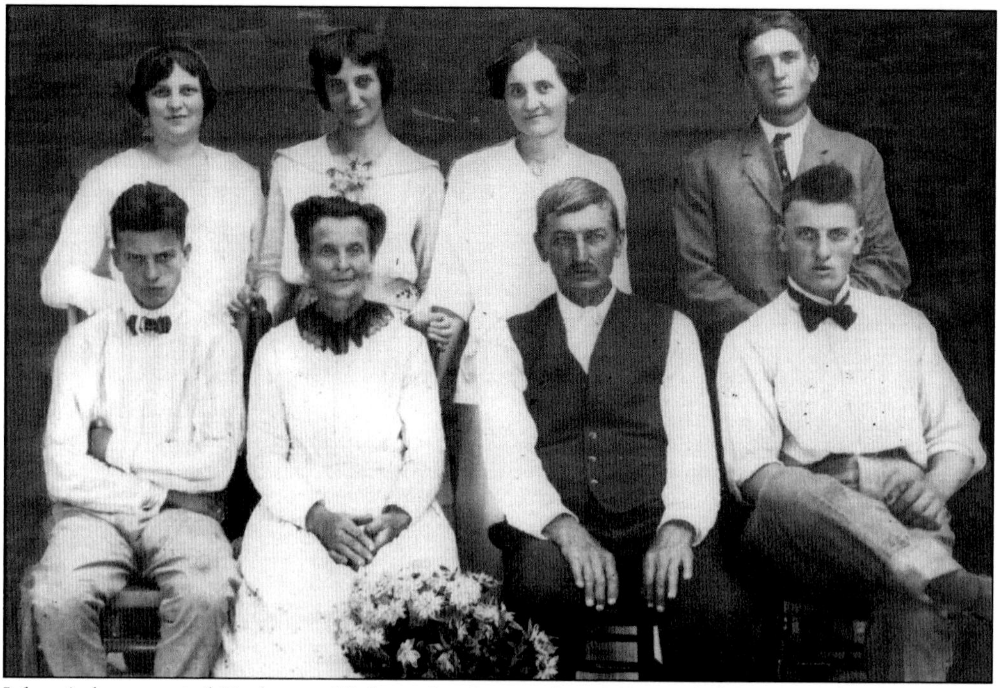

John Acker married Katherine Philipensky during the 1880s, and they raised 10 children on the Acker farm at 10023 South Ninety-second Street. The offspring included Angeline, Hattie, Mamie, Frank, Lawrence, Louie, John Jr., Sarah, Charles, and Florence, who died as an infant.

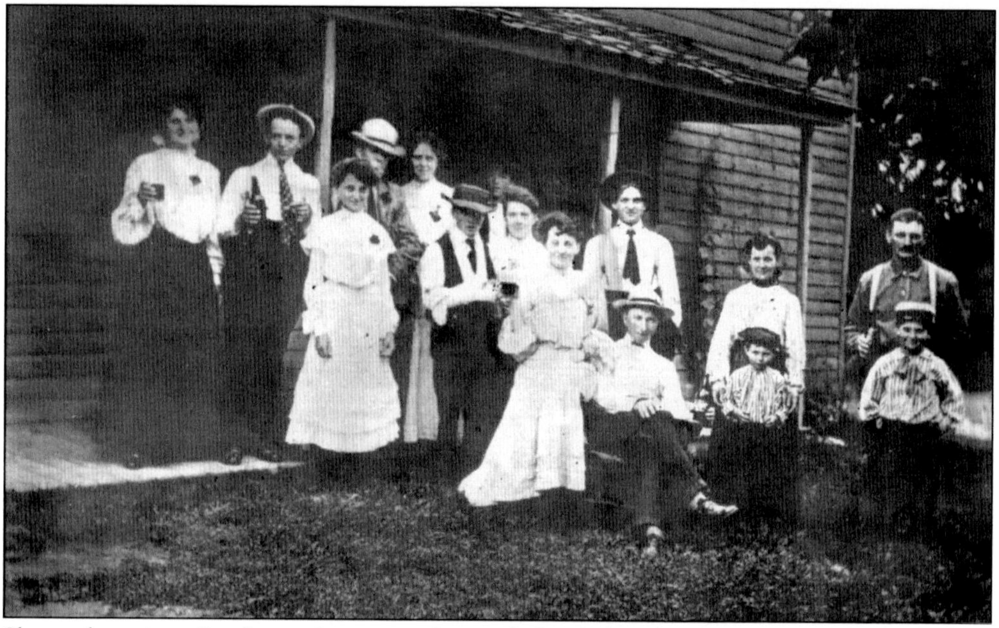

Shown here is a Sunday gathering in front of the Acker farmhouse in 1906. The group includes, from left to right, (first row) Mamie Acker and her boyfriend and Kate and John Acker standing behind sons Lawrence and Louie; (second row) Hattie Acker, Charlie Acker (with broken arm), Sarah Acker, and Frank Acker; (third row) Angie Acker, John Keyoth, and three unidentified friends.

One of the tasks familiar to Franklin farm families was growing crops of wheat, hay, corn, and soybeans. Shown in the field here is Kate Acker, who at the age of 83 was still strong enough to pick and remove husks from bushels of corn in 1939.

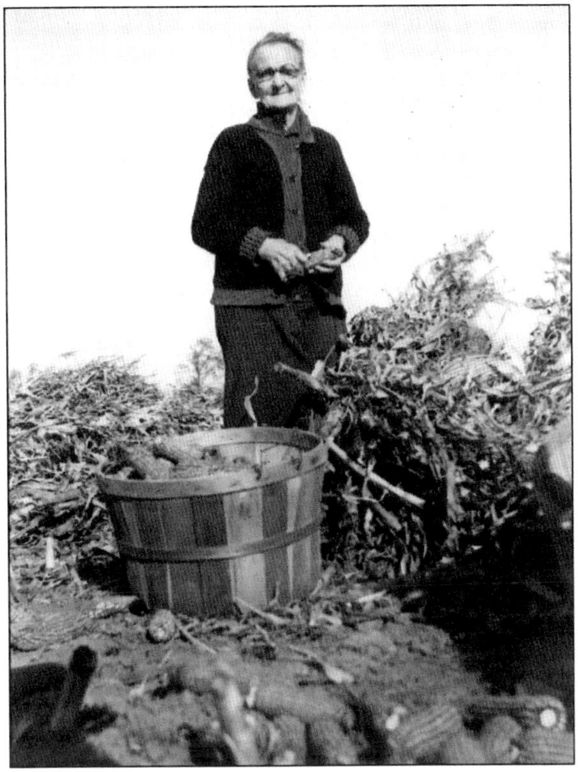

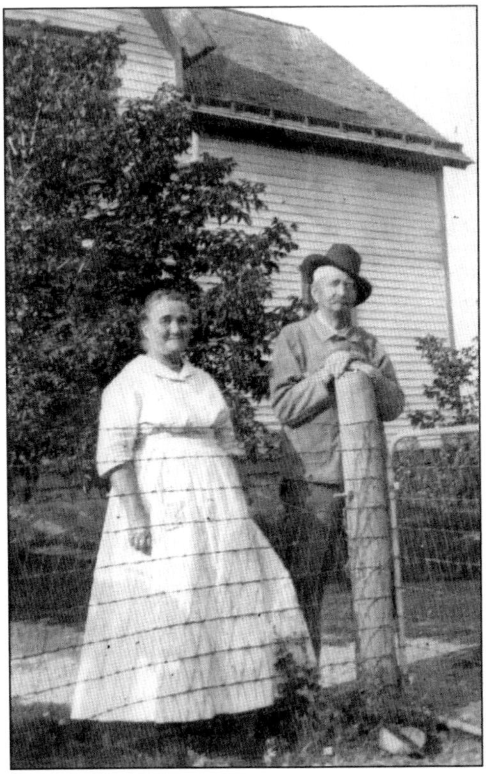

Born in 1854, Fred Ludwig emigrated from Germany to Franklin in 1875 and purchased an 80-acre farm on Colby Road (8520 South Sixty-eighth Street). Five years later, he married Mary Riebe, the stepdaughter of Fred Mueller, who owned a farm across the street. Fred and Mary raised five children, John, William, Sam, Robert, and Sarah, before Fred paid $6,400 to purchase another farm a half mile up the road at 7979 South Sixty-eighth Street in 1902. This became the Ludwig homestead after a barn was built in 1906 and a house in 1908. (Author's collection.)

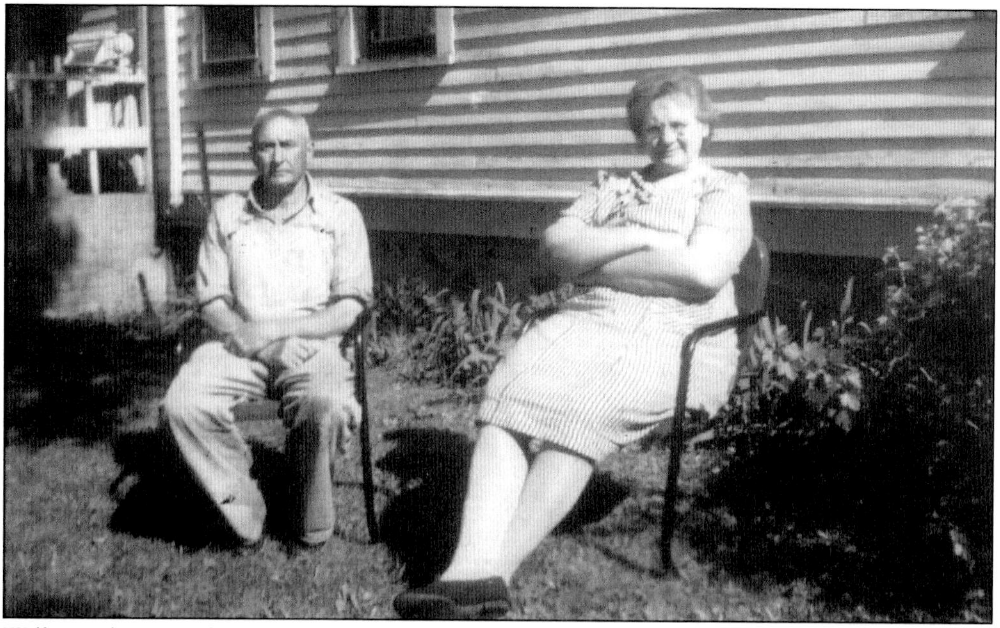

William, the second-oldest son of Fred and Mary Ludwig, married Emma Wendt in 1912, and they ran the Ludwig farm at 7979 South Sixty-eighth Street from 1919 until William's death in 1955. Helping with the chores were five children, Clarence, Marie, Grace, Lucille, and Fred "Fritz" Ludwig. William also had a milk route, which he started in 1912 while working on his dad's farm. He later turned it over to his sons, Clarence and Fritz. (Author's collection.)

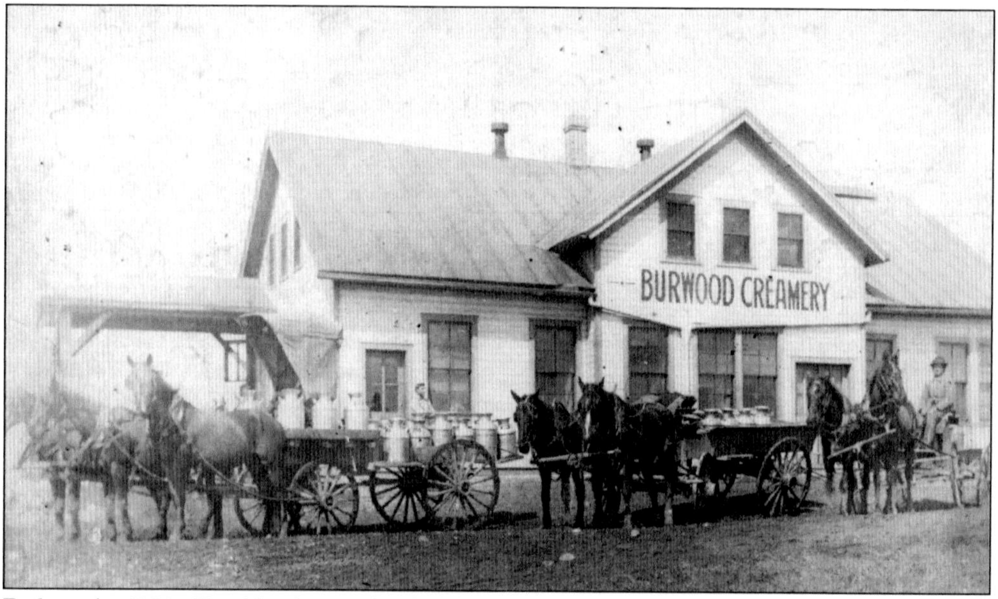

Early in the 1900s, Franklin farmers hauled their milk to the Burwood Creamery on horse-drawn wagons. The dairy was located at the intersection of Colby Road (Sixty-eighth Street) and Ryan Road. Transporting milk could sometimes prove challenging after a snowstorm when country roads went unplowed. Some farmers were known to drop off their milk at Julius Jecke's service station located along two county highways, Loomis Road and Ryan Road. Since county trunks were the first to be plowed, Jecke's was easier for the milk haulers to reach.

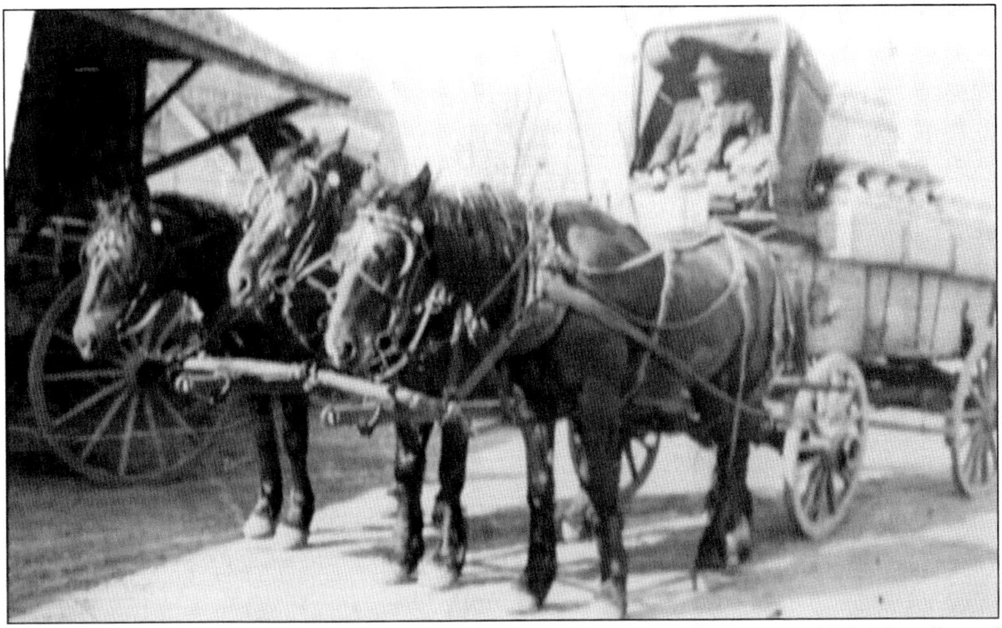

Using a team of three horses, William Ludwig began operating a milk wagon in 1912. He collected milk cans from local farmers and hauled them to the Burwood Creamery. The horse-drawn wagon was later replaced by a series of milk trucks that transported the milk to the Gridley Dairy in downtown Milwaukee and the Layton Park Dairy on Forest Home Avenue. He continued to deliver milk to the dairy during a strike in 1932 and slept with a shotgun next to his bed. (Author's collection.)

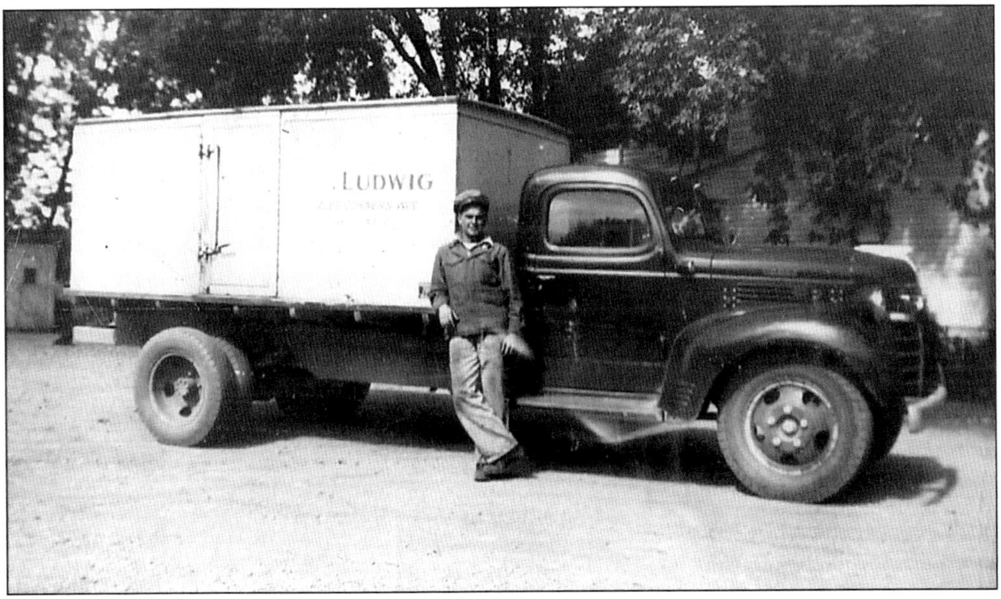

The milk route was a Ludwig family tradition carried on by William's youngest son, Fritz. He took over his dad's route in 1947 but was interrupted in 1950 when he was called to serve in the army during the Korean War. Fritz resumed the milk route in 1952 and continued it until Franklin dairy farming began to wane in 1962. Fritz and his wife, Louise, continue to live in the farmhouse. (Author's collection.)

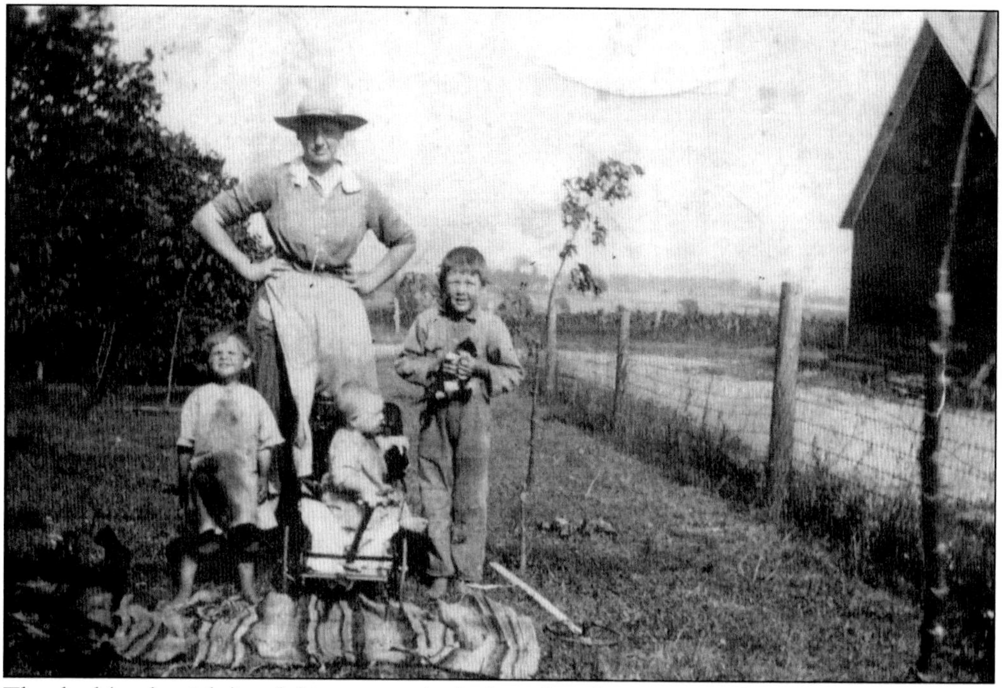

The shed (to the right) and driveway to the Ludwig farm have remained unchanged for the past 100 years. In this 1921 photograph, Emma Ludwig shares some time in the front yard with her three children at the time, Marie, four; Grace, two; and Clarence, eight. (Author's collection.)

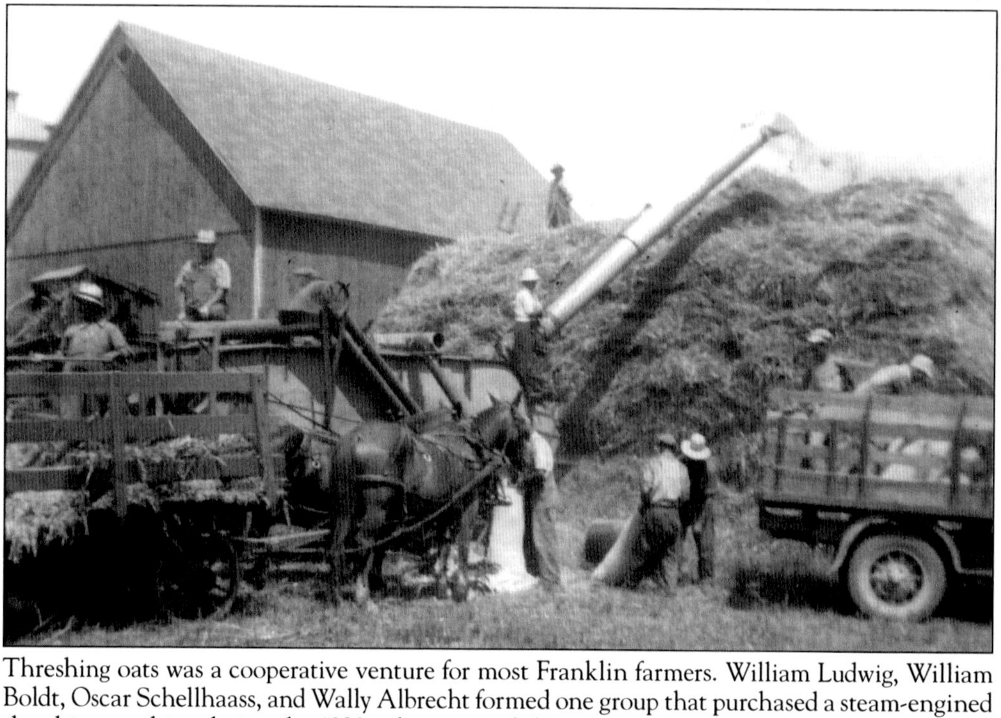

Threshing oats was a cooperative venture for most Franklin farmers. William Ludwig, William Boldt, Oscar Schellhaass, and Wally Albrecht formed one group that purchased a steam-engined threshing machine during the 1930s, then rotated their equipment and manpower from farm to farm to harvest one another's crops in the fall. (Author's collection.)

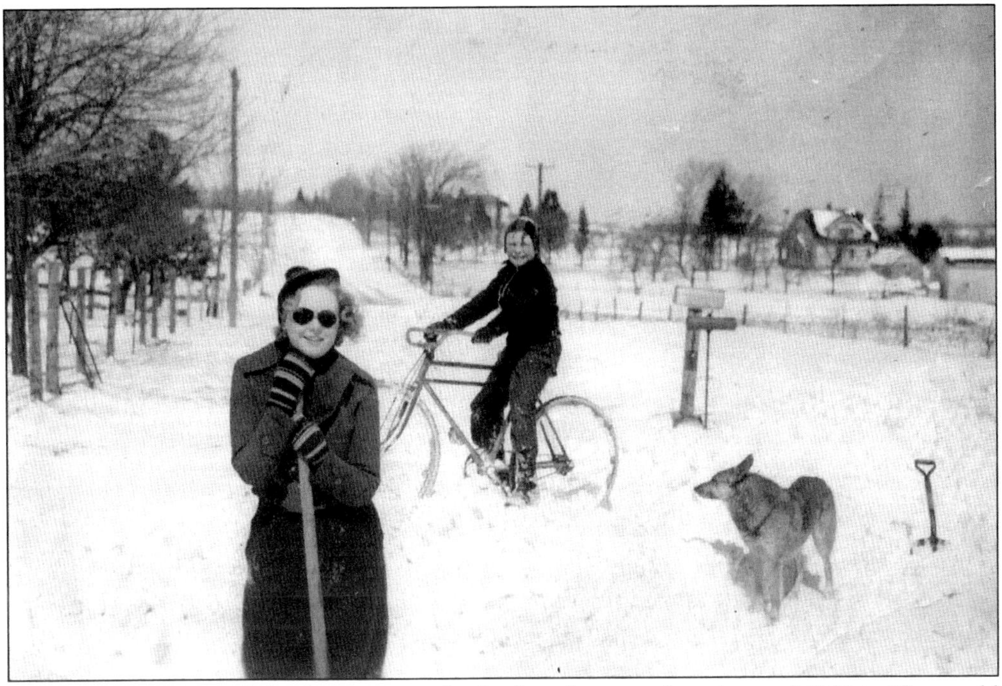

Shoveling snow out of the driveway on the Ludwig farm in the winter of 1937 is 18-year-old Grace Ludwig while her brother Fritz, 10, watches from his bicycle. This photograph is looking north toward the intersection with Drexel Avenue where the Hilbert Gennerotzke farmhouse can be seen. (Author's collection.)

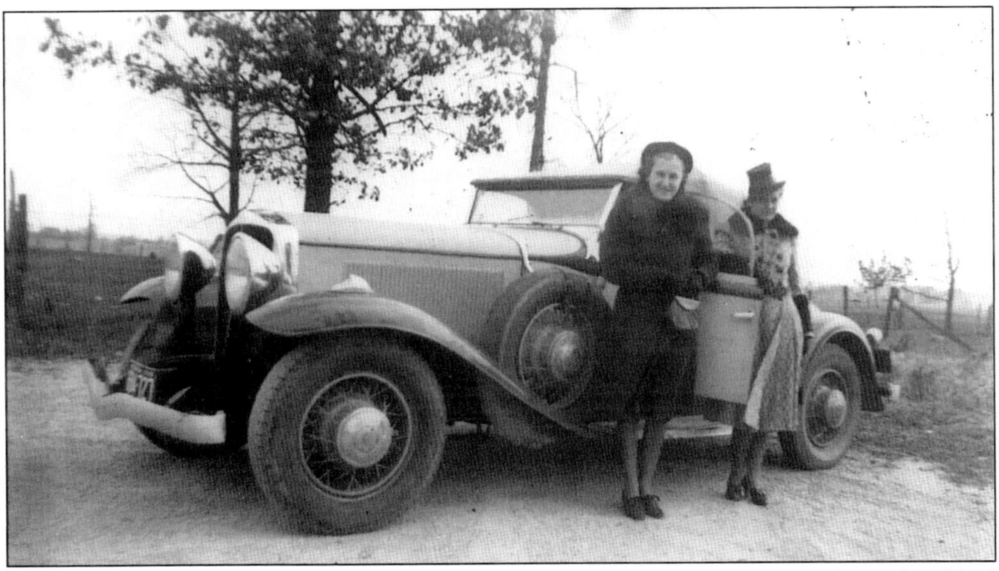

Ready for a ride into town wearing their Sunday best in 1939 are sisters Dorothy and Mildred Kneser. Their grandfather August Kneser owned farmland on both sides of Seventy-sixth Street just north of Loomis Road. In 1941, Mildred married Edwin Bertram, who grew up on the Max Bertram farm down the road on Loomis at Sixty-eighth Street.

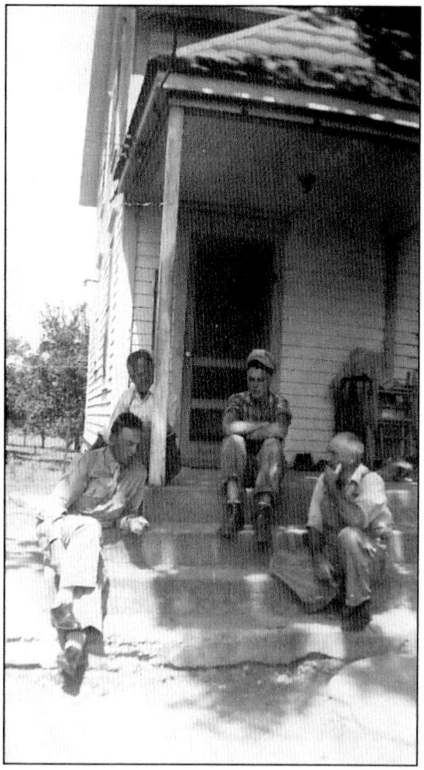

The front porch was a popular gathering place when visitors stopped in at the Ludwig farm on Sixty-eighth Street. Here Otto Bertram (top left) and his son Elmer (in uniform) visit Fritz and William Ludwig. Elmer Bertram was home on leave from the U.S. Army in August 1943. (Author's collection.)

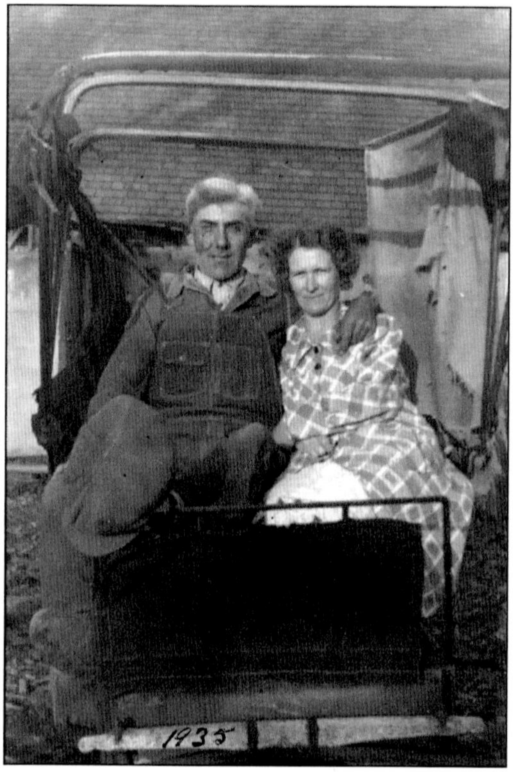

Relaxing in a buggy seat in 1935 are Alfred and Lydia Kneser on the Kneser farm along Loomis Road.

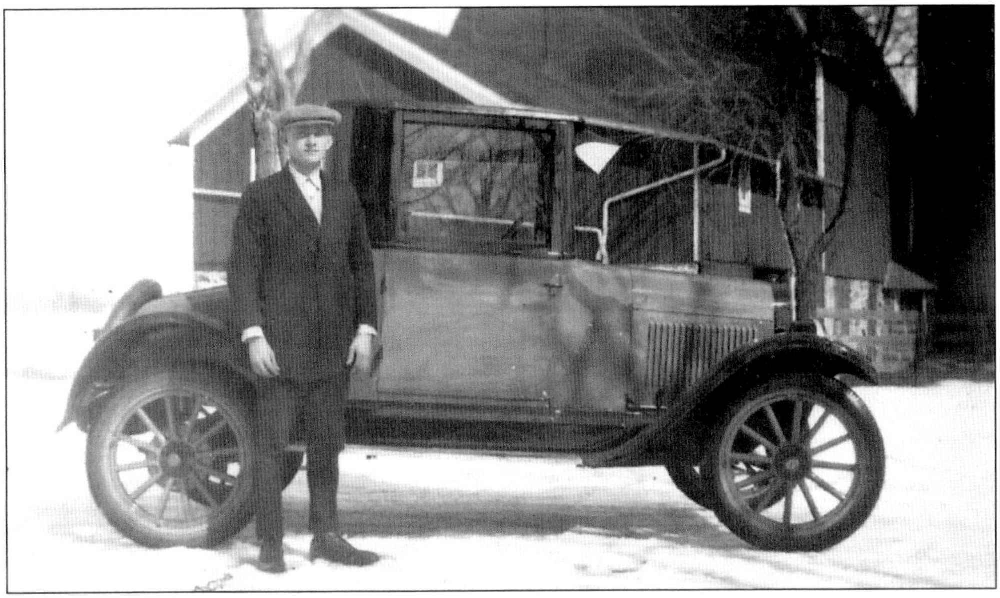

Wilhelm "William" Boldt is shown here next to his 1925 Ford Model A. He was a third-generation Boldt in Franklin. His grandfather Friedrich Boldt, who married Anna Maria Huckstorf, arrived from Germany in 1868. The Boldts established a farm on Central Street (South Seventy-sixth Street) where they raised six children. One of them, Wilhelm Johann Carl Boldt, married Bertha Paap, and they had one son, William, who married Lillian Tretow in 1930. William Boldt became a member of Franklin's first school board in 1951.

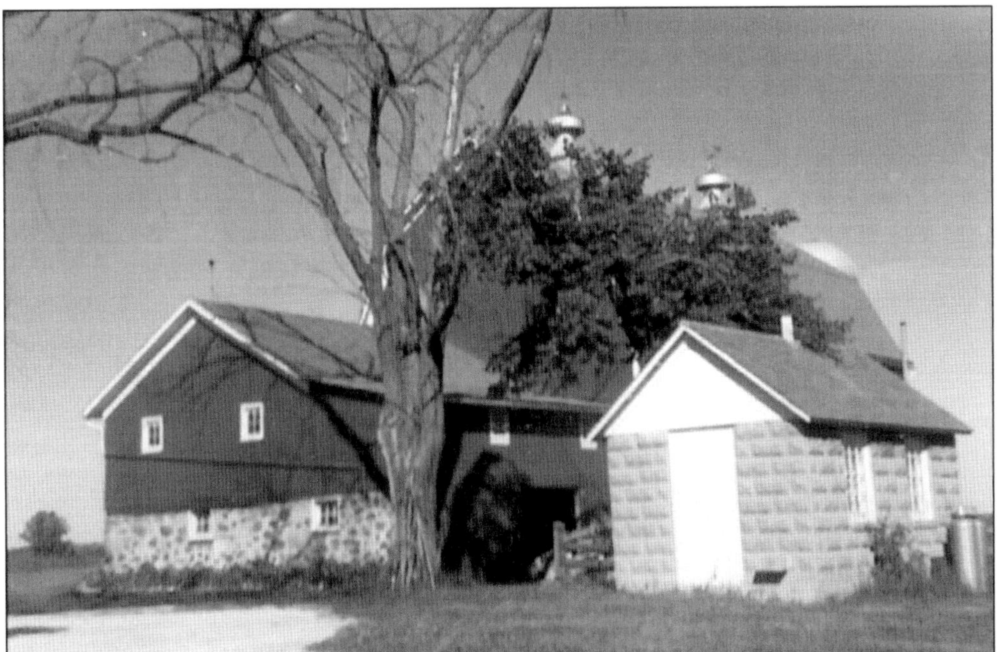

This is the Boldt barn and milk house on South Seventy-sixth Street. The barn was used for storage of golf course maintenance equipment after the Boldts sold five acres of the farm to Tuckaway Country Club in 1966.

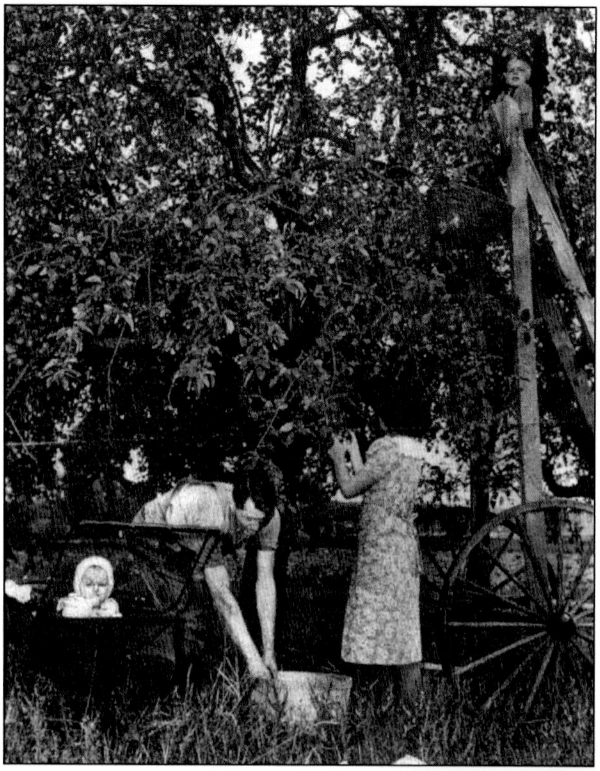

Apple orchards were commonplace on Franklin farms throughout the first half of 20th century. It was serious business on the John Schweitzer farm at South Seventy-sixth Street and Oakwood Road in 1941. Here John Schweitzer and his wife, Gwen, begin filling a basket while son David, eight, picks apples from atop a ladder mounted on wagon wheels. Showing little interest in the chores is nine-month-old Lois in the baby carriage. (Courtesy of Milwaukee Journal.)

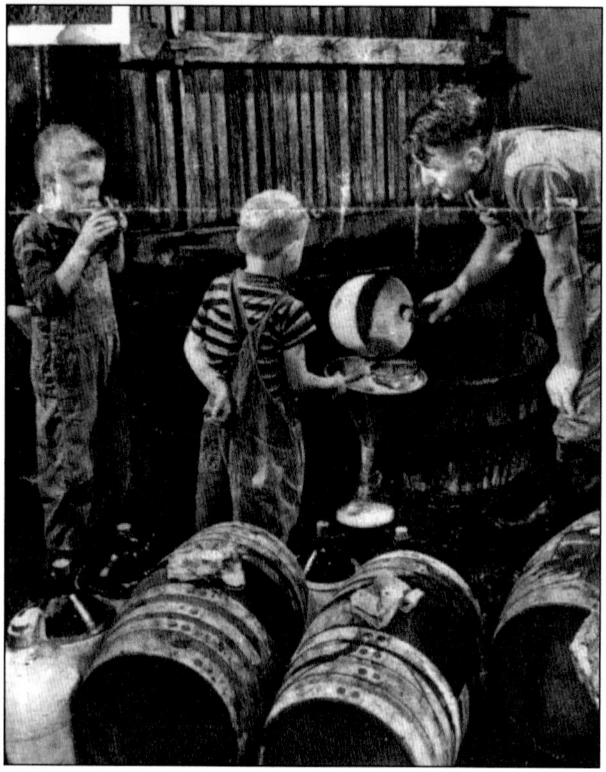

A cider press made fermenting apple juice a labor of love for John Schweitzer. A homemade screw press strained and funneled the apple juice into jugs and barrels. Other farmers in the area availed themselves of Schweitzer's services to turn apples into cider. Farmers sold apple cider for 50¢ a gallon at roadside stands. Here Schweitzer's son Billy, six, samples the juice while Jackie, four, holds the strainer. (Courtesy of Milwaukee Journal.)

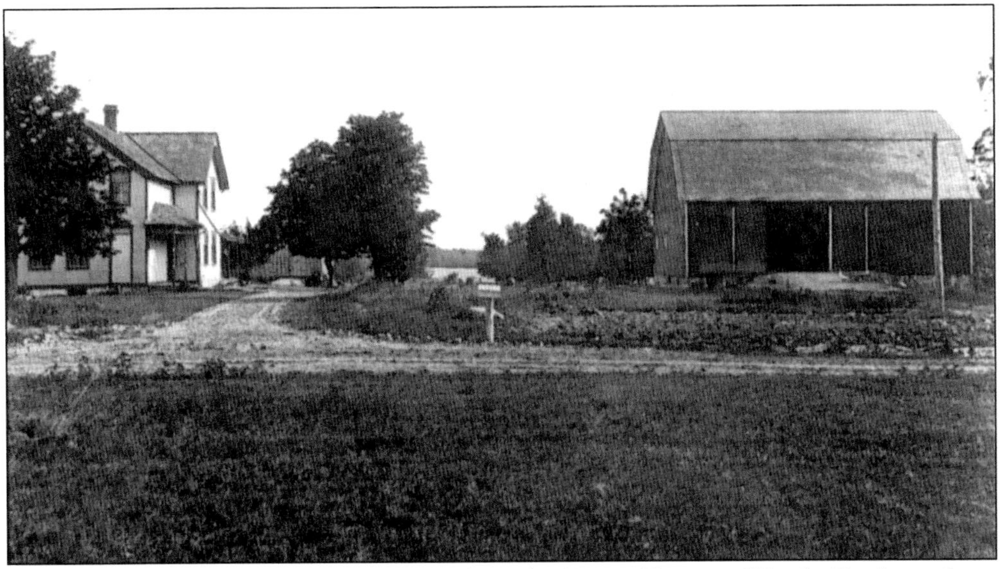

Located in the 4700 block of West Ryan Road was the 80-acre Henry and Bertha Prochnow farm, about a mile west of Highway 41. Also living in the farmhouse were their son-in-law and daughter Alfred and Hattie Peters with their three children, Delbert, Derald, and Dale. The Prochnows raised 25 dairy cows, 500 chickens, and 200 ducks, along with fields of cash crops. Today the property is part of Franklin's business park, and Ryan Road is a four-lane divided thoroughfare.

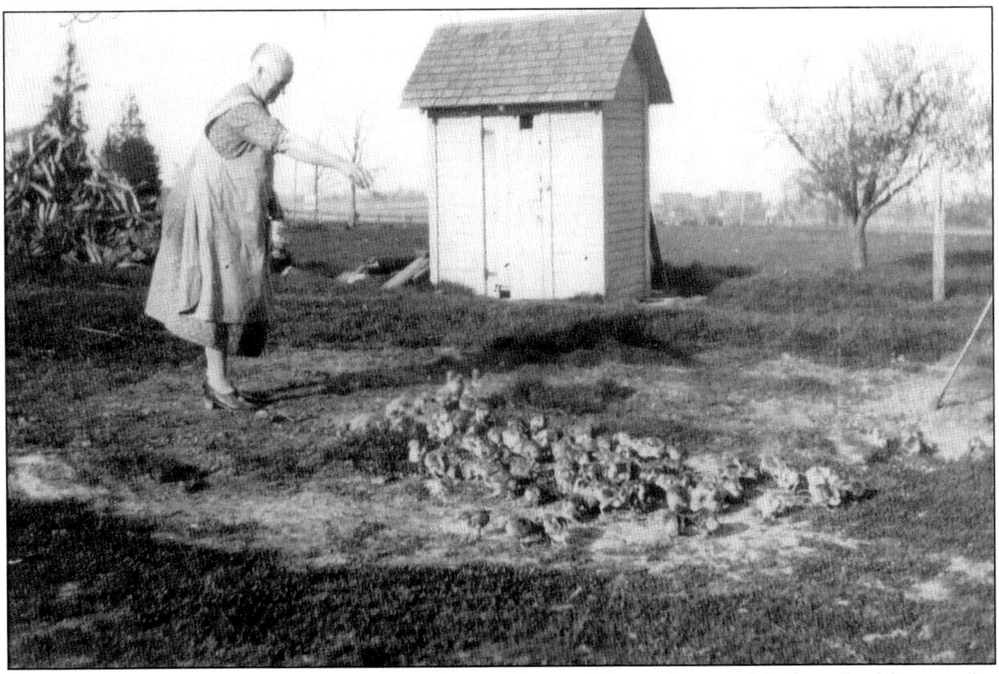

Feeding the ducklings on the farm is Bertha Prochnow. The indispensable farm building in the background is the outhouse.

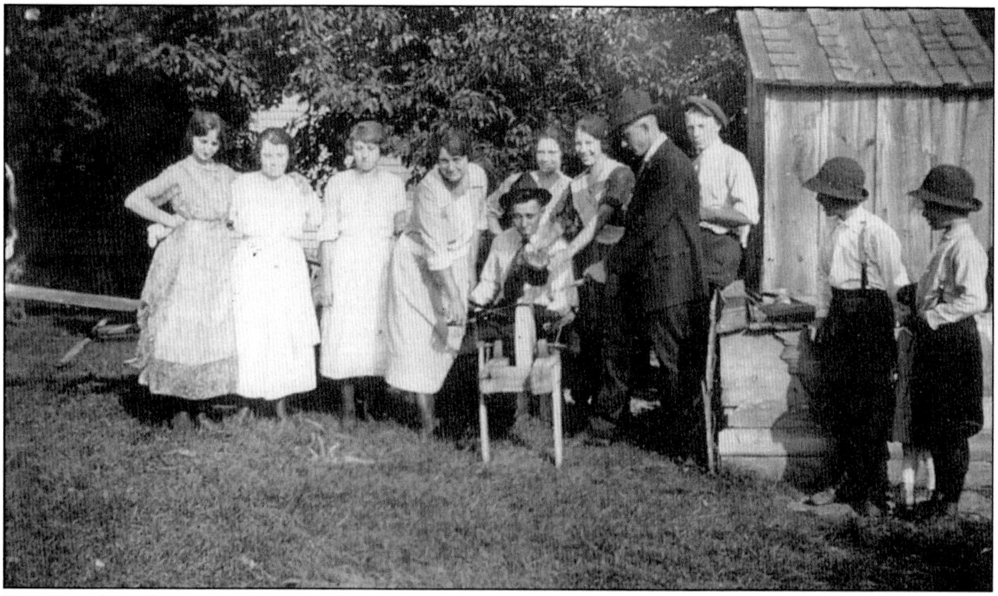

Families found inventive ways to amuse themselves on Sunday afternoons. Shown here on the Herman Yunker farm in 1925 is Gus Friebel (seated) sharpening a blade on the grindstone while Elizabeth Friebel turns the crank. Other family members pictured are Hattie Acker, Ida Yunker, Elsie Sellhorn, Josie Friebel, Gus Salchow, Bill Friebel, and Otto Friebel. The farm was established on Forest Hill Avenue by Herman's father, Ernst Yunker, who arrived in Franklin during the 1850s.

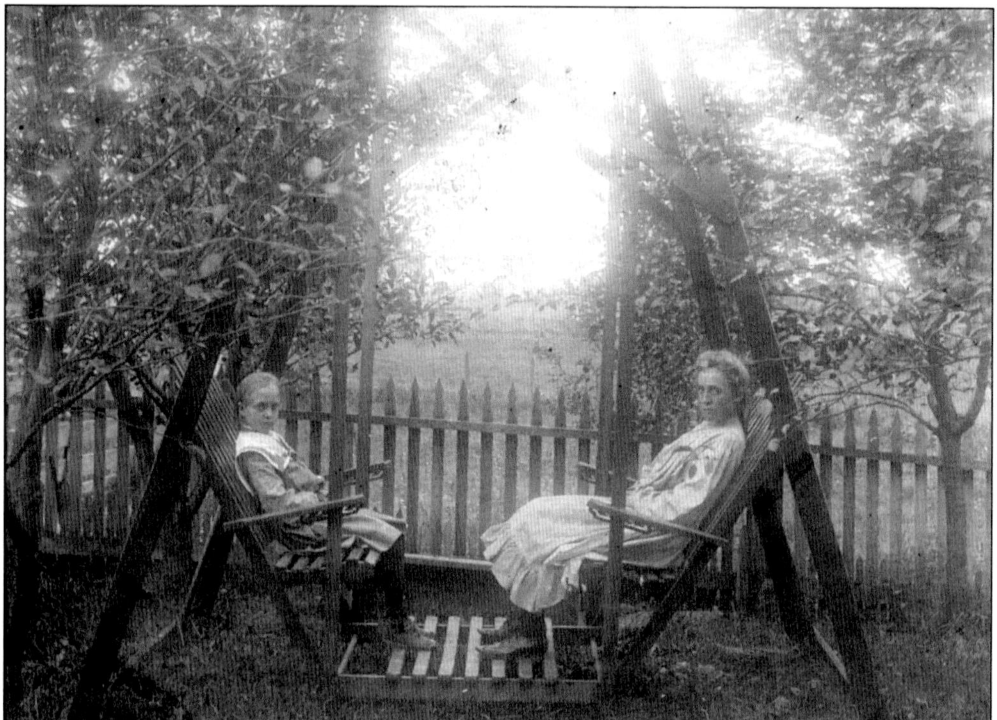

An unidentified mother and daughter relax on a backyard glider during the 1920s.

Three

LIFE OUTSIDE THE FARM

With farms spanning out over 34 square miles, Franklin never really developed a commercial district. Consequently, businesses reflected the needs of the farmers and their families.

For farm supplies ranging from tractors and machinery to animal feed and plant seed there were the J. F. Herda and R. A. Mayer implement stores in St. Martins. Home necessities could be purchased at Vanden Boom's on the corner of Swiss Street and St. Martins Road and Peter Poths's general store on Rawson Avenue near Seventy-sixth Street.

The most abundant businesses were service stations and taverns. Taverns such as the Buckhorn and White Dove began as post office stops. The White Dove and Walter Heiden's tavern, both located along Seventy-sixth Street, featured dance halls that offered space for school functions such as Christmas pageants and graduation ceremonies. Other popular taverns were the Harrisburg Inn and Ollie Pederson's in St. Martins, along with Jack Dillman's, Lizzie Schmidt's, and John Sem's in other parts of Franklin.

Gas and service stations were the most plentiful. The intersection of Loomis Road and Ryan Road, in fact, featured gas stations at all four corners. Ervin Tretow established the first automobile repair business on Loomis Road in 1927, and Julius Jecke followed in 1932. Over time, Jecke's business on Loomis and Ryan Roads evolved from automobile repair and gas to include a tavern, an ice-cream parlor, and a dance hall.

Franklin also had room for a stone quarry, which opened in 1941 and continues in operation today.

Sunday was a day of rest from farm chores, and most Franklin immigrants maintained strong Christian values, so churches evolved to reflect their Protestant or Catholic faith. Some congregations raised funds to build their own parochial schools.

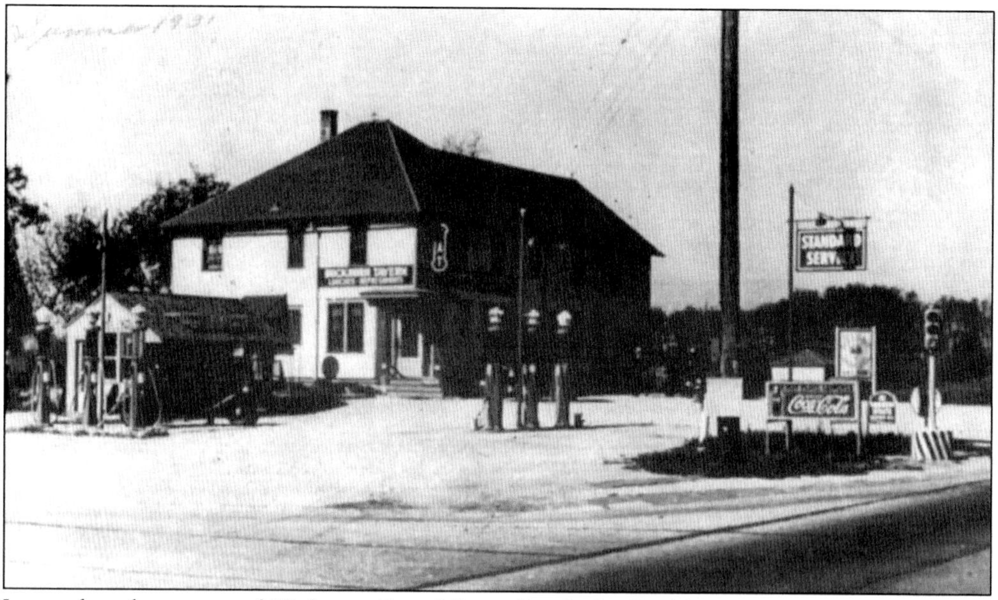

Located at the corner of Highway 41 and Ryan Road, the Buckhorn Tavern has had a long, colorful history since it was opened by Paul Noe in 1843. The Buckhorn got its name in 1899 when owner Adam Doerr, who married Paul Noe's daughter Maria, shot a buck from his upstairs window and mounted the antlers under the window. The original inn was torn down and rebuilt with a second-floor dance hall by new owners Herman and Della Karstens in 1906.

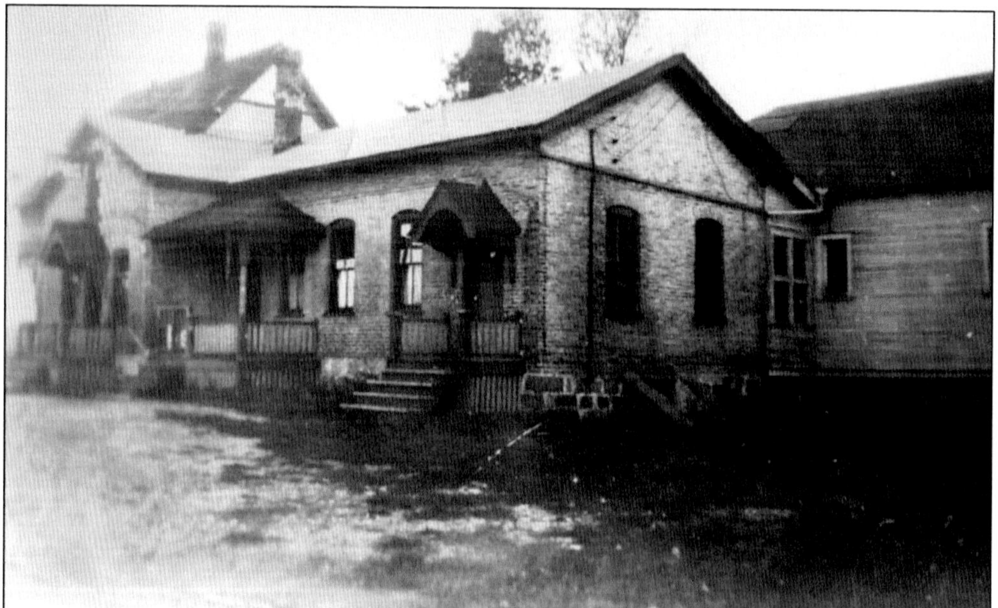

A tavern and dance hall built by Lizzie Schmidt occupied the pie-shaped corner of Colby Road (Sixty-eighth Street) and Loomis Road during the 1920s and 1930s. She turned the business over to her sons, Fred and Herb Schmidt. Future proprietors were Pete Socha and Bill Reinhardt. Early in the 1930s, the coat-check room was removed and transported to the William Ludwig farm where it was converted into a chicken coop. The corner was later annexed by the Village of Greendale, and the tavern was torn down in 1941.

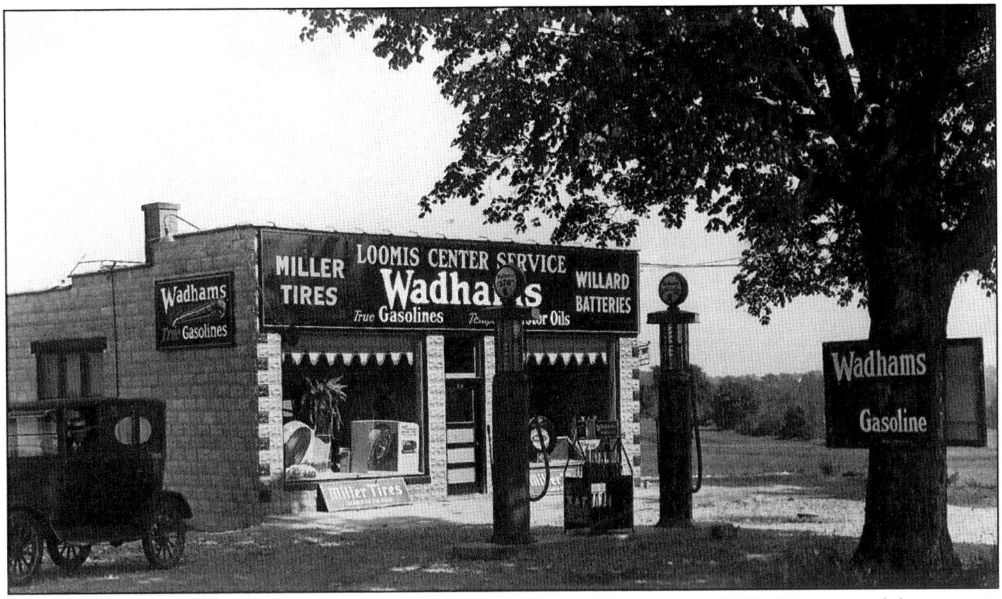

The Loomis Center Garage was established by Ervin Tretow in 1927. He named his repair shop after the intersection of streets where it was located, Loomis Road and Center Street (Seventy-sixth Street). Automobile repairs remain a family tradition at Loomis Center Garage, except that it is now located on Old Loomis Road. The shop was bypassed when the state carved out a new divided Highway 36 in 1970. Ervin ran the shop until 1955, and his son Vernin ran it until 2000. Today the garage is operated by Ervin's grandson Tom Tretow.

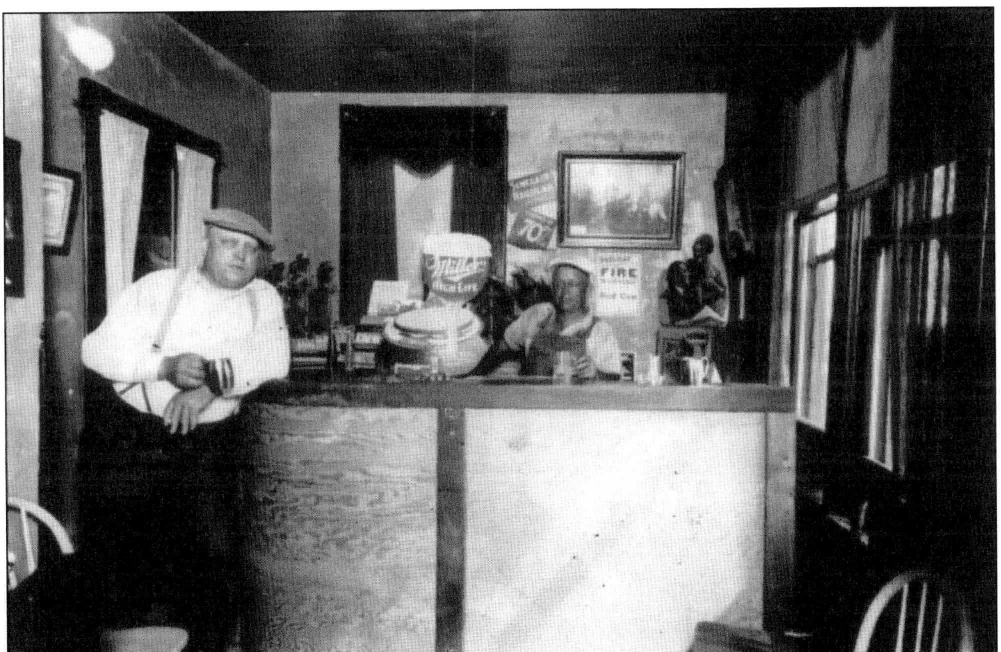

Seated behind the bar is owner Julius Jecke, who talks with his brother-in-law Mike Dropp over a beer in 1932. The small tavern was located inside Jecke's gas station. On Saturday nights the barroom was expanded into the kitchen to accommodate more customers.

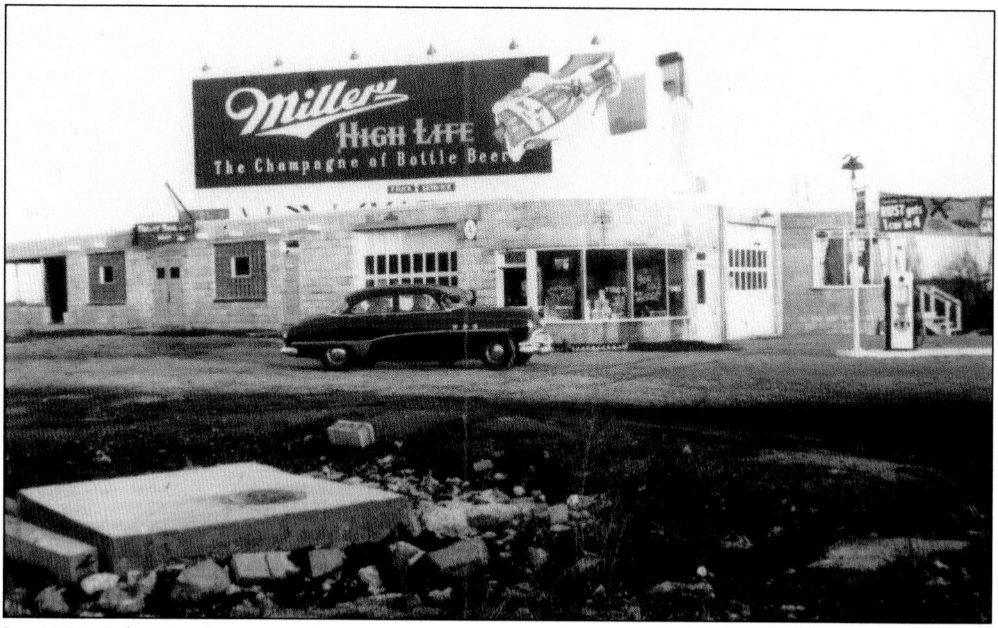

In 1953, Julius Jecke opened a new multiuse facility at the intersection of Loomis Road (Highway 36) and Ryan Road. Jecke's Sinclair service featured an automobile repair shop, a tavern, and, to the far right, an ice-cream parlor. A dance hall on the far left was still under construction. In the foreground is a well that was capped after the original building was removed to widen the highways.

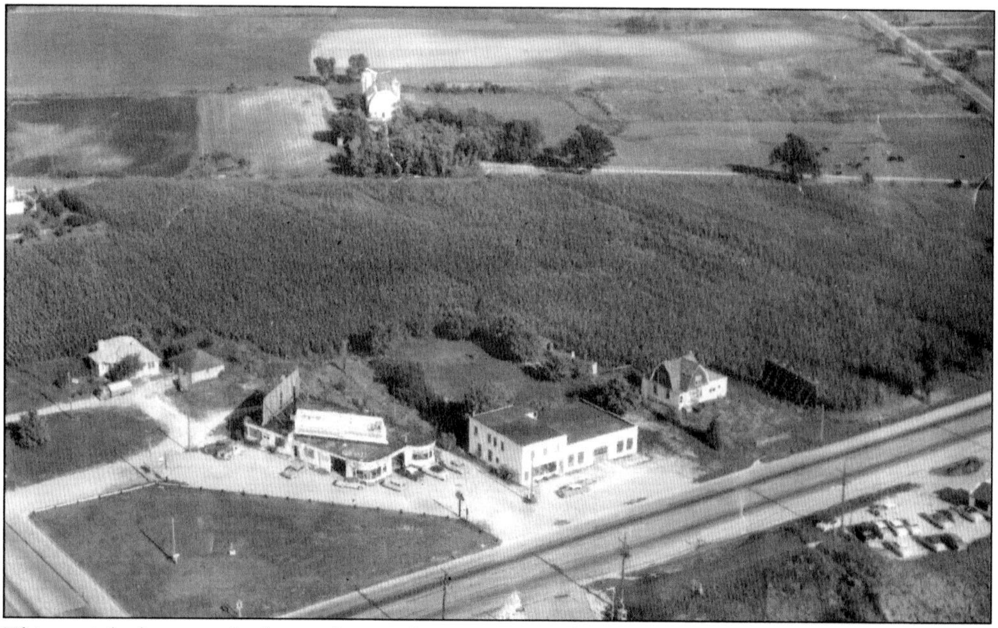

This aerial photograph shows the northeast corner of Loomis Road and Ryan Road in 1956 with Jecke's Sinclair station in the center. Julius Jecke's new home is to the left. His original home was moved east along Ryan Road, past Carl Jensen's Garage, which was built in 1941. For decades this busy intersection featured four gas stations, Sinclair, Pate, Shell, and John Dillman's Standard service. Jensen's Garage offered Texaco gas.

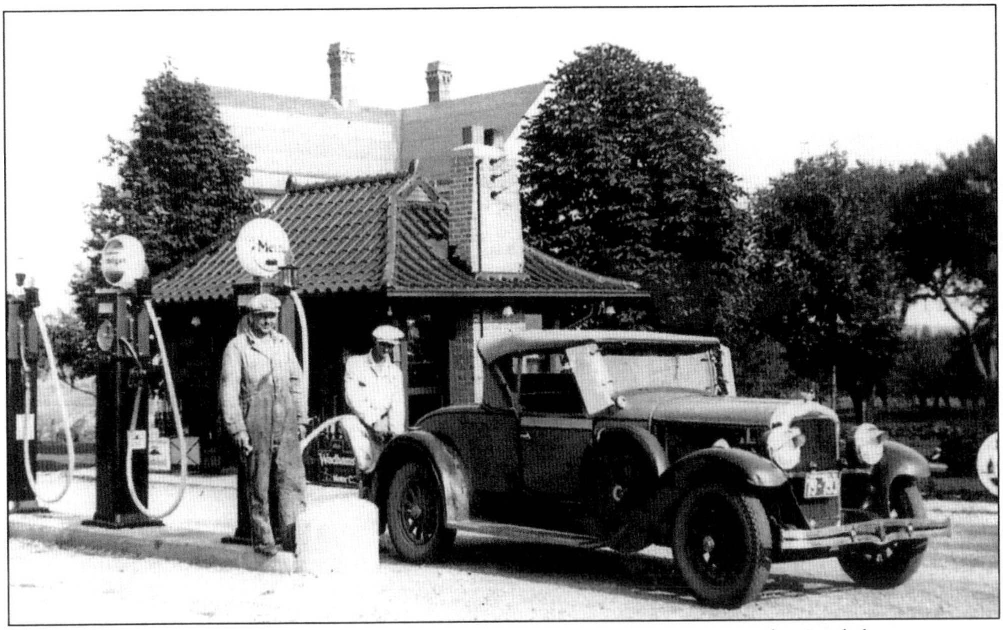

Standing in front of a gas pump is proprietor Joseph Acker. He opened a Mobile gas station during the 1920s on Ryan Road, just east of Center Street (South Seventy-sixth Street). The service station featured one of the period's unique red pagoda-style roofs. The business remained open into the 1960s when it was purchased by the State of Wisconsin for $10,500 to widen Ryan Road.

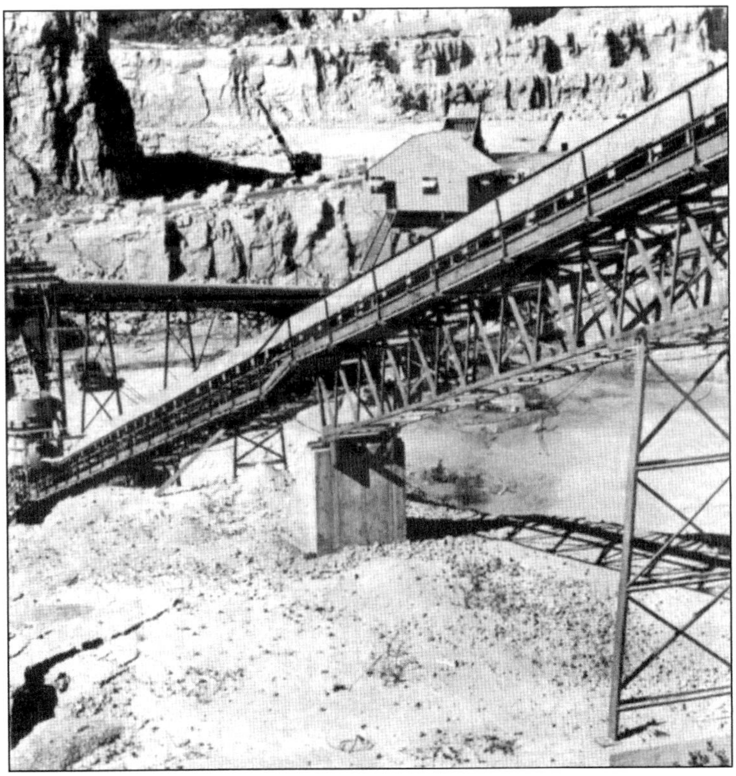

A huge conveyor carried crushed limestone to the top of this Franklin quarry located south of Rawson Avenue. The sand and gravel pit was located behind the William Folack farm on South Sixty-eighth Street and was opened by Jim Buckley in 1941. Buckley paid Folack a percentage for every yard of gravel removed. After a dispute, Folack turned his operation over to Dale Dawson and Elmer Garrity, who named it Franklin Stone.

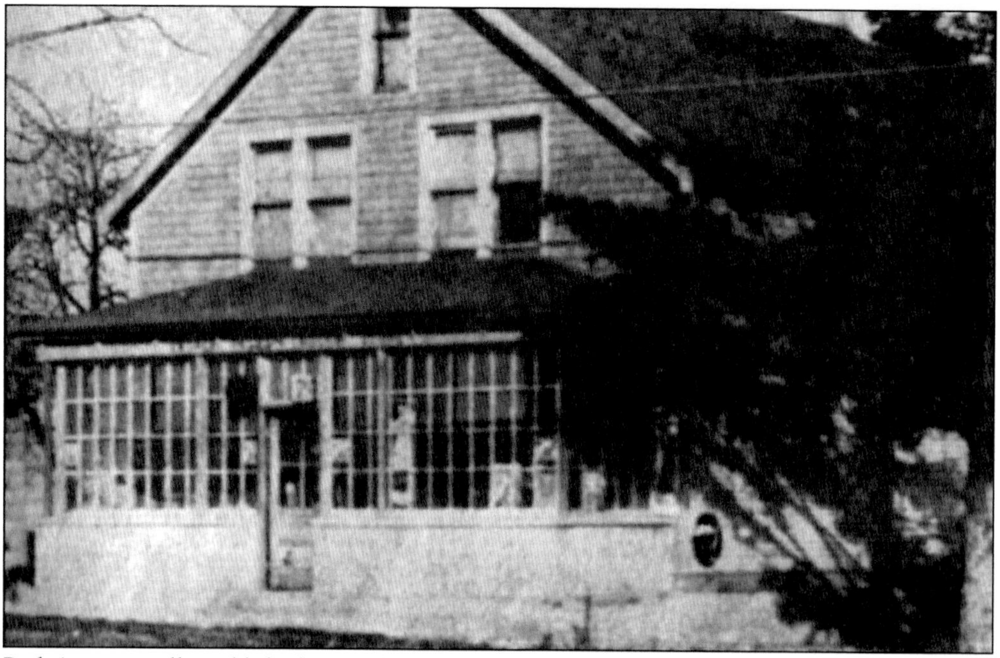

Poths's was a well-established general store on the corner of Rawson Avenue and Seventy-sixth Street from 1916 to 1955. Operated by Andrew Poths and his wife, the store carried all varieties of nonperishable items, from kerosene and vinegar to canned foods, coffee, and penny candy. (Courtesy of Tri-Town News.)

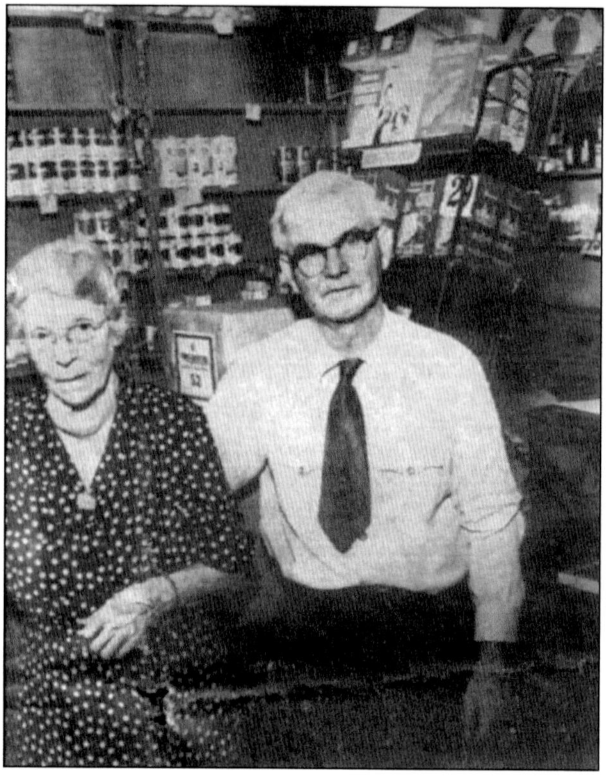

After Andrew Poths died in 1938, the store was run by his son, Peter, and Mrs. Poths's sister, Jennie Bierbach. The store was finally forced to close in 1955 when it was torn down for the widening of Rawson Avenue. (Courtesy of Tri-Town News.)

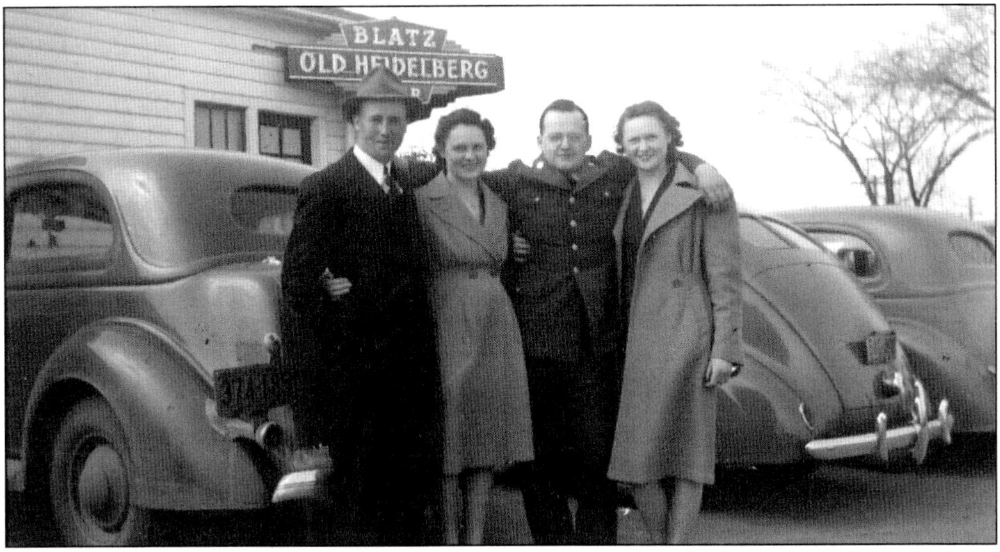

The White Dove was a popular Franklin hangout for decades. On leave from the U.S. Army in 1941, Delbert "Butch" Schmidt poses with his girlfriend, Lucille Ludwig (far right), her sister Marie, and Marie's husband, Harold Schumacher. Marie and Lucille, who grew up on the Ludwig farm on Sixty-eighth Street and attended Green Valley School, both had their eighth-grade graduation ceremonies held at the White Dove.

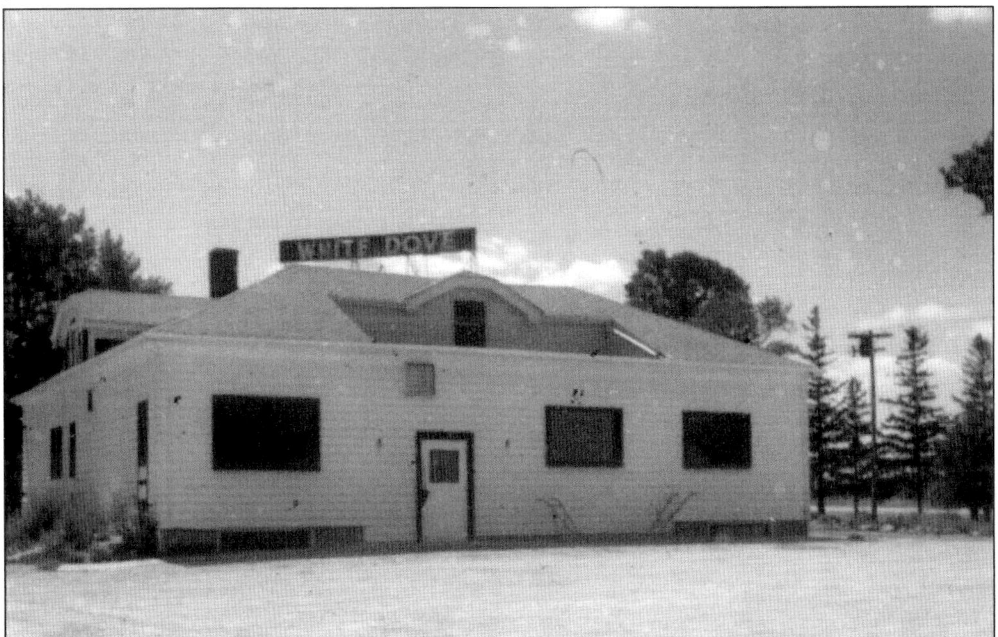

Undergoing a face-lift in 1964 is the White Dove located at Loomis Road and South Seventy-sixth Street. The tavern and dance hall were built in 1928 by Ed and Marie Stremke. The location was originally a post office where a Native American, White Dove, picked up mail on his pony express route to Waterford. It then became the site of Hoppel's Blacksmith Shop before the Stremkes built the tavern. It was torn down after the department of transportation decided to widen Seventy-sixth Street.

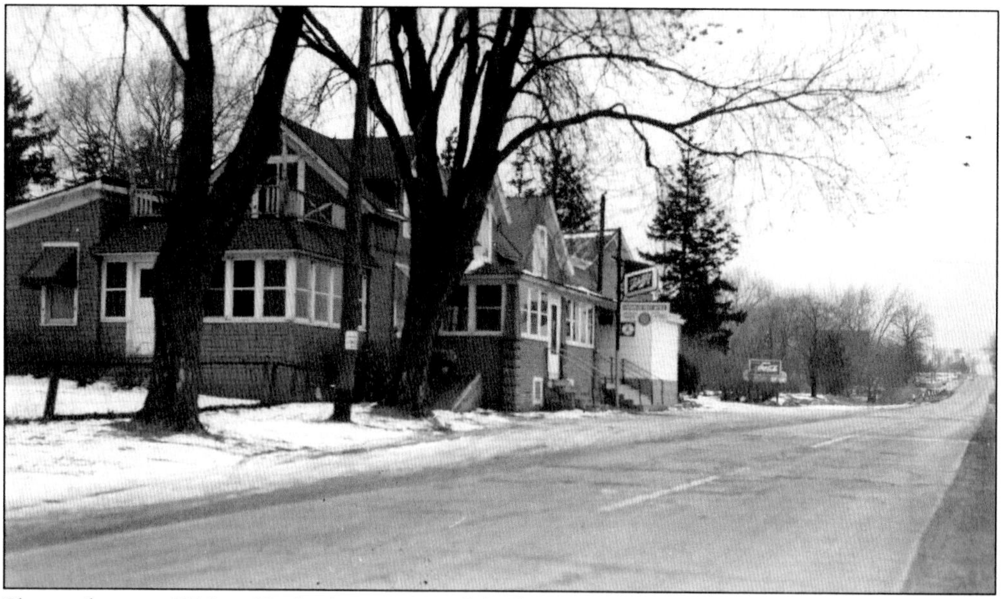

Shown here is Walter Heiden's tavern and hall in 1924. It was built along Center Street (Seventy-sixth Street) just south of Ryan Road and served several purposes, including eighth-grade graduation ceremonies for children attending one-room schools. During the 1950s, it became the Wildwood Inn, and Elmer Acker's barn to the north housed Franklin's first fire engine. Emergency calls went to Heiden, who would dispatch calls to Chief Acker and his volunteer firemen. Today the Wildwood Inn is known as the Hideaway.

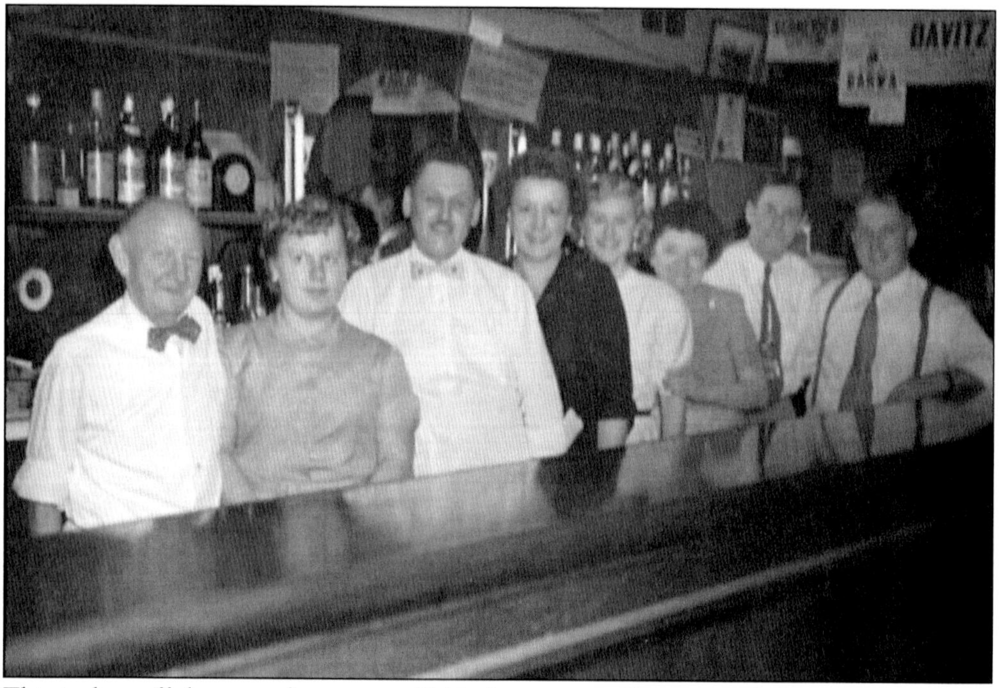

This is the staff that served patrons at Heiden's tavern on Seventy-sixth Street in 1957. They are (from left to right) Ben Gross, Joanne Kania, Walter Grusnick, ? Grusnick, an unidentified woman, Hilda Heiden, owner Walter Heiden, and Roy Klingbeil.

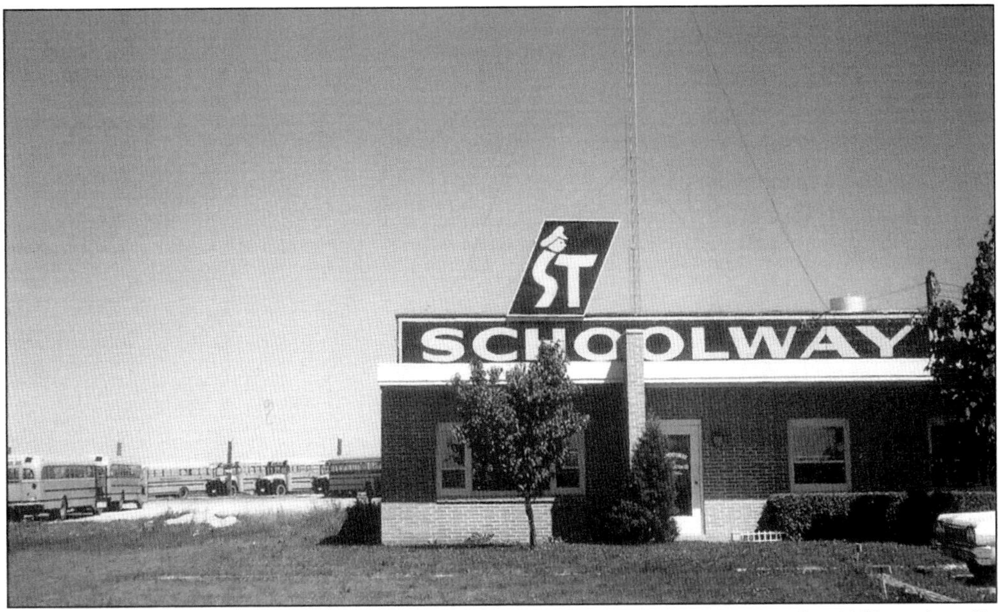

The Schoolway Bus Company was established on Forest Home Avenue in the 1950s to handle transportation of students in the newly created Franklin School District 5 in 1953. Schoolway buses served the Franklin, Greendale, Greenfield, and Hales Corners School Districts for over 30 years.

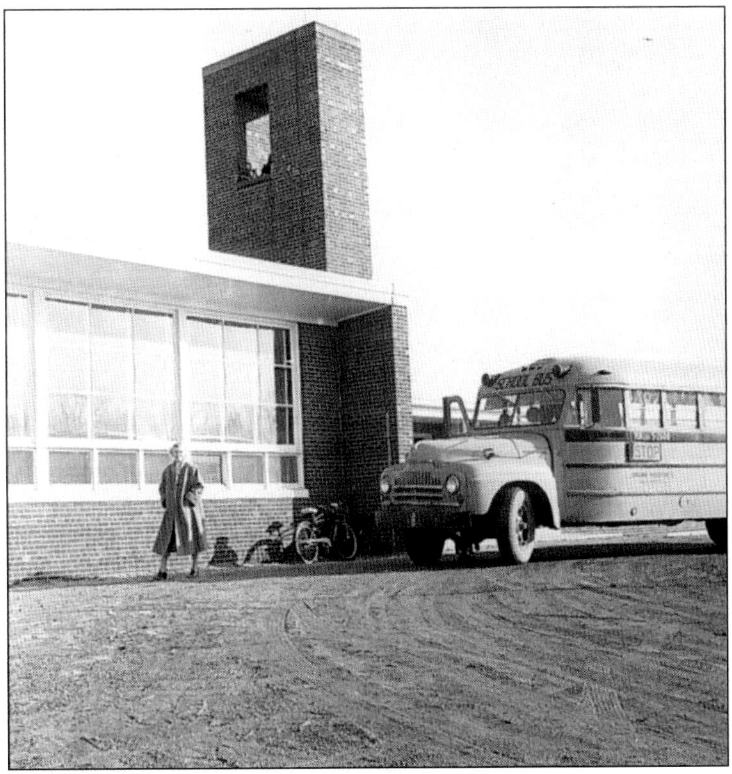

Getting picked up at home and dropped off at school was a new experience for Franklin students who were used to walking prior to the 1950s. Here a Schoolway bus delivers kids to the front door of Ben Franklin School in 1953 before the new school had a paved driveway.

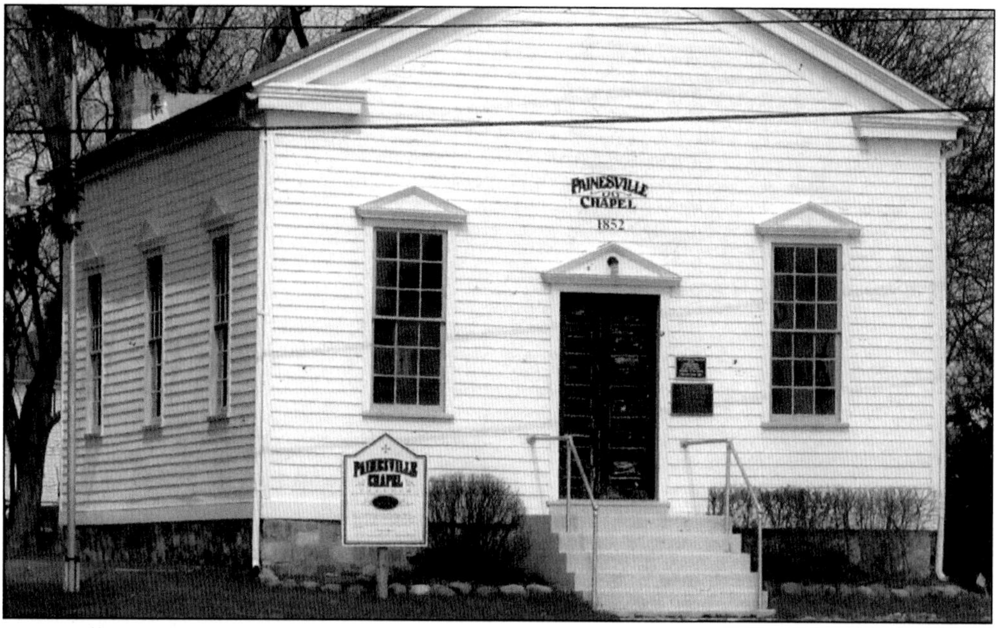

Painesville was a community surrounding the crossroads of Highway 41 (South Twenty-seventh Street) and Highway 100 (Ryan Road). The Painesville Chapel was built by the First Free Christian Congregation on one and one-eighth acres where a cemetery was started in February 1851. It was decided to name the meeting hall after Thomas Paine. The hall cost $370 to build and was restored in 1942 at a cost of $1,200, which included a basement.

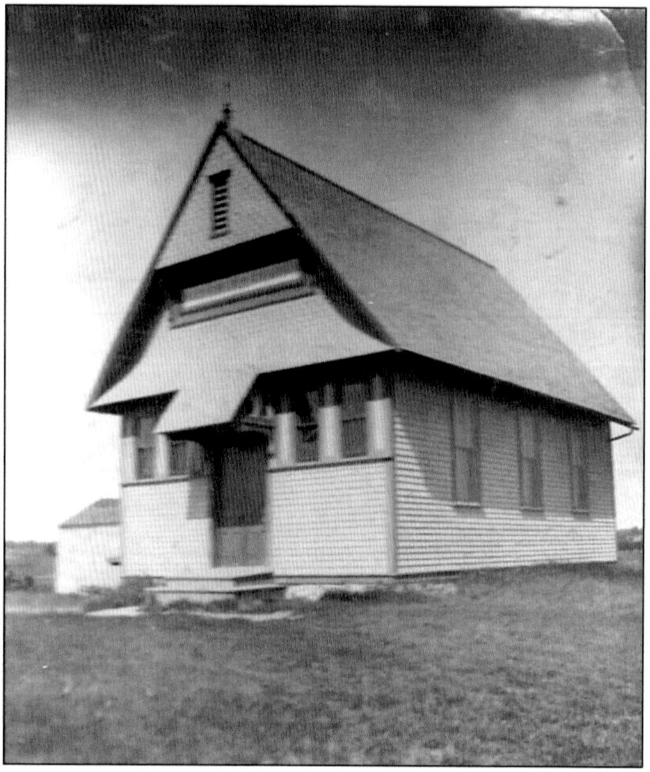

This building located at 9910 South Seventy-sixth Street began as the Reformed Church. It was constructed on property donated by Benjamin Baden in the late 1800s to serve a group of Dutch settlers in Franklin. In 1890, it was rebuilt by Cornelius Leenhouts, but over the next 25 years, the congregation dwindled until services were discontinued. The building reverted back to the Baden estate and was converted into a private residence.

St. James Catholic Church was established along Highway 41 (South Twenty-seventh Street) by a group of Franklin and Oak Creek farm families in 1857. Initially built on the east side of the street, St. James moved to the west side after seven acres of land were purchased in Franklin. The building shown here was the administration building for a World War II prisoner of war camp at the county airport. In 1966, a new St. James church was built.

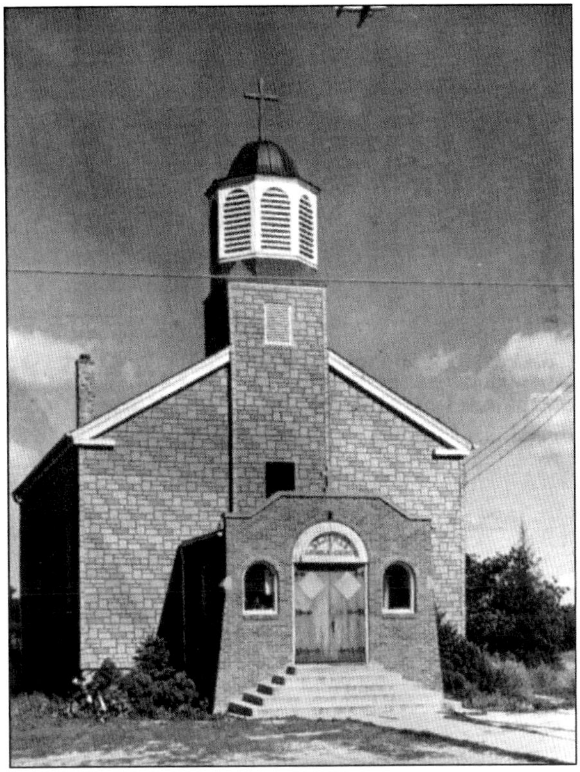

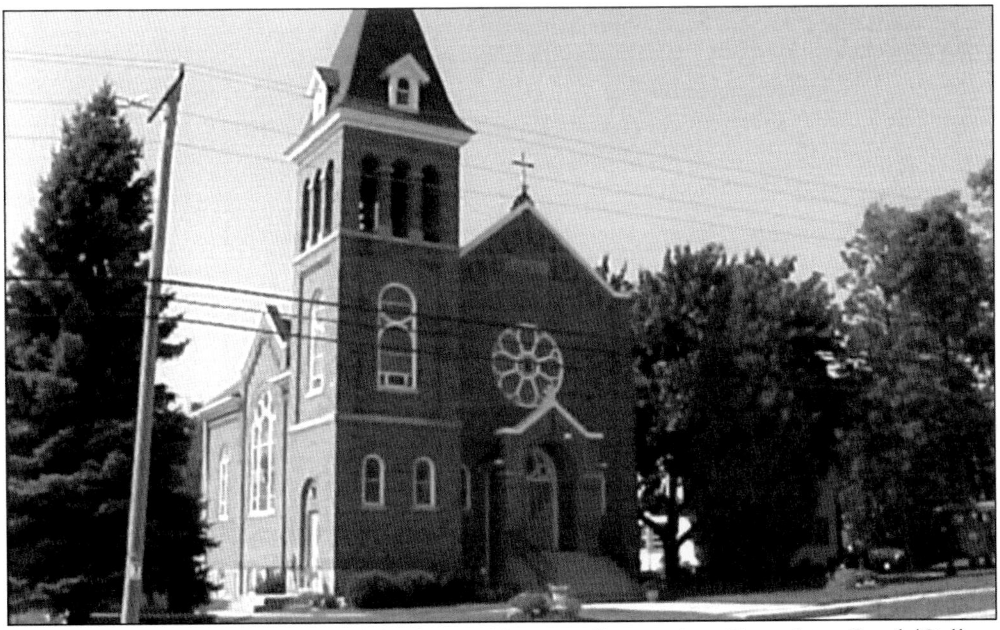

St. Paul's Lutheran Church, established in 1865, originally stood on Town Line Road (College Avenue). A German-language school was added in 1887. In 1916, the congregation voted to build a new church (shown here) on Smith Road (South Fifty-first Street), and the old school was moved to that location in 1950. The first English-speaking services were conducted in 1925. In 1964, St. Paul's began raising funds to build a new school, which opened in 1966.

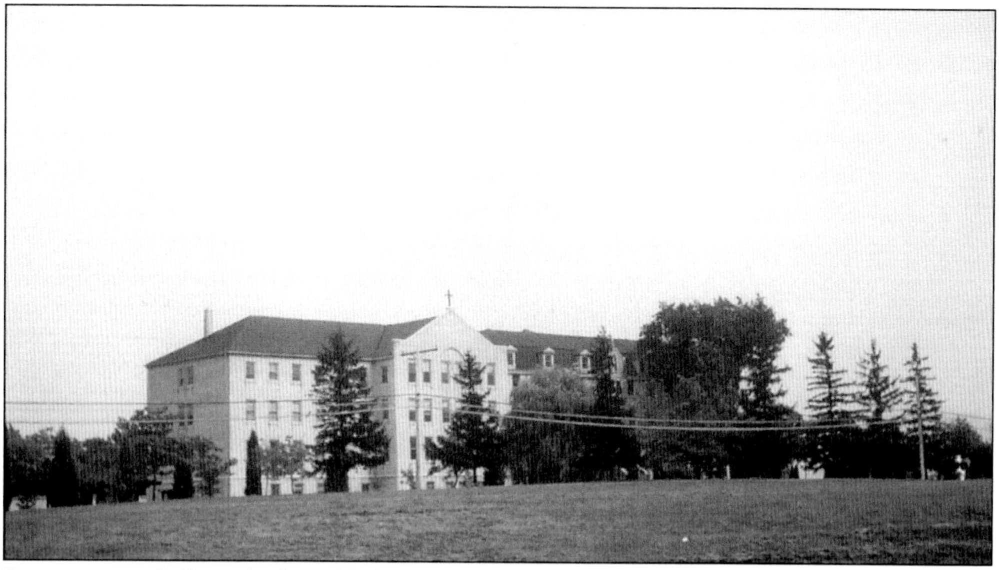

Sitting atop a hill overlooking Highway 100 was the Sacred Heart Monastery located south of Rawson Avenue along Lovers Lane Road. Originally the Perpetual Rosary Convent for the Dominican Sisters, it was purchased by the Sacred Heart Fathers and Brothers in 1925. The third floor was added during the 1930s and a north wing in the 1940s. It served as a seminary for men pursuing priesthood until a monastery was built across from it in 1968.

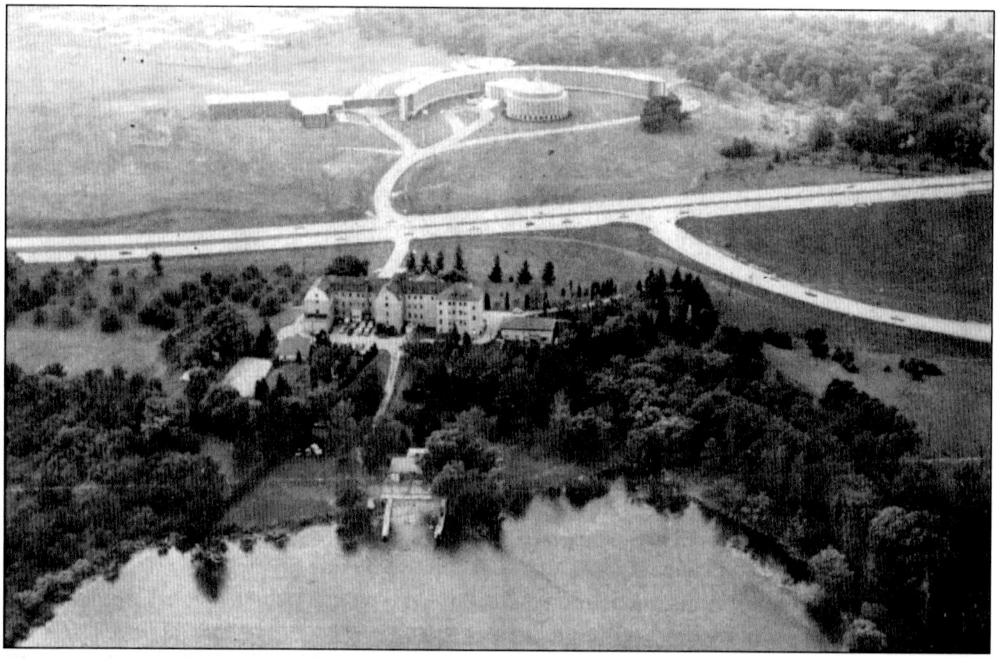

This aerial view shows the old Sacred Heart Monastery (bottom) and the one that replaced it in 1968. Located west of Highway 100, the distinctive new monastery with the imposing gold crown was designed by Henry R. Slaby Architects of Milwaukee. Slaby incorporated rounded walls to utilize the contour of the land and avoid the long straight corridors usually found in institutional buildings. In 1972, the name was changed to Sacred Heart School of Theology. It is the largest of two U.S. seminaries devoted to preparing men for the priesthood.

Four

POLITICS AND PROTECTION

Franklin's first town meeting was held in the home of J. C. Loomis on April 5, 1842. Town meetings continued to be held in private homes or public buildings until 1884 when town administrators pledged $900 to construct a town hall along Ryan Road.

Franklin was essentially a network of farm families until the 1950s. In August 1956, Franklin residents voted to incorporate as a city, and that October they elected their first mayor, Robert G. MacDonald, along with three aldermen and two justices of the peace. A fire and police commission was established in 1957.

A volunteer fire department was formed under Chief Elmer Acker, but law and order remained under the domain of the Milwaukee County Sheriff's Department. Franklin's roads were patrolled by Constable George Davitz, much like Sheriff Andy Taylor of Mayberry. A police department was established in 1964.

As an offshoot of the cold war, the United States Department of Defense embarked on an antinuclear defense system around major cities and Milwaukee was one of them. During the 1950s, Franklin had the distinction of serving as one of the sites. Nike missiles were stored underground in concrete silos off Sixtieth Street south of Ryan Road. A radar tracking station was set up on grounds next to the Milwaukee County House of Correction.

As Franklin struggled to balance growth with economic development, the city often found itself making headlines in Milwaukee newspapers under the turbulent leadership of Mayor Ted Fadrow during the 1960s. He stepped aside in 1970 but ran again in 1976 and remained in office until he lost the 1986 election to Mark Miazga by 128 votes.

During the 1980s, Franklin's population expanded by nearly 5,000, but commercial and economic growth was not keeping pace. Fred Klimetz sought to give the city direction and was elected mayor in 1990. Like Fadrow, Klimetz stepped down in 1998 but returned as mayor from 1999 to 2005. Since then Tom Taylor has supervised Franklin's economic expansion. The population has surpassed 32,500 with a median household income of $78,470. The city's home ownership rate is 78 percent, which is 10 percent higher than the state average.

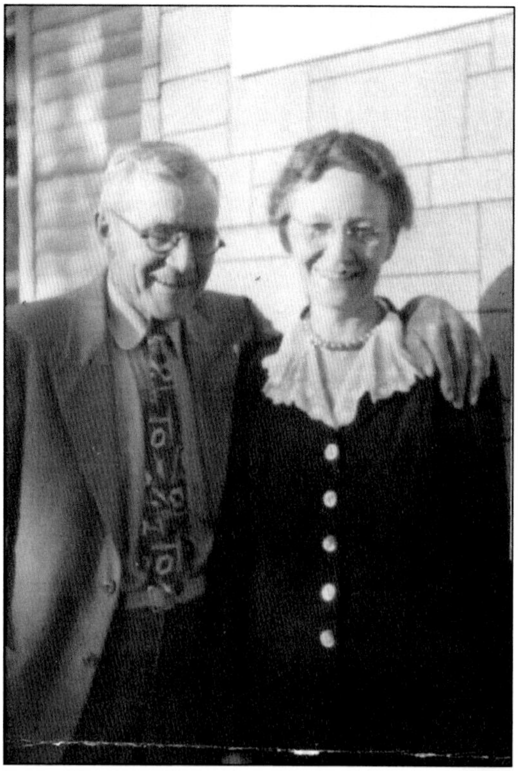

Edward Barg and his wife, the former Annette Meyer, ran a farm on Smith Road (Fifty-first Street) and celebrated their 50th wedding anniversary in July 1958. Edward Barg played a key figure in Franklin politics, serving as town clerk for 34 years.

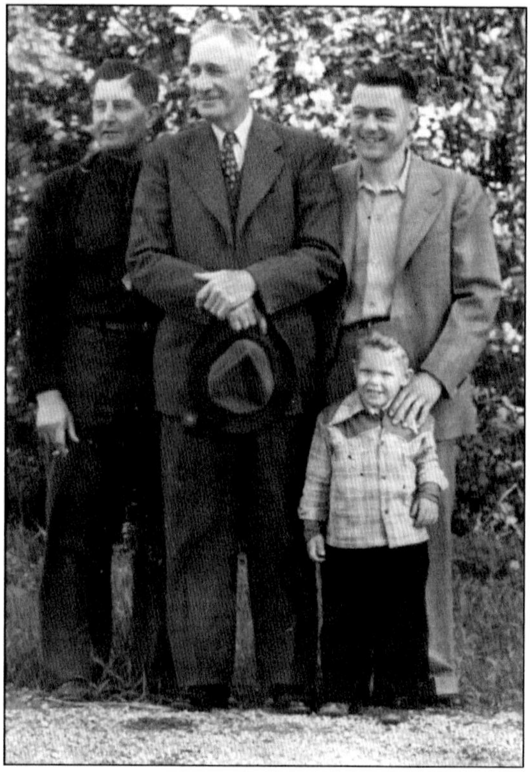

Serving as administrators for the Town of Franklin during its formative years in the 1940s were (from left to right) supervisor Joseph Schweitzer, town chairman George Shields, and supervisor David Mayer with his son. Shields was town chairman from 1928 to 1930 and again from 1940 to 1952. Mayer was elected to the town board in 1948 and served on various city boards and commissions for more than 40 years. Franklin's public works facility was named in his honor.

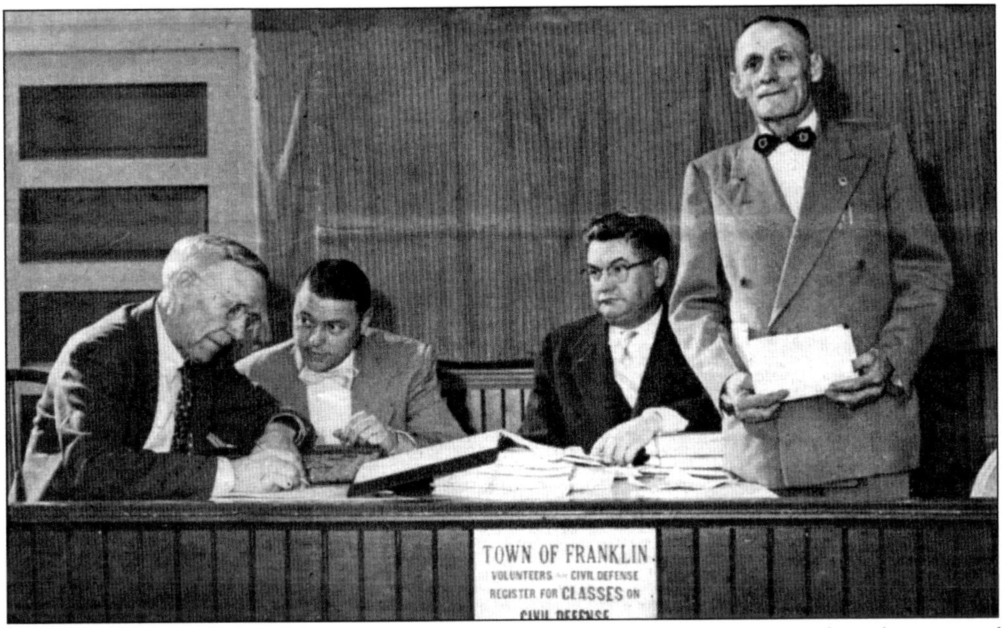

Presiding over a town meeting in April 1954 is Thomas Godsell, who served as chairman of the Franklin town board from 1952 until 1956. He would call the meeting to order by rapping his knuckles on a wooden railing. Joining Godsell on the town hall stage are (from left to right) town clerk Edward Barg, town supervisor David Mayer, and town attorney C. J. O'Brien. (Courtesy of Milwaukee Journal.)

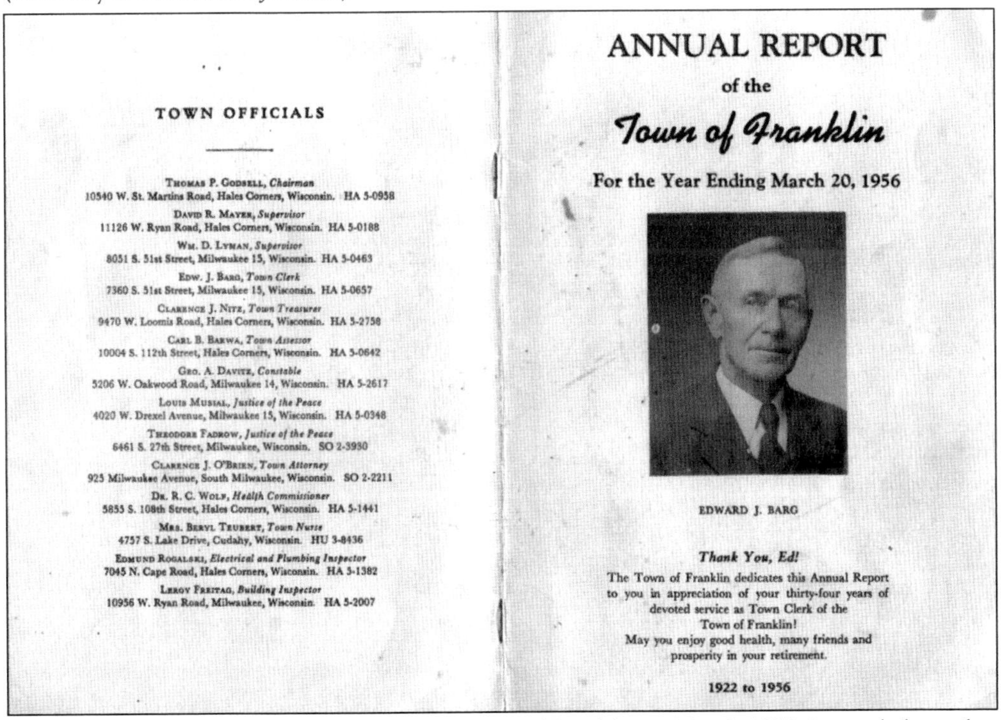

TOWN OFFICIALS

THOMAS P. GODSELL, *Chairman*
10540 W. St. Martins Road, Hales Corners, Wisconsin. HA 5-0958

DAVID R. MAYER, *Supervisor*
11126 W. Ryan Road, Hales Corners, Wisconsin. HA 5-0188

WM. D. LYMAN, *Supervisor*
8051 S. 51st Street, Milwaukee 15, Wisconsin. HA 5-0463

EDW. J. BARG, *Town Clerk*
7360 S. 51st Street, Milwaukee 15, Wisconsin. HA 5-0657

CLARENCE J. NITZ, *Town Treasurer*
9470 W. Loomis Road, Hales Corners, Wisconsin. HA 5-2758

CARL B. BARWA, *Town Assessor*
10004 S. 112th Street, Hales Corners, Wisconsin. HA 5-0642

GEO. A. DAVITZ, *Constable*
5206 W. Oakwood Road, Milwaukee 14, Wisconsin. HA 5-2617

LOUIS MUSIAL, *Justice of the Peace*
4020 W. Drexel Avenue, Milwaukee 15, Wisconsin. HA 5-0348

THEODORE FADROW, *Justice of the Peace*
6461 S. 27th Street, Milwaukee, Wisconsin. SO 2-3930

CLARENCE J. O'BRIEN, *Town Attorney*
925 Milwaukee Avenue, South Milwaukee, Wisconsin. SO 2-2211

DR. R. C. WOLF, *Health Commissioner*
5855 S. 108th Street, Hales Corners, Wisconsin. HA 5-1441

MRS. BERYL TEUBERT, *Town Nurse*
4757 S. Lake Drive, Cudahy, Wisconsin. HU 3-8436

EDMUND ROGALSKI, *Electrical and Plumbing Inspector*
7045 N. Cape Road, Hales Corners, Wisconsin. HA 5-1382

LEROY FREITAG, *Building Inspector*
10956 W. Ryan Road, Milwaukee, Wisconsin. HA 5-2007

ANNUAL REPORT

of the

Town of Franklin

For the Year Ending March 20, 1956

EDWARD J. BARG

Thank You, Ed!

The Town of Franklin dedicates this Annual Report to you in appreciation of your thirty-four years of devoted service as Town Clerk of the Town of Franklin!
May you enjoy good health, many friends and prosperity in your retirement.

1922 to 1956

Shown here is the last annual report for the town of Franklin in March 1956. It was dedicated to Edward Barg in recognition of his 34 years as town clerk from 1922 to 1956.

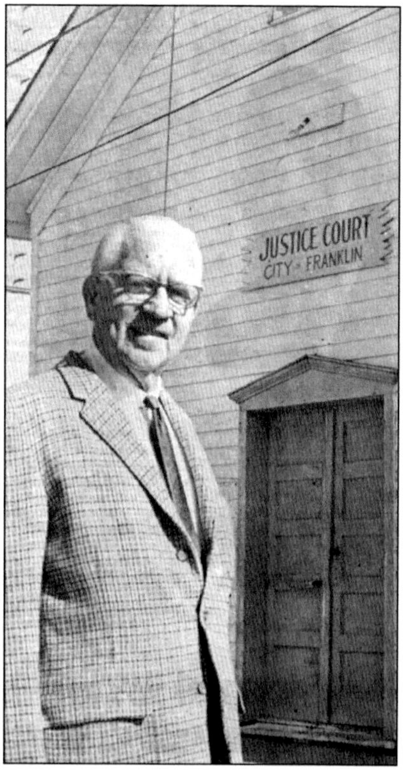

Elected Franklin's first mayor in 1956 was Robert G. MacDonald, who upset Thomas Godsell in the October election, 1,124 votes to 779. A vice president for the Heil Corporation, MacDonald used his administrative skills to guide Franklin through its formative years as a city. He served as mayor until 1960. (Courtesy of Franklin Hub.)

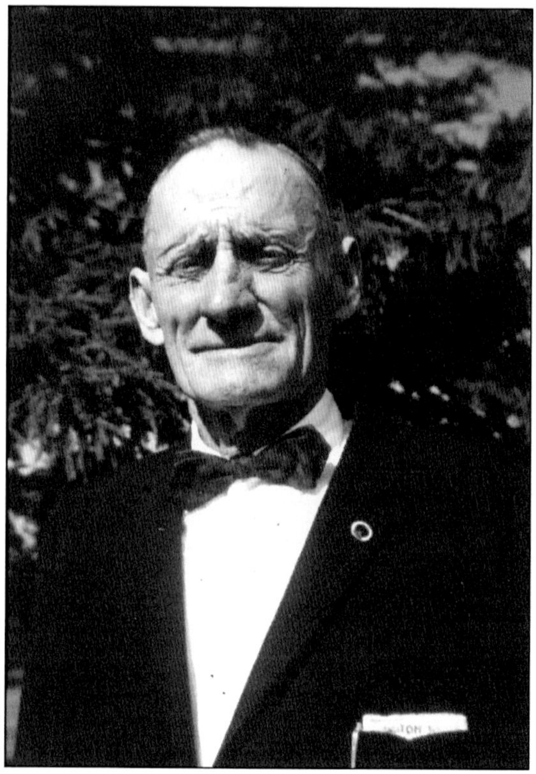

Thomas Godsell followed George Shields as town chairman in 1949 and had a long career in Franklin politics. He helped lead efforts to incorporate Franklin as a city, organize Franklin's first fire department, and move the Hales Corners Fair to St. Martins in 1958. He lost a bid to become Franklin's first mayor to Robert G. MacDonald, however, in 1956.

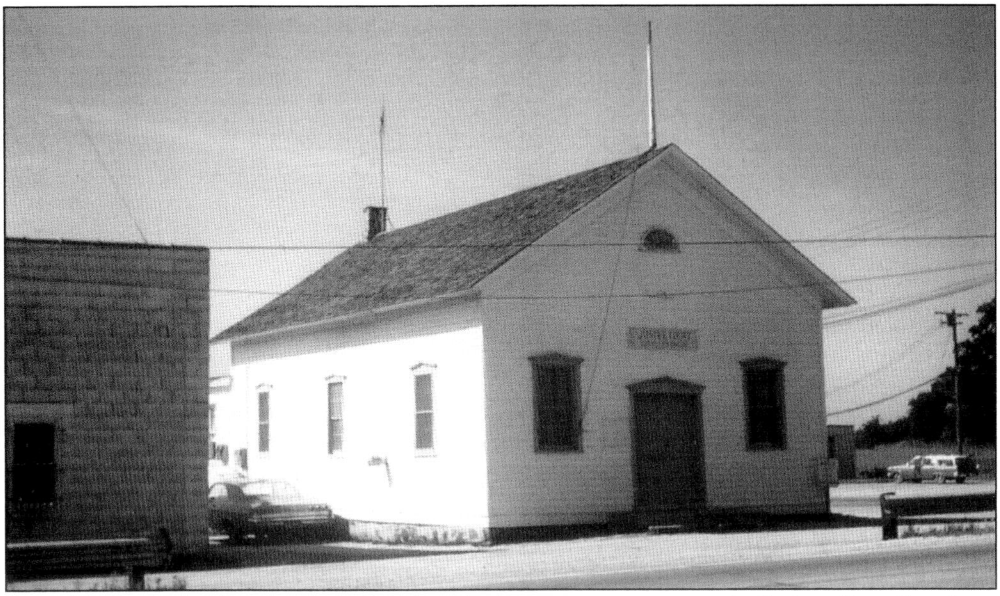

In November 1884, the town board pledged $900 to construct a town hall along Ryan Road just west of Center Street (Seventy-sixth Street), and Franklin began holding government activities there on April 6, 1886. It ceased to function as a local government meeting place after Franklin was incorporated as a city on August 15, 1956, but continued in other capacities such as the engineering department, police department, and justice court. It was closed for good in 1970 and was moved to Lions Legend Park in 1976 by Franklin's bicentennial commission.

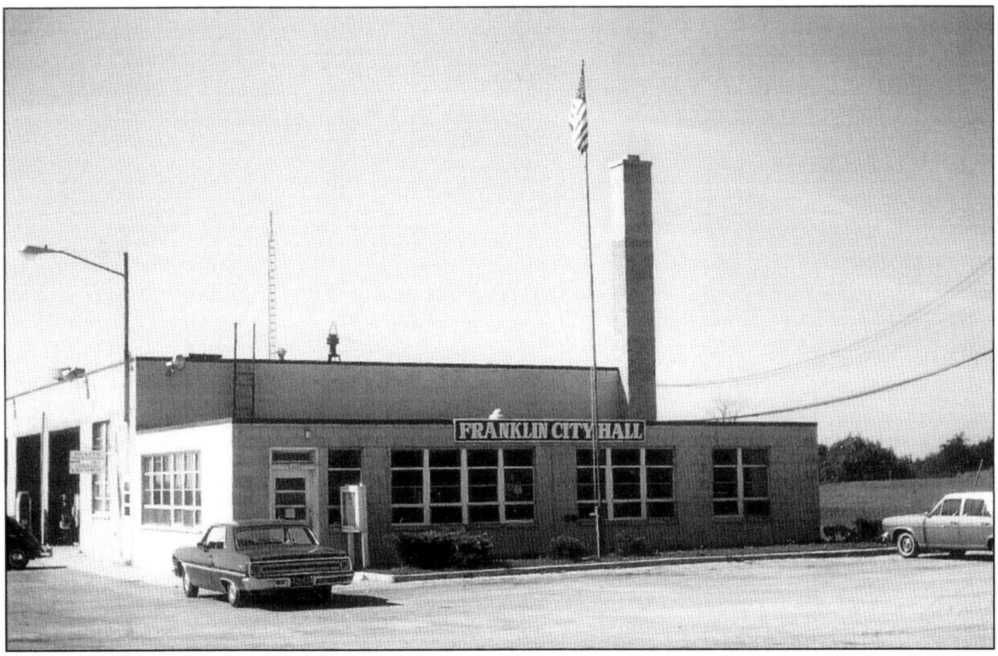

After Franklin incorporated as a city in 1956, government activities shifted from the old town hall to this new municipal building next door that served Franklin government for 14 years. When a new civic administration building opened along Loomis Road in 1971, this building became the public works garage.

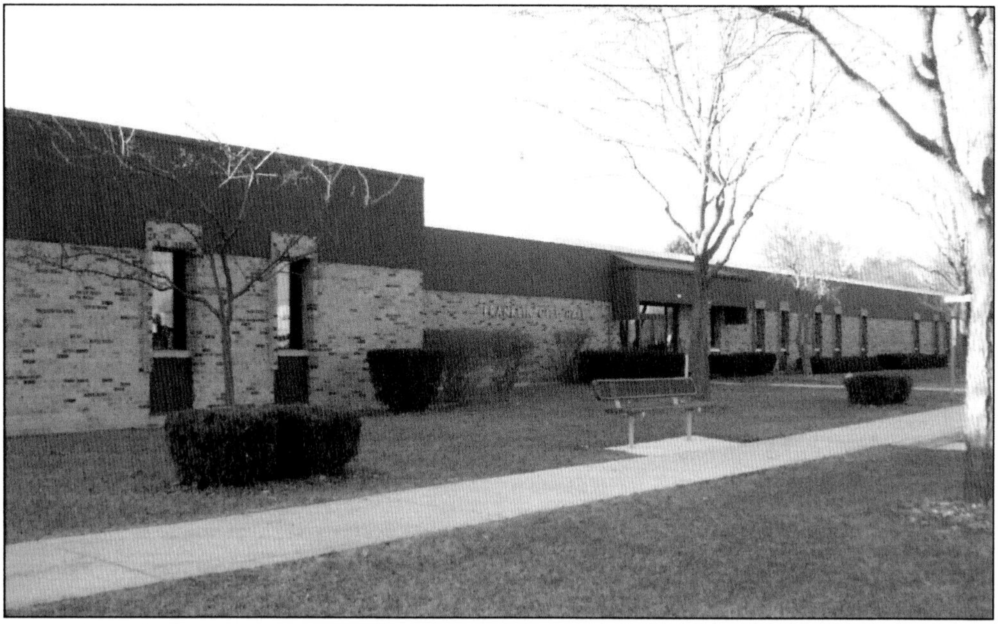

Ground was broken for a new two-level Franklin administration building in 1970 on Loomis Road just south of Drexel Avenue, and it opened a year later when John Hyde was elected mayor. The building reflected the needs of a growing city. It included offices for the mayor, engineering department, police department, health department, and assessor, along with a common council chambers/municipal court, community meeting room, and library.

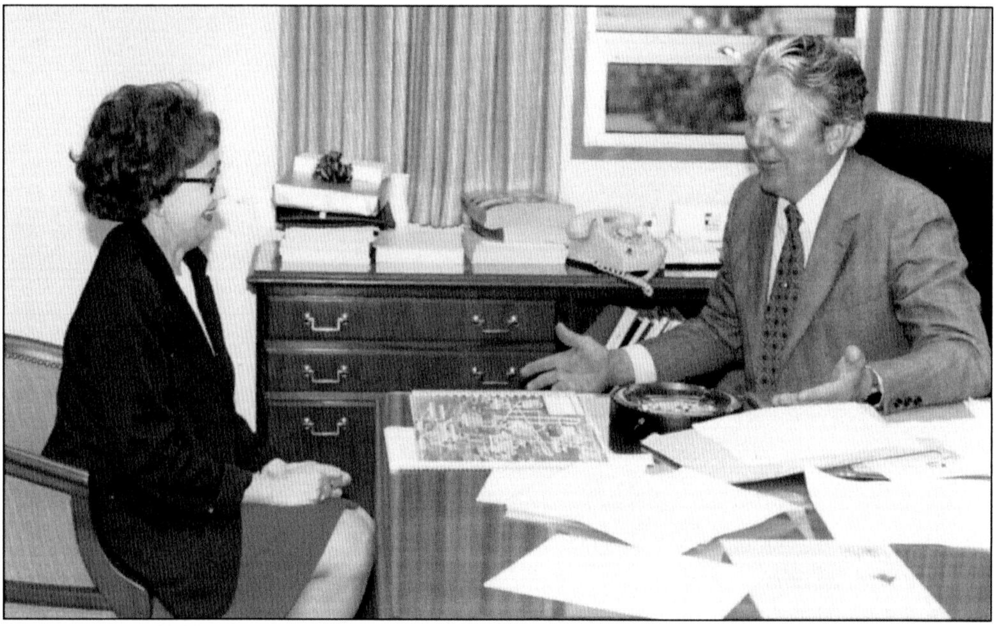

Conferring with deputy city clerk Frances Jecke-Meyer is Franklin mayor Ted Fadrow. Generally acknowledged as Franklin's most colorful politician, Fadrow was elected alderman in 1958 and became mayor in 1962 when the city was still 80 percent farmland. He was reelected mayor in 1976 and served another 10 years before he was unseated by his harshest critic on the common council, Mark Miazga, in 1986.

An attorney, Fred Klimetz moved to Franklin in 1981 and ran for mayor in 1990 with the goal of developing a master plan to balance the city's commercial and industrial growth. He defeated incumbent Mark Miazga and held the office until announcing his retirement in 1998. However, Klimetz returned as mayor through a recall election in 1999 and held the post until 2005. During his second term, Franklin built a new library, police station, and fire station.

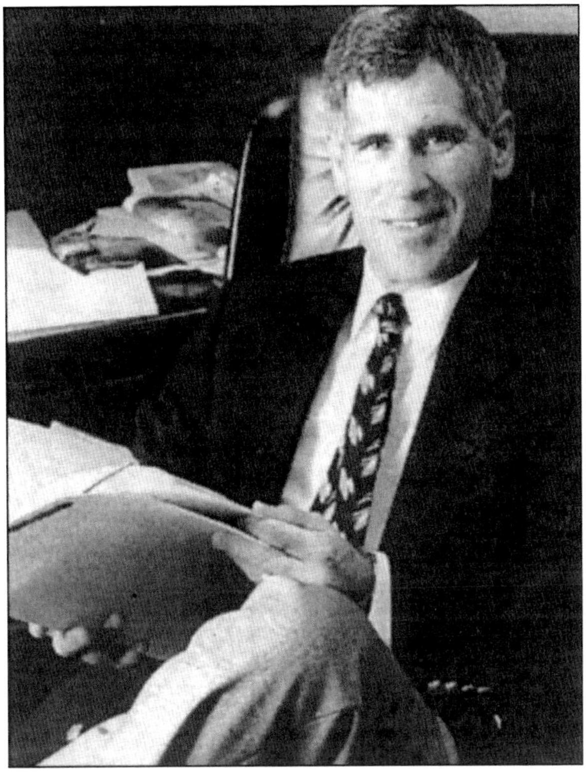

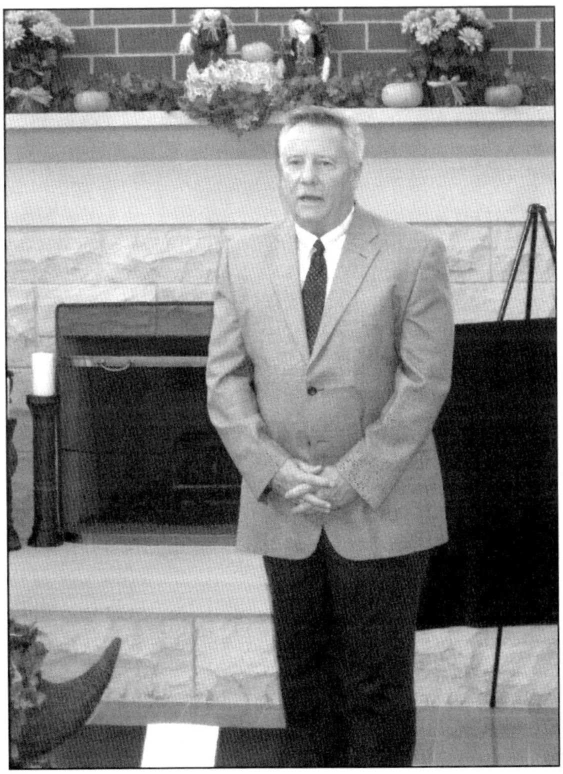

After serving as an alderman, Tom Taylor was elected Franklin mayor in 2005. He served as chairman of the plan commission and worked to improve city services as Franklin's population surpassed 32,000. In 2006, Taylor promoted Franklin's 50th anniversary as a city and continued to support the community's historical preservation efforts. He was elected mayor for a second term in 2008.

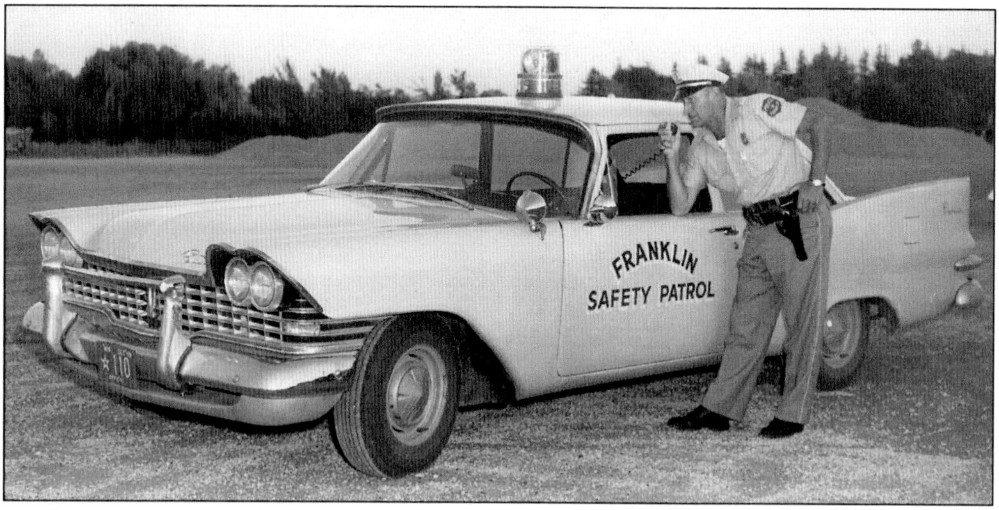

Until the city established its own police department in January 1964, law and order on Franklin roads was the solitary domain of Constable George Davitz. Throughout the 1950s, he was well known as the town's law enforcement agent. Second- and third-shift patrol officers were furnished by the Milwaukee County Sheriff's Department.

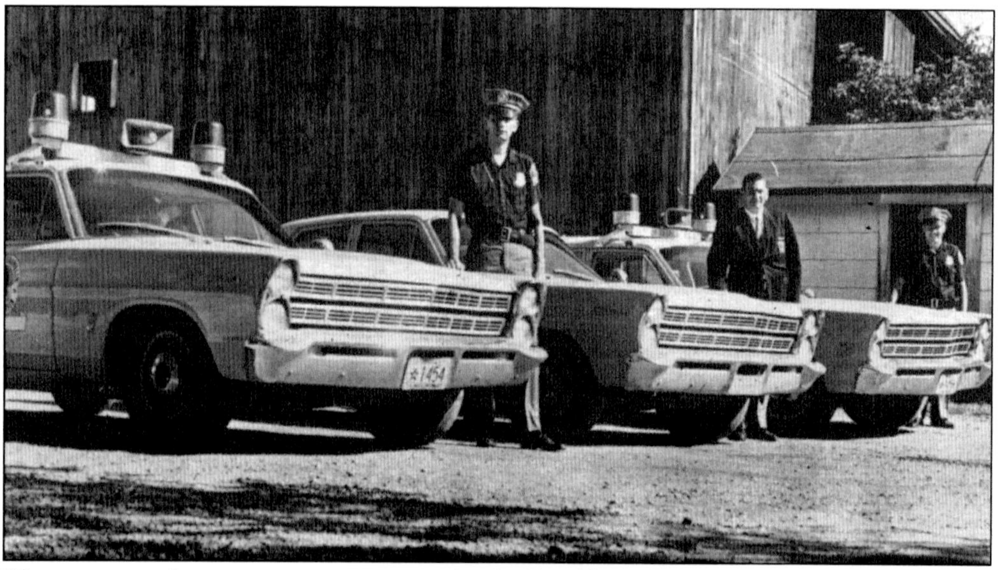

Three new squad cars were put into service by the Franklin Police Department in August 1967. Posing with the cars are (from left to right) patrolman Robert Petermann, police chief Harold Roach, and patrolman Doug Luttrell. Budgeting enough patrol cars and officers was a constant battle for Franklin's government. Roach had six officers when he became police chief in 1964. By 1971, the number had grown to 26. (Courtesy of Franklin Hub.)

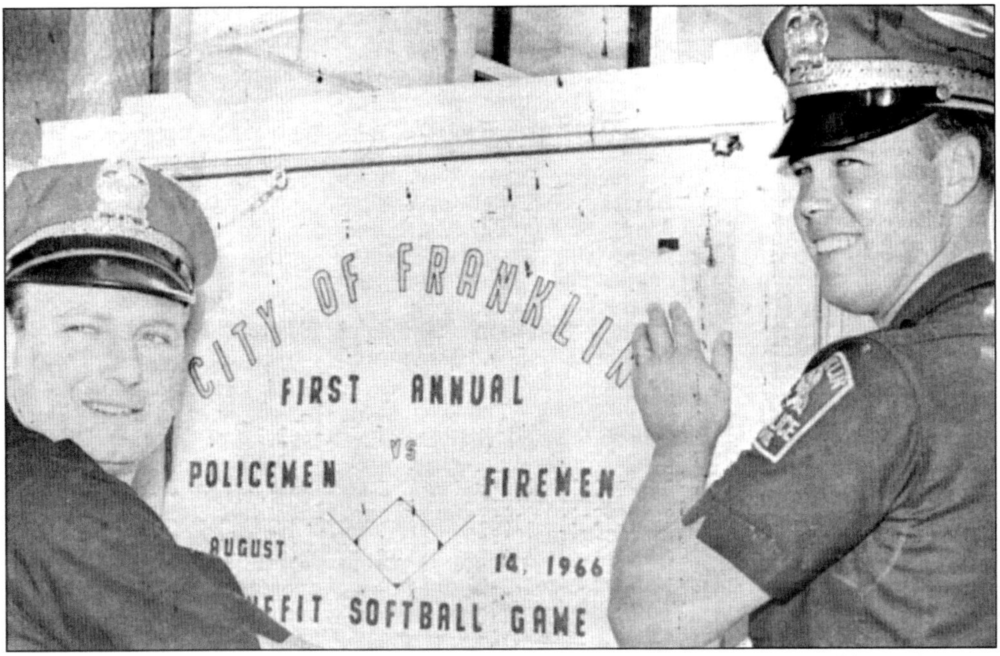

Putting up a poster to promote the first benefit softball game between Franklin policemen and firefighters are officers Dan Loomis (left) and Don Hareng. The interdepartmental event was scheduled for August 14, 1966, on the Little League diamond behind the Franklin Fire Department. (Courtesy of Franklin Hub.)

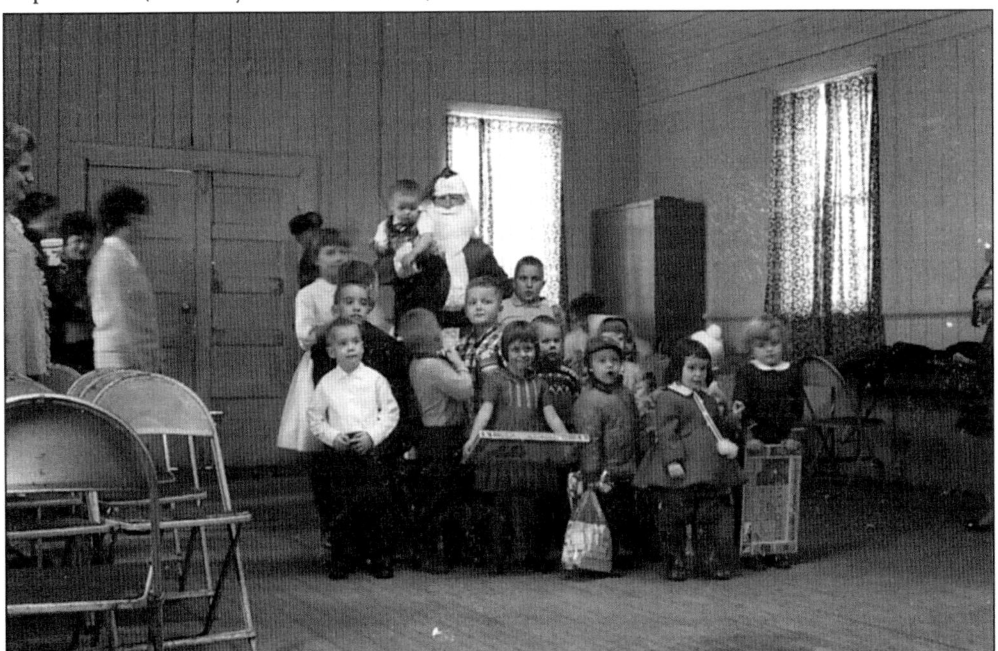

Santa Claus visited Franklin's old town hall in December 1965 as the guest of the Franklin Police Department. He presented gifts to children of the police officers. (Courtesy of Franklin Police Department.)

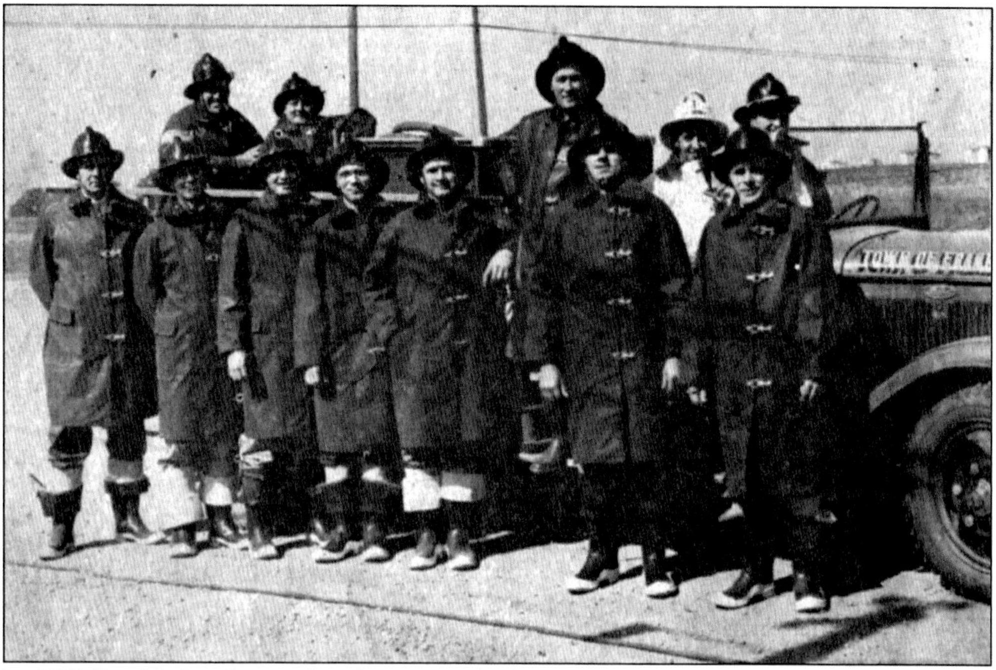

In 1955, Franklin's volunteer fire department had one engine, a 1934 Ford purchased from the Union Grove Fire Department. It was stored in a barn owned by Fire Chief Elmer Acker. Posing proudly with the fire truck are, from left to right, (first row) Elmer Delikat, James Ashley, Erwin Bosch, William Houtler, Myron Benning, Joe Mainus, and Robert Lindner; (second row) Harvey Mahr, Clement Piotrowski, Marvin Hareng, Fire Chief Acker, and Glen Zamjahn. (Courtesy of Tri-Town News.)

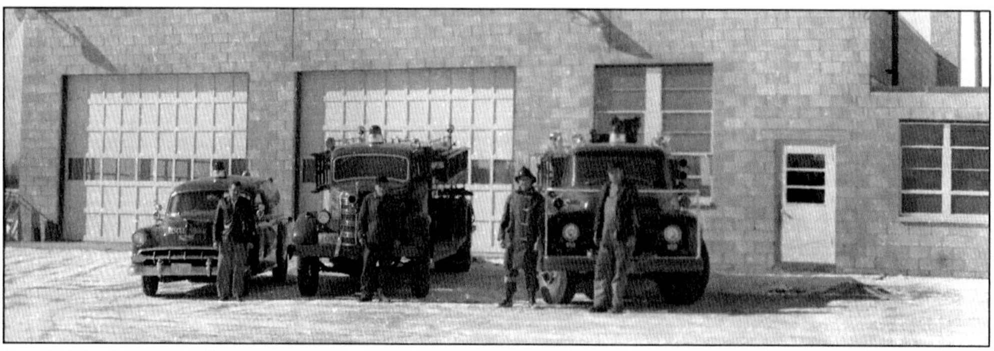

By 1960, the Franklin Fire Department had upgraded to owning three vehicles, including a rescue squad, and had a new fire station built next to city hall on Ryan Road.

Five

Sports and Leisure

One of the advantages of living in the rural community is that it allows plenty of space for various forms of recreation not confined by city blocks. As the farms achieved their limits of utility, Franklin's wide expanse gave rise to recreational activities not found in neighboring communities. Covering 36 square miles, Franklin featured two airports, three golf courses, a racetrack, baseball fields, and two outdoor theaters.

Among them was Rainbow Airport based along Seventy-sixth Street south of Ryan Road, a base for small privately owned aircraft. Franklin also became home to the Experimental Aircraft Association (EAA) located along Forest Home Avenue. The facility housed an air education museum.

Two popular Franklin venues on Saturday nights were the 41 Twin Outdoor Theater and the Hales Corners Speedway. The 41 Twin, located along Highway 41 (South Twenty-seventh Street) north of Drexel Avenue, was a popular destination for decades. Franklin, in fact, even had another smaller drive-in theater hidden off Ryan Road for a time, but it could not match the popularity of the 41 Twin, which actually added a third, separate screen. The 41 Twin also featured a go-kart track during the 1960s.

Sportsmen who enjoyed golf first had the option of playing a beautiful county course, Whitnall Park, and later Oakwood. During the 1960s, farmland between Sixty-eighth and Seventy-sixth Streets was sold and developed into the Tuckaway Country Club. From 1973 through 1994, Tuckaway hosted an annual professional tournament, the Greater Milwaukee Open.

For gearheads and race fans, the dirt track at Hales Corners Speedway on Highway 100 was a favorite venue and made local legends of area drivers who drove for the thrill of competition more than for monetary gain. For residents living near the speedway, the roaring engines on Saturday could be deafening and on a clear night could be heard miles away.

By the 1950s, most young boys were no longer tied to farm chores and often gathered in open fields or pastures to play pickup games of baseball. Organized ball became a reality when the Franklin Lions Club and the Franklin Volunteer Fire Department each developed a diamond and formed their own Little Leagues.

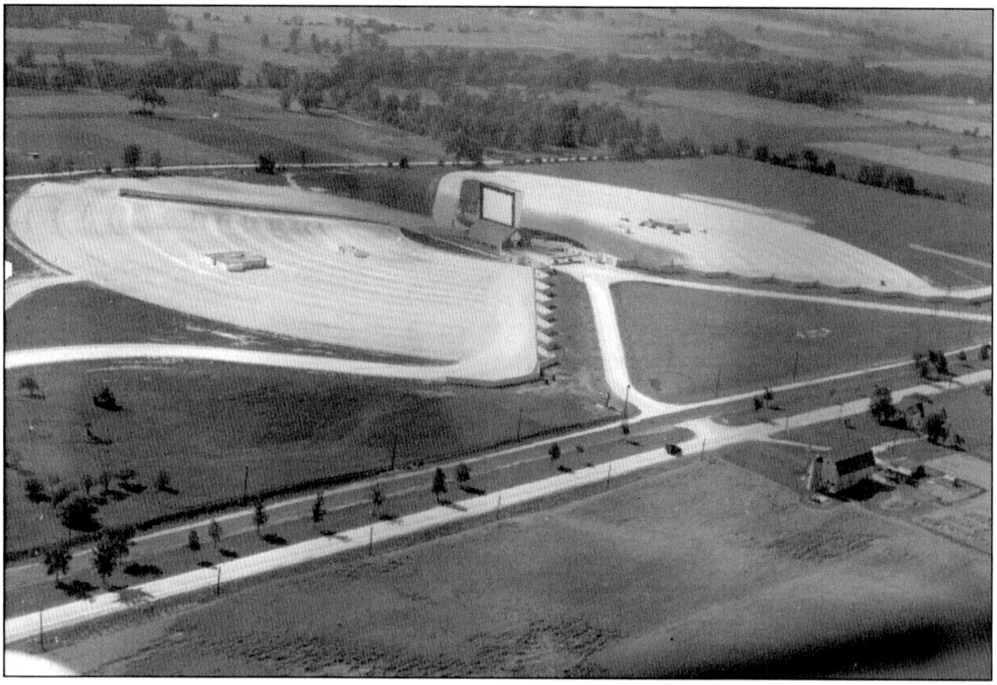

This is an aerial view of the 41 Twin Outdoor Theater as it appeared around 1950. At this point the screen tower had not been lengthened for CinemaScope film. To the south is Twenty-seventh Street (Highway 41). (Courtesy of Dale Lindner.)

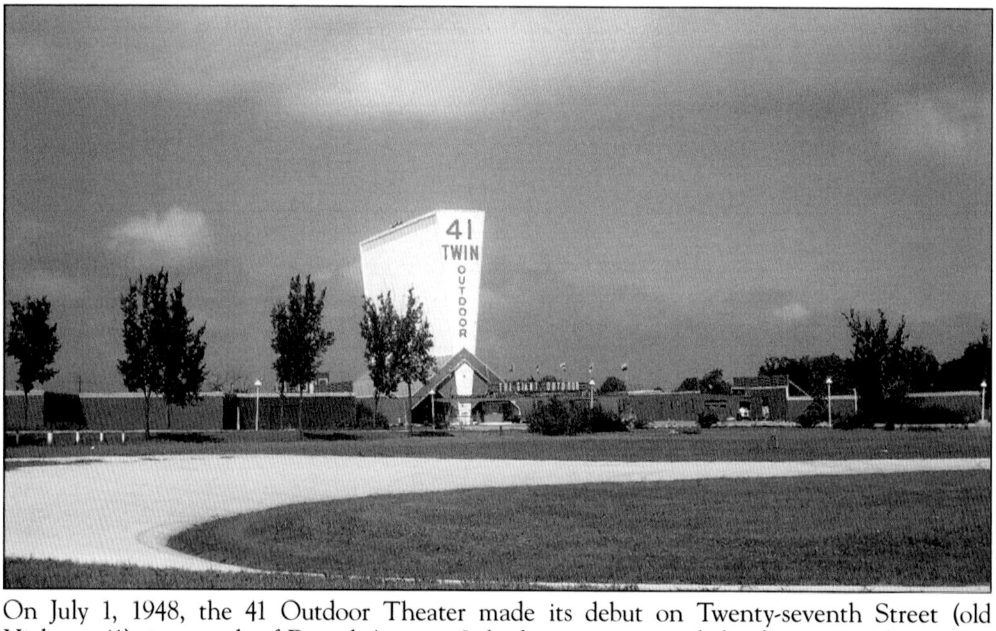

On July 1, 1948, the 41 Outdoor Theater made its debut on Twenty-seventh Street (old Highway 41), just north of Drexel Avenue. It had one screen, and the first movie shown was *Four Faces West*. Within two years it had screens facing north and south with concession stands in both parking lots. Two more screens were added in 1981. The 41 Twin remained Wisconsin's second-oldest outdoor theater until the property was purchased by the Northwestern Mutual Life Insurance Company and showed its last double feature in September 2001.

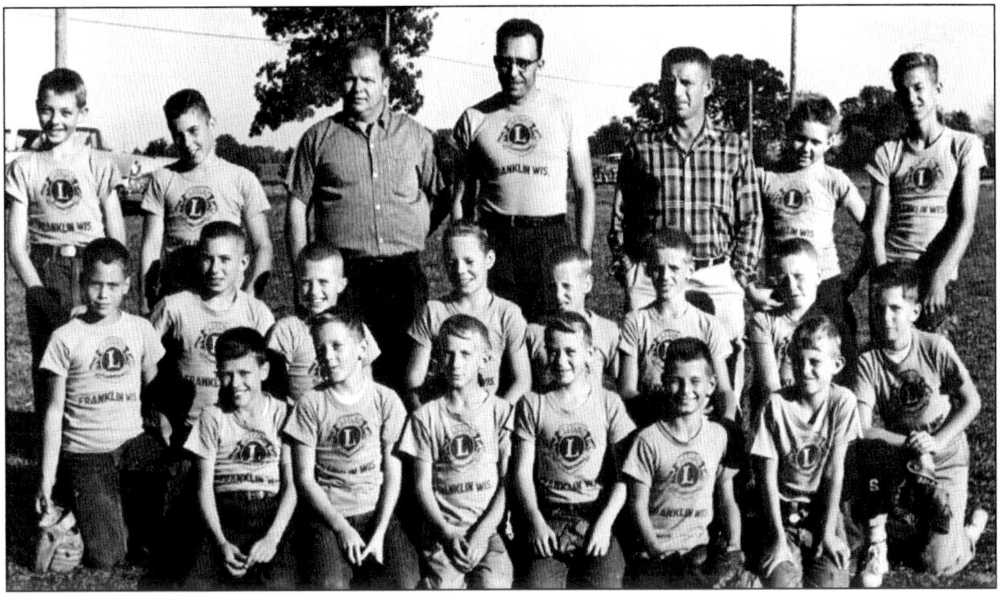

Little League baseball came to Franklin in the late 1950s. The 1960 Lions Club champions were Santo Mason Contractors, which included, from left to right, (first row) Marko Gerovac, Mike Swan, Gene Grant, Robert Schultz, Tom Schleuter, and unidentified; (second row) Monty Podevels, Dan Schreiner, Gary Greene, Jim Marx, Ron Marx, Dennis Glass, Kent Kosibucki, and Pat Murray; (third row) Bill Grant, Kerry Smith, sponsor Don Santo, manager Mel Podevels, coach Tom Greene, Monte Swan, and Mike Bruce.

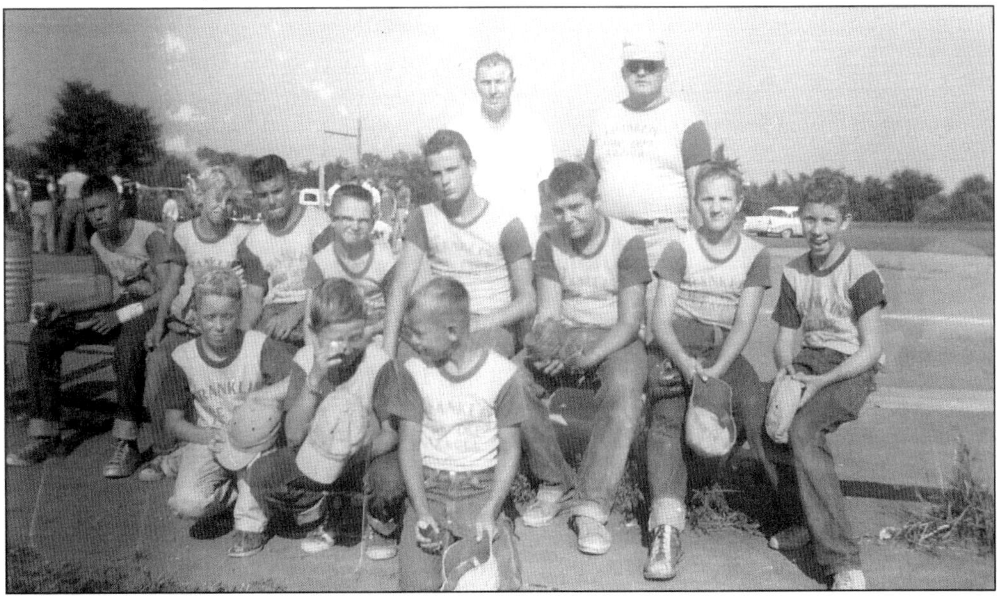

Franklin featured a second Little League sponsored by the Franklin Volunteer Fire Department. The field was built behind the fire station on Ryan Road in 1959. The White Dove sponsored the 1960 champions, who included, from left to right, (first row) Jim Rosenwirth, Ernie Vretnar, and Carl Raether; (second row) Greg Everett, Dennis Radler, Ken Toutant, Doug Schmidt, Tom Babcock, Albert Ormsby, Mark Weissbrodt, and Bill Brody; (third row) coach Bob Radler and manager Butch Schmidt. (Author's collection.)

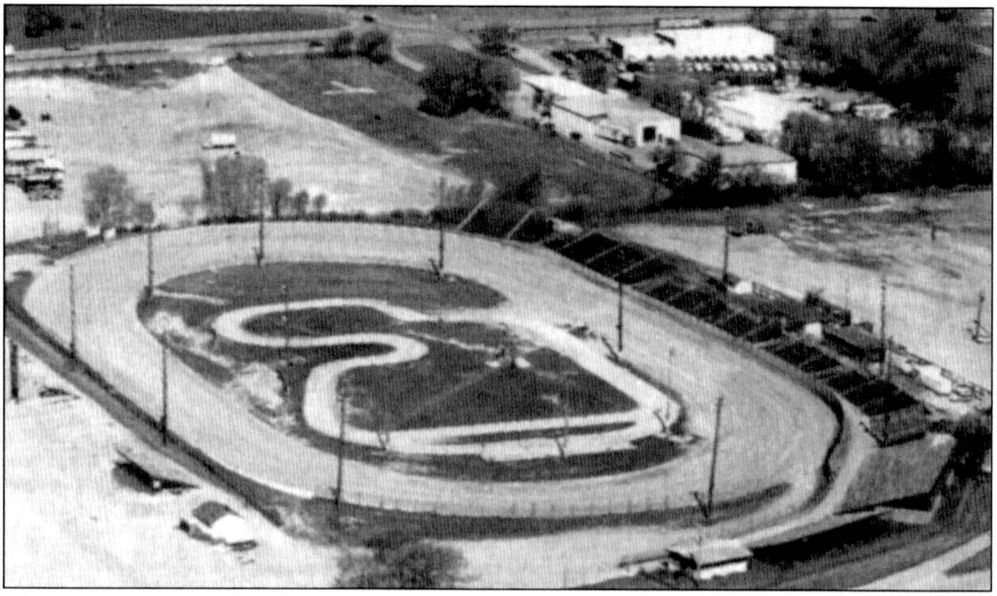

This is an aerial view of the Hales Corners Speedway, located west of Highway 41. The one-third-mile dirt track also featured a go-kart track in the infield. Saturday, August 30, 2003, was the last night races were scheduled at the venerable one-third-mile clay oval track, and over 8,000 fans turned out. However, a power outage engulfed the area in darkness and the races were rescheduled for the following night. After one last hurrah on August 31, the speedway closed for good and was demolished to make room for a Menards superstore.

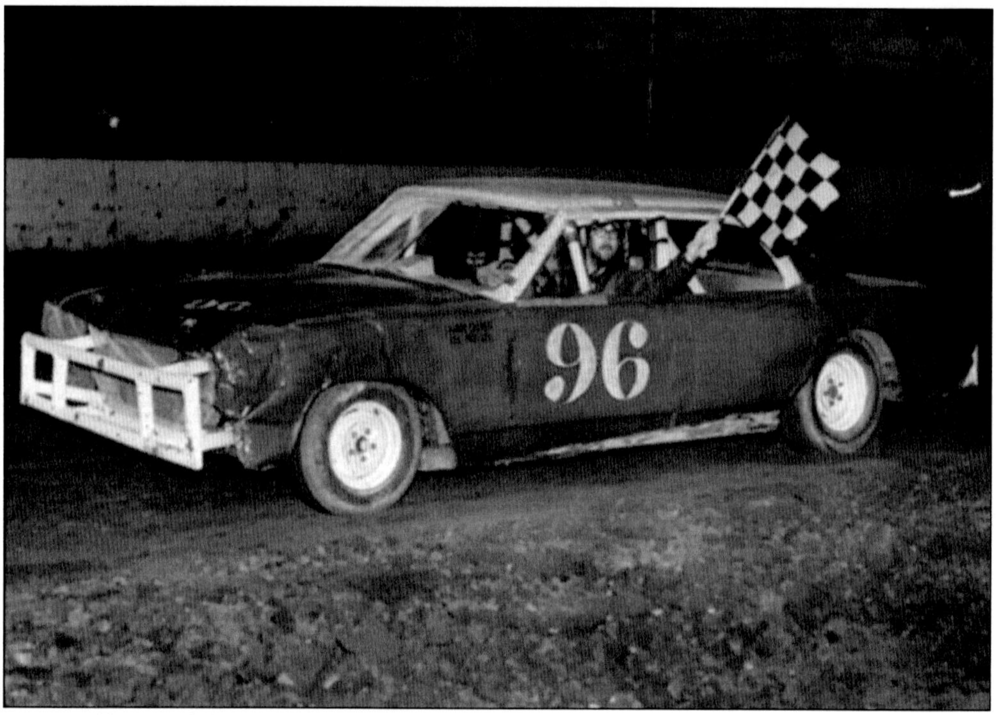

Driver Bill Preitzel does a victory lap after winning the feature race at Hales Corners Speedway in 1974. (Courtesy of R.P.M.)

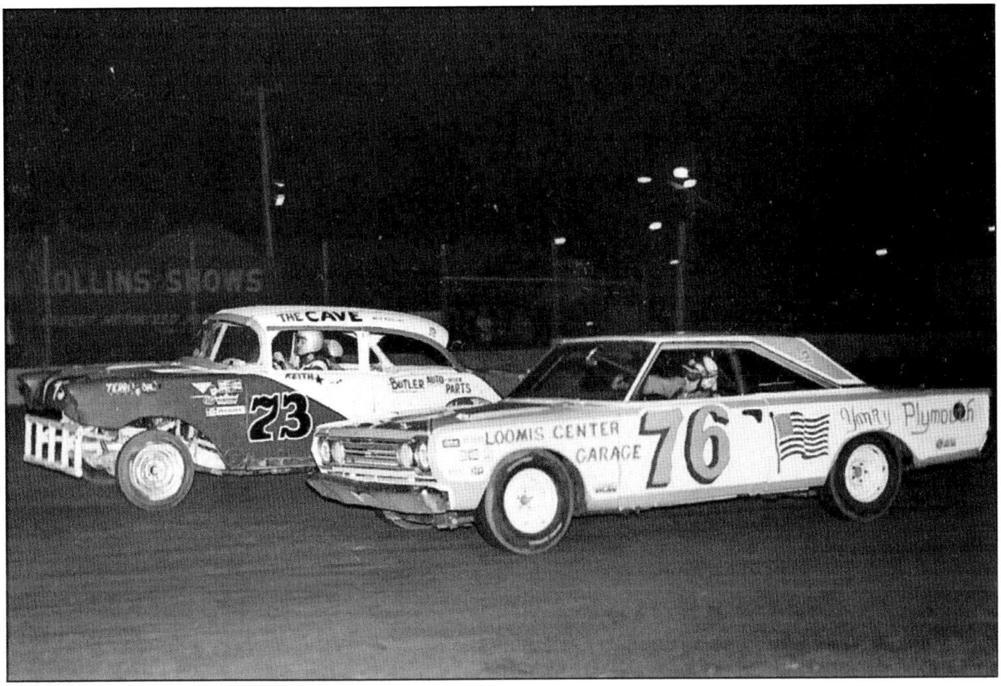

Passing an opponent on the inside of the main straightaway at Hales Corners Speedway in a 1976 Sportsmen Division race is Wally Benning (76) in a Plymouth sponsored by Loomis Center Garage. (Courtesy of Jon Benning.)

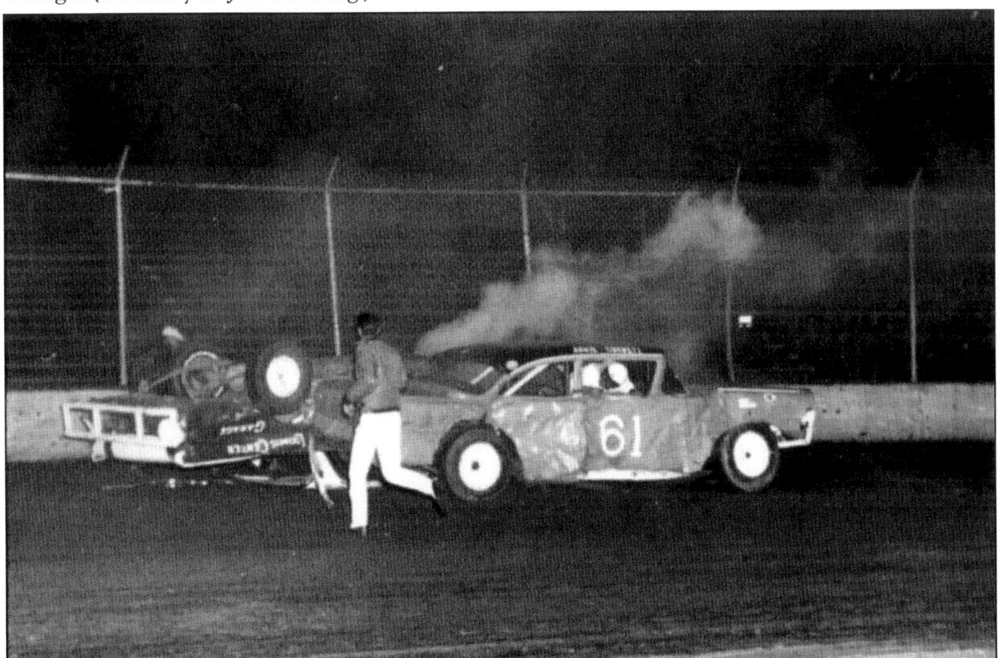

Spinouts and collisions like this one in 1976 were part of the excitement every Saturday night at the Hales Corners Speedway for 56 years. The speedway opened in 1949 and remained a popular stop for short-track drivers and their fans until it closed in 2003. (Courtesy of Jon Benning.)

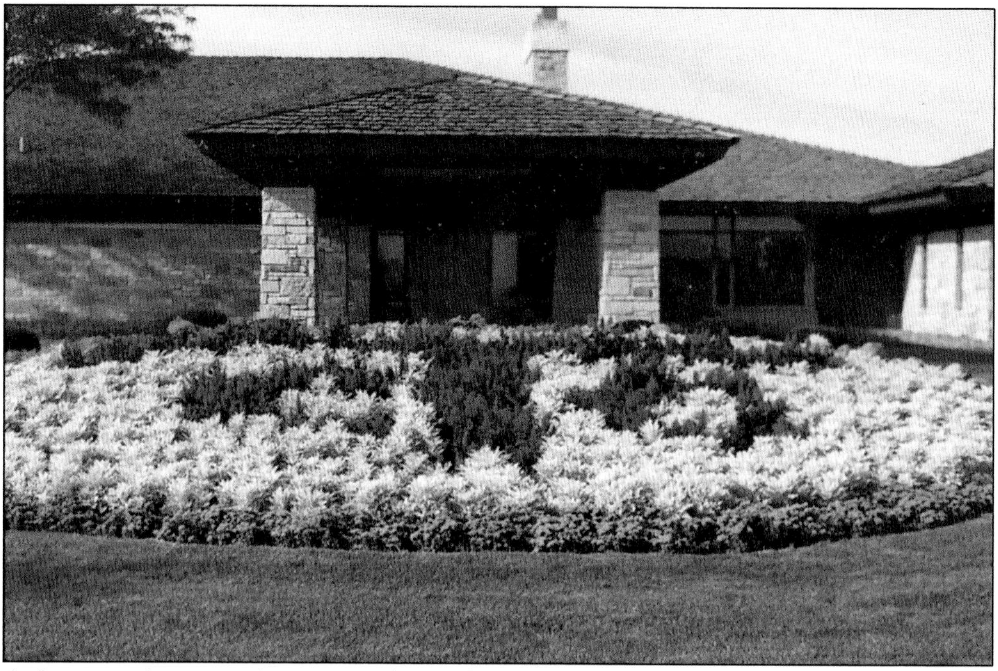

A flower garden greeted guests to the Tuckaway Country Club in 1988. The private club has made Franklin its home since moving from Greenfield in 1968. (Courtesy of Tuckaway Country Club.)

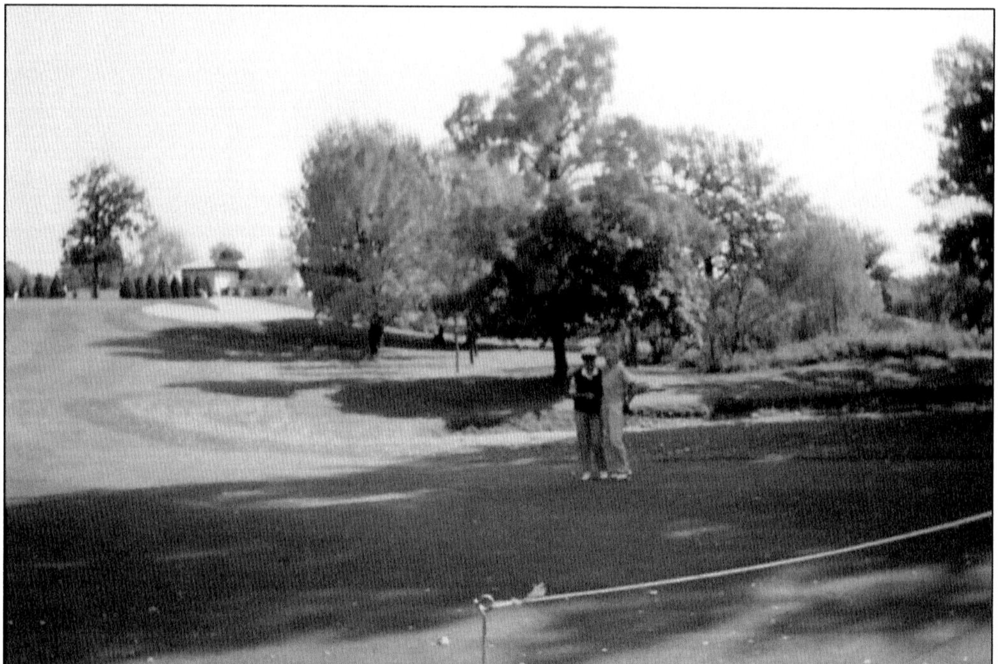

Two ladies take time out from their round of golf to pose along a fairway facing north toward the Tuckaway clubhouse in October 2001. (Courtesy of Tuckaway Country Club.)

The Tuckaway Country Club was carved out of the former William Boldt, William Ludwig, Fred Mueller, and Alfred Meyer farms sandwiched between Sixty-eighth and Seventy-sixth Streets south of Drexel Avenue. Grading began in 1966, and the course opened in 1968. From 1973 through 1993, Tuckaway hosted the Greater Milwaukee Open professional golf tournament. (Courtesy of Franklin Hub.)

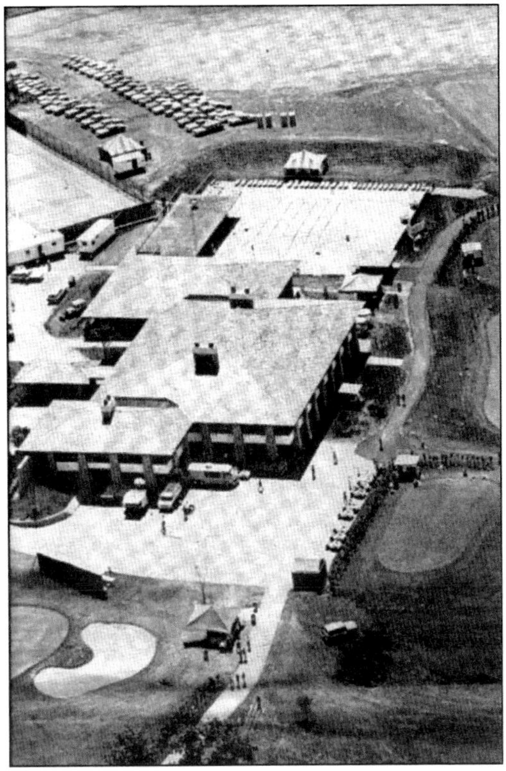

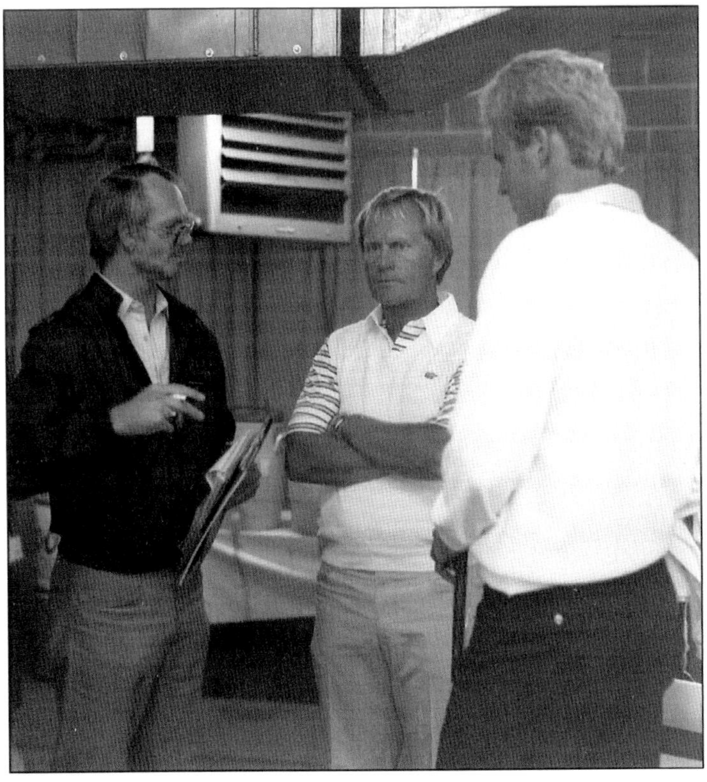

Interest in the Greater Milwaukee Open tournament peaked when PGA legend Jack Nicklaus made his lone appearance at the Tuckaway Country Club in 1985. Nicklaus is shown here being interviewed by *Franklin Hub* sports editor Doug Schmidt while his son, Jack Jr., looks on. Nicklaus agreed to compete in the Greater Milwaukee Open provided his son receive a two-year exemption to play in the tournament. (Courtesy of Jack Plale.)

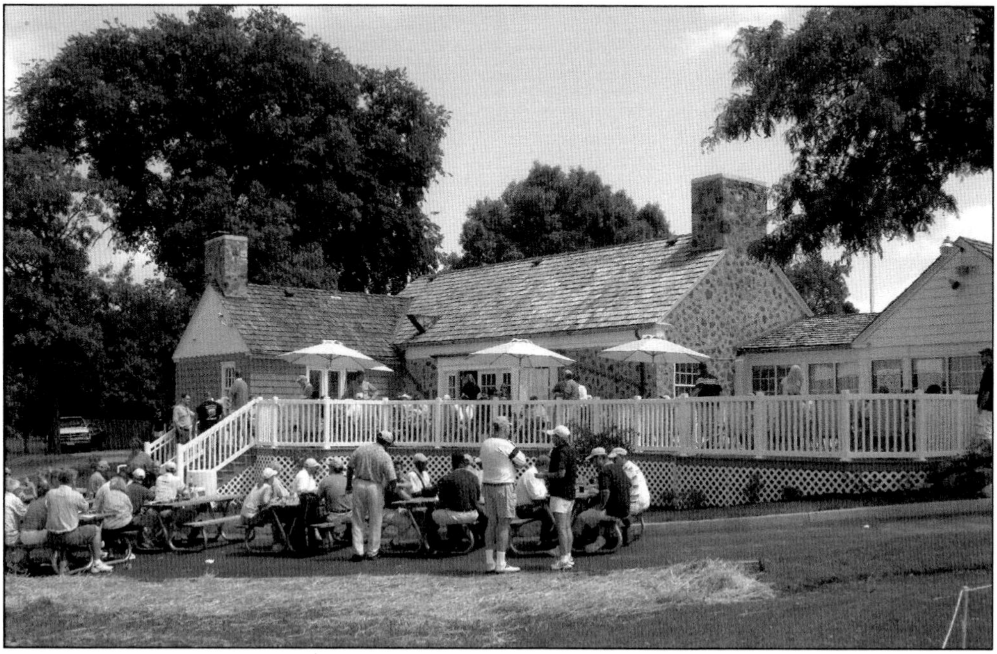

One of Milwaukee County's most scenic parks is Whitnall, which is wedged between the western border of Franklin and eastern edge of Hales Corners. Along with an 18-hole golf course and clubhouse, Whitnall Park features the Charles A. Whitnall Botanical Gardens, picnic areas, and a lagoon.

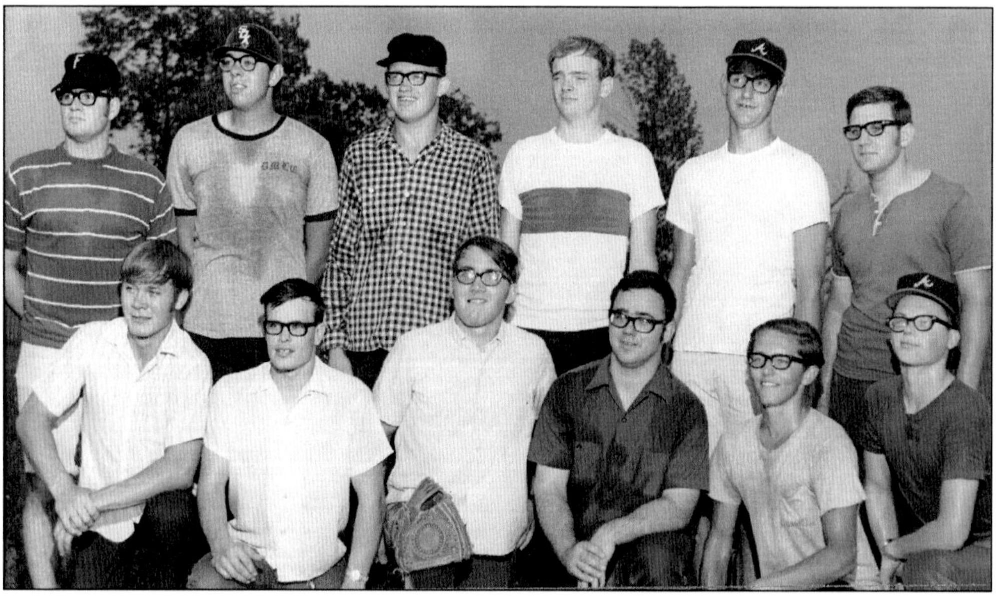

The Franklin Recreation Department organized a men's softball league behind Pleasant View School in 1969, and the first championship was won by the Franklin High School alumni team with an 8-2 record. The players are, from left to right, (first row) Dave Czerniejewski, Bill Hill, Roy Kruegel, Herb Reuteler, Dale Martin, and Doug Schmidt; (second row) George Johnson, Hartley Dus, Dave Ross, Kevin Manske, Mark Lindner, and Bill Nelson. Other members not shown are Paul Bergmann, Bill Gregor, and Alfred Mahr. (Courtesy of Franklin Hub.)

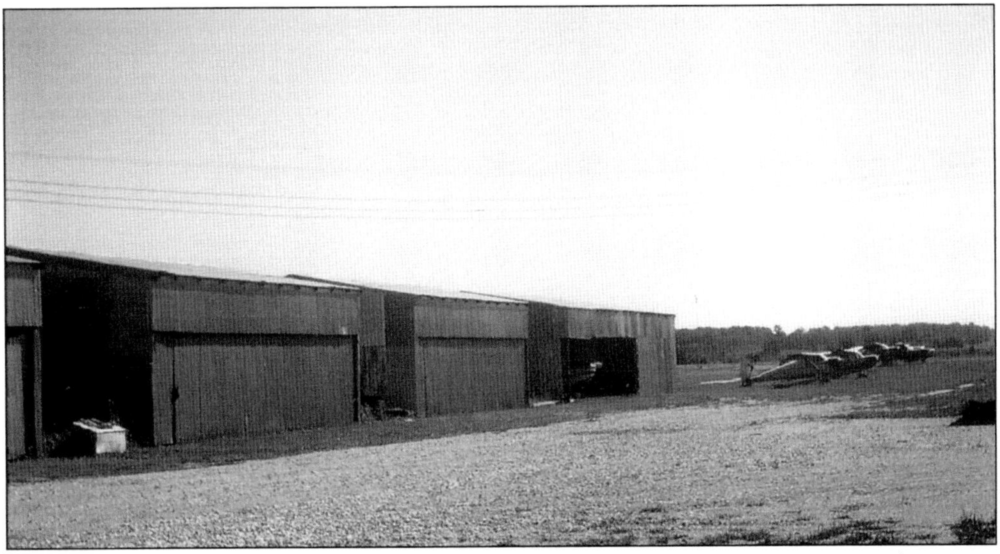

Rainbow Airport opened along Seventy-sixth Street a half mile south of Ryan Road in 1946. Originally called Cronin Field, it was started by Ed Rediske and Roy Dietz. They began with just two planes, a Piper J-3 Cub and a Piper Super Cruiser PA-12. Dietz was bought out by Harvey Fowles, who worked with Rediske to expand the business, and Rediske renamed the airport after sighting a rainbow. Ed's son, Leon Rediske, offered flight training lessons until the airport was forced to close by the Milwaukee County Park Commission in November 1996.

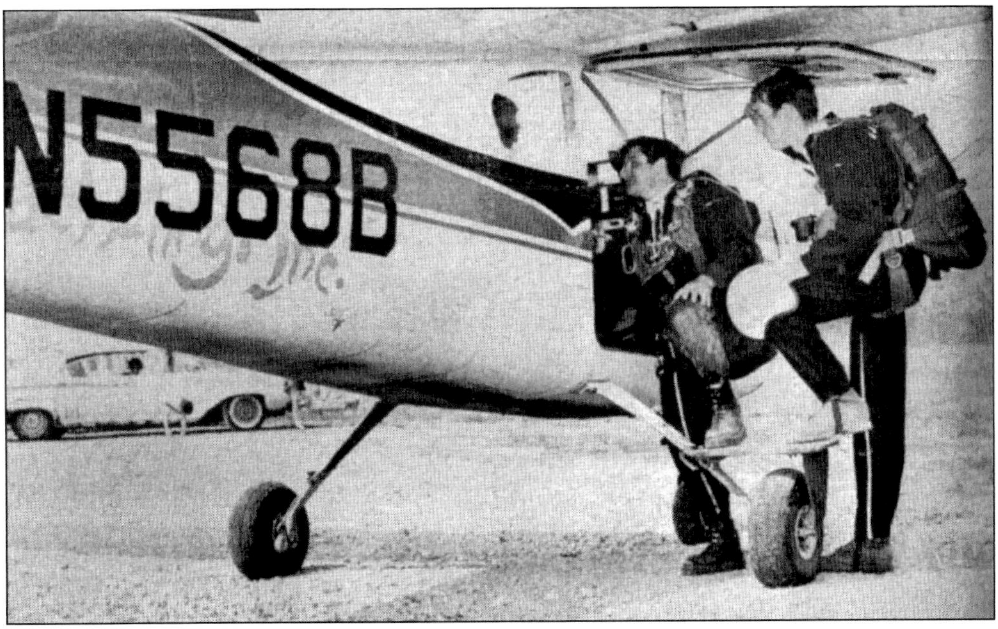

Skydiving was one of the activities afforded to aviators at the Rainbow Airport. Boarding a plane here on such an adventure are Ray Maguire (left) of South Milwaukee and Harry Gorski of Greenfield. (Courtesy of Franklin Hub.)

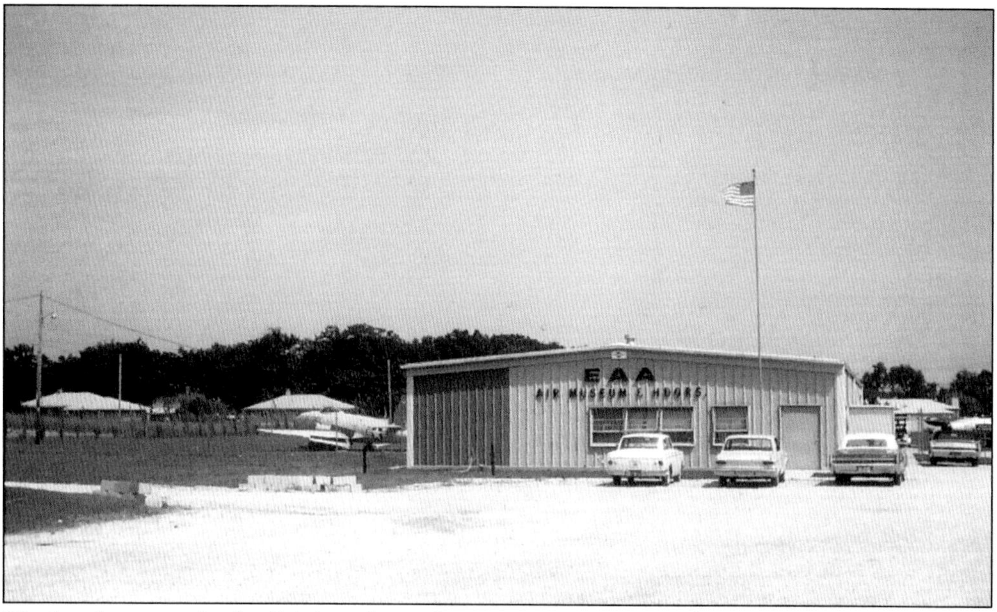

The headquarters for the EAA and air education museum opened in June 1964 on seven and one-half acres at 11321 West Forest Home Avenue to restore and preserve vintage aircraft. A new $250,000 building began housing vintage aircraft in 1966. The founder and president of the EAA was Paul Poberezny.

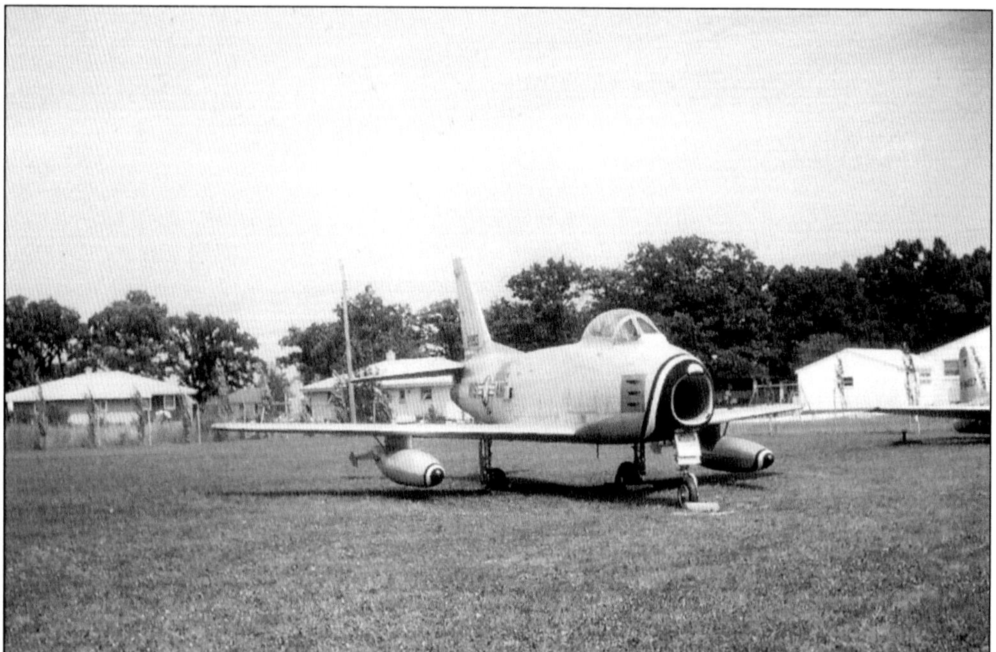

A World War II vintage aircraft was displayed on the grounds of the EAA museum during the 1970s.

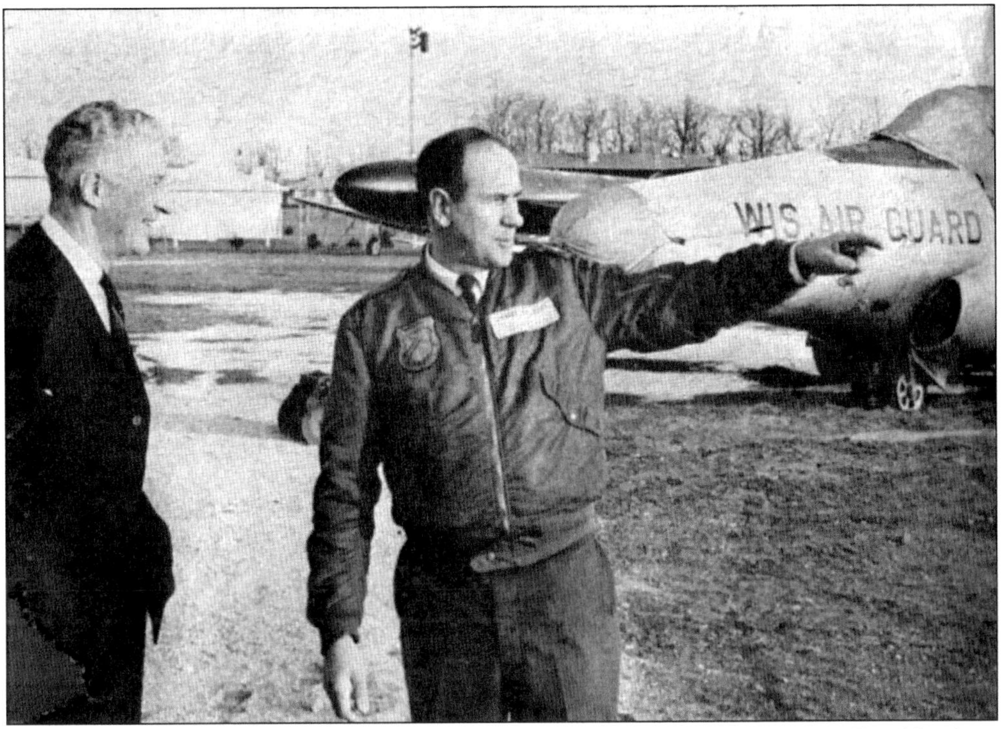

In January 1966, Gov. Warren P. Knowles received a tour of the EAA museum in Franklin from EAA president Paul Poberezny. One of the aircraft on display was an F-89 Scorpion used by the Wisconsin Air National Guard. (Courtesy of Franklin Hub.)

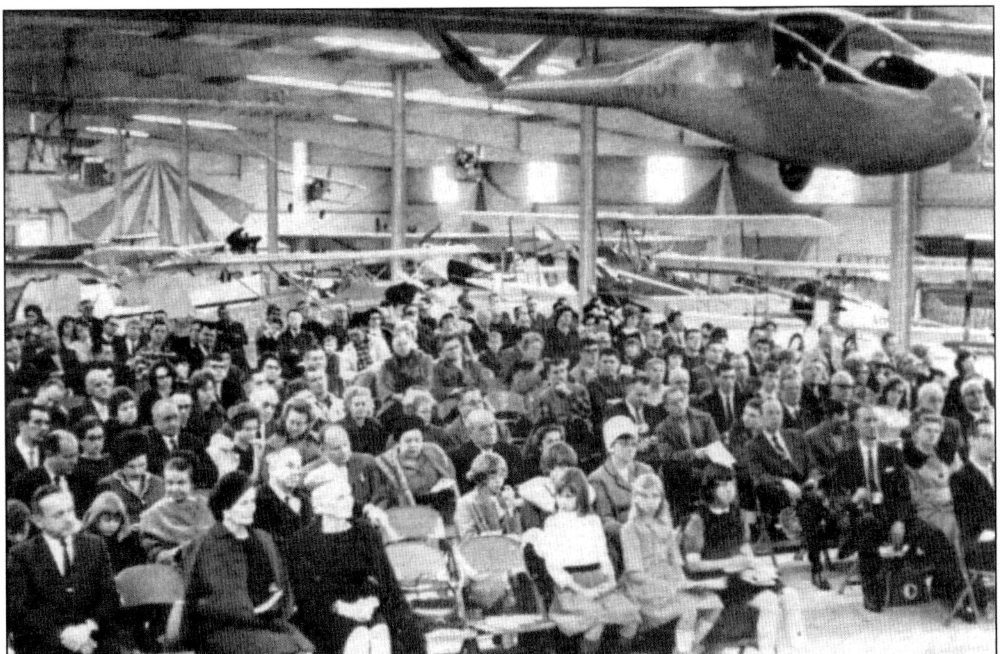

Spectators filled the EAA hanger for the air museum's formal dedication coordinated by EAA president Paul Poberezny in 1966. (Courtesy of Franklin Hub.)

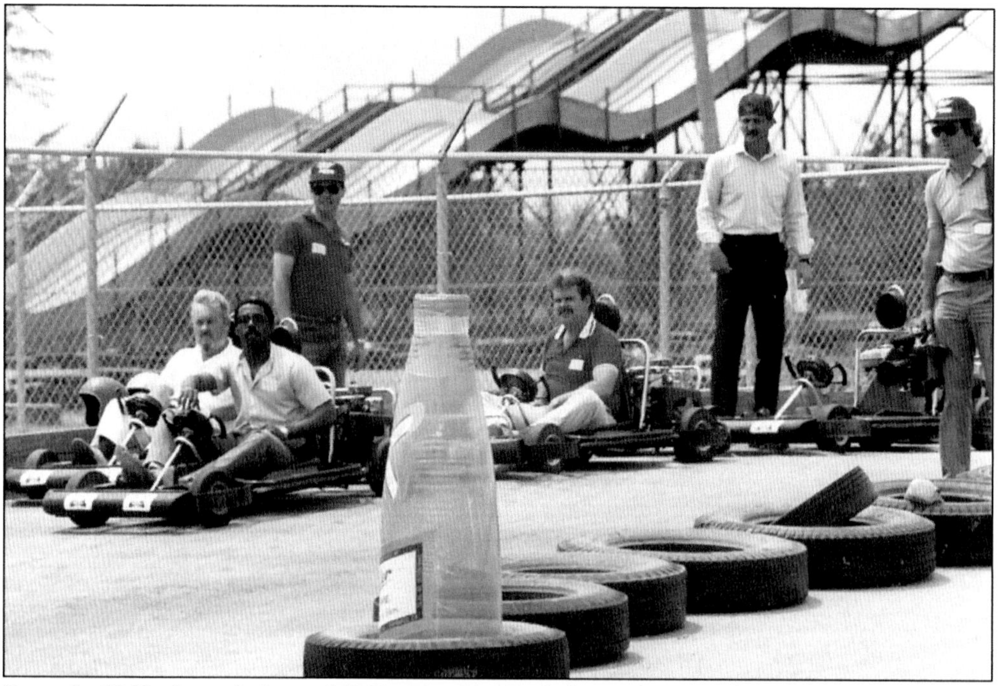

From the 1960s through the mid-1980s, Franklin Park, located on South Twenty-seventh Street, featured a variety of recreational outlets, including a miniature golf course, a driving range, slides, and the go-kart track shown here. (Author's collection.)

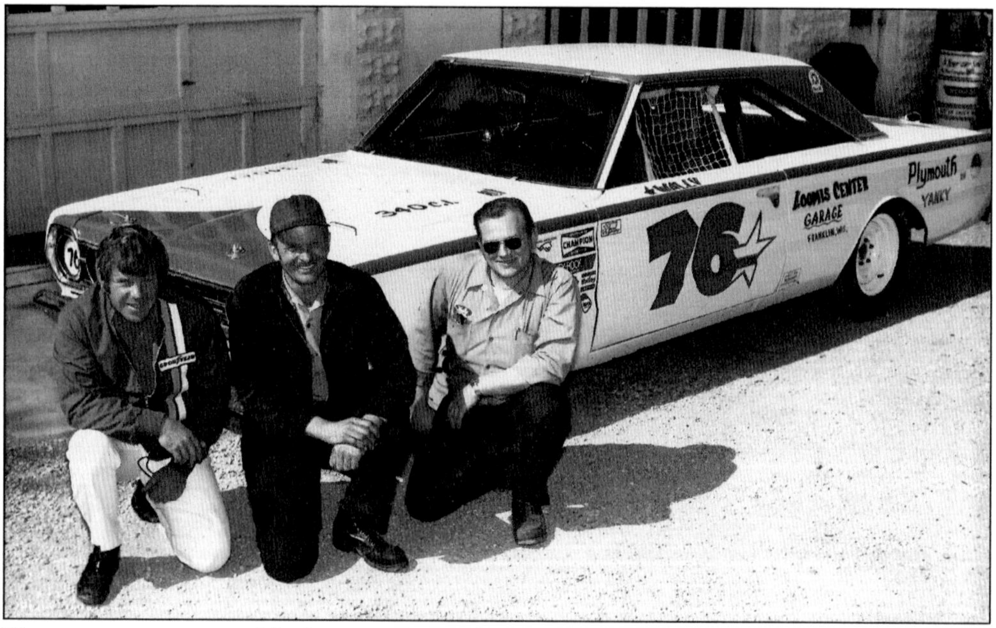

The race team sponsored by Loomis Center Garage was a regular entry in the Saturday night sportsmen competition at Hales Corners Speedway for nearly a decade beginning in 1968. The team consisted of (from left to right) Al Tietyen, Vernin Tretow, and Wally Benning. Tietyen and Benning were both mechanics who worked for Tretow, who owned Loomis Center Garage and drove the race car. (Courtesy of Vernin Tretow.)

Six

ONE ROOM, EIGHT GRADES

As a spacious farm community during the 1800s, the town of Franklin began offering educational opportunities in a series of one-room schools where a single teacher was contracted to teach the basics—reading, spelling, arithmetic, language, and geography—to all children in grades one through eight.

Initially the school year lasted no longer than three months and corresponded to the needs of farming life—classes began after the fall crops were harvested and ended when spring planting started. The teacher's salary for an entire three-month term was $24. Over time the school year expanded and teacher salaries ranged from $60 to $125.

Schools were heated by a potbellied stove, and boys took turns carrying in logs from the wood bin to start the fire each morning. Hot lunches were the result of placing bag lunches next to the stove. Boys also were required to pump buckets of water from an outside well while girls washed chalkboards, cleaned erasers, and worked with younger students.

The first school erected in Franklin was Riverside (located near the Root River) on Ryan Road in 1850. Seven other public schools emerged over the next 80-plus years. They were Whelan (1851), Stargard (1852), Oakwood (1883), Green Valley (1894), St. Martins (1907), Willow Edge (1929), and Kilbourn (1934). Some families felt a close kinship to their church and sent their children to one of the three parochial schools in Franklin, St. Paul's Lutheran, St. James Catholic, or Sacred Heart Catholic.

In April 1951, Franklin consolidated Riverside, Stargard, Green Valley, and Whelan into a single district. The following year, construction of a new elementary school, Ben Franklin, began on property purchased from the William Ludwig and William Boldt farms along Seventy-sixth Street south of Drexel Avenue. When Ben Franklin School opened in 1953, the four one-room schools were closed. Another merger took place in 1957 when Willow Edge and Country Dale were consolidated with Ben Franklin to form School District No. 5. Country Dale was transformed into the community's first middle school. But until 1962, a high school education required students to venture outside Franklin.

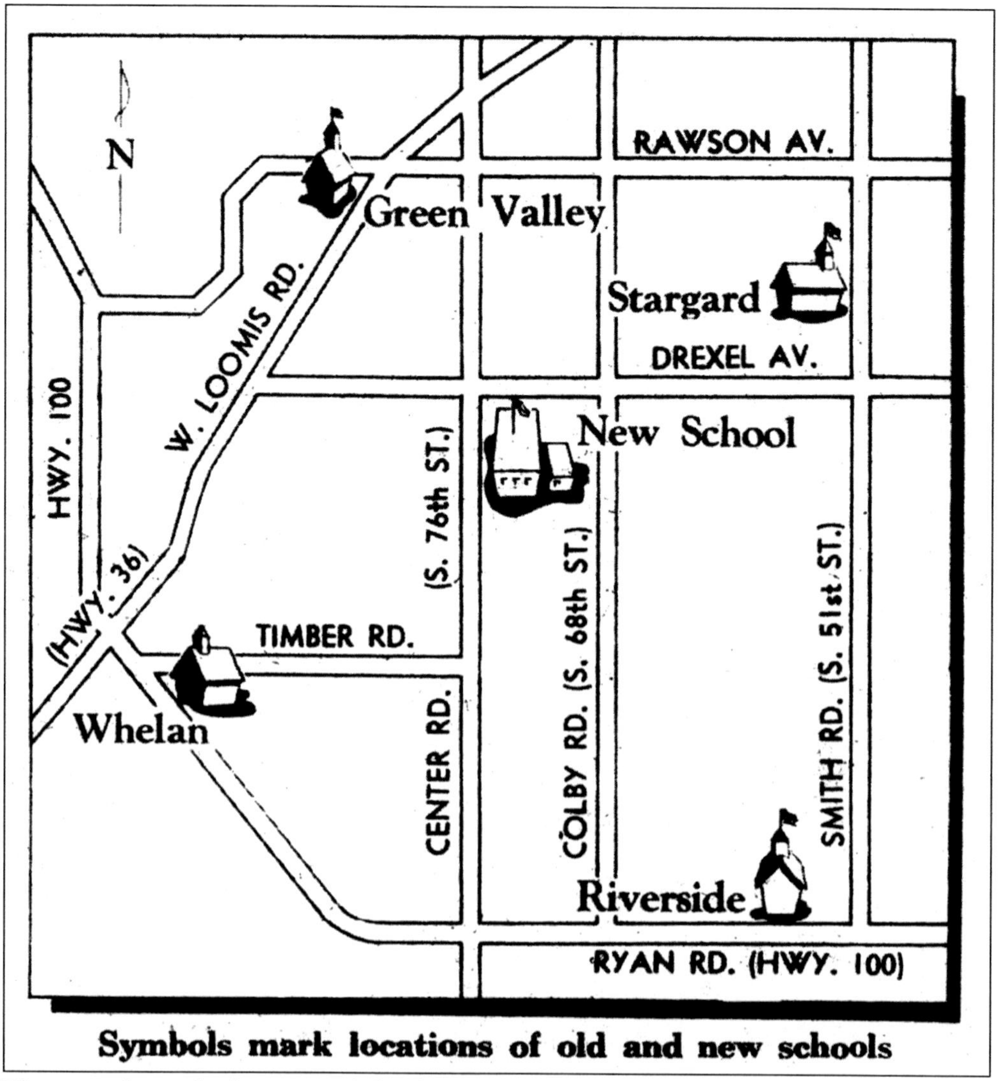

This map shows the locations of the four one-room public schools, Whelan, Green Valley, Stargard, and Riverside, that served Franklin youth between 1852 and 1952. In 1953, Ben Franklin School (new school) opened on Seventy-sixth Street and signaled the beginning of a new era in Franklin's educational facilities.

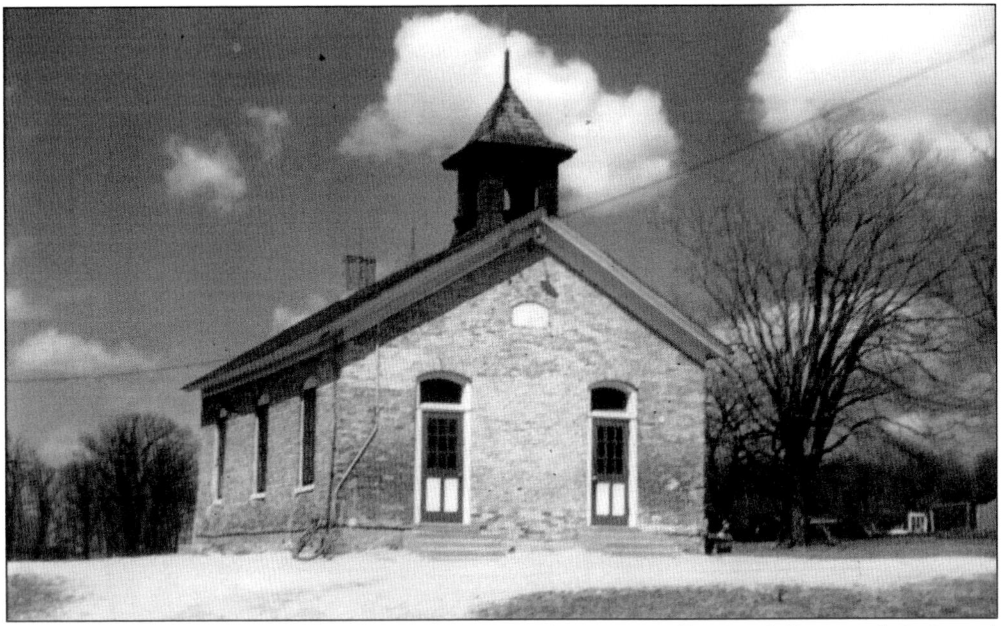

Built along Ryan Road just east of the Root River between Colby Road (Sixty-eighth Street) and Smith Road (Fifty-first Street), Riverside School opened in October 1852 with a school term of three months. The first teacher was S. Beardsley, who was paid $12 per month. Children were allowed to start attending Riverside at age 4 and continue to age 20. In 1877, the old frame school was enlarged and covered in brick. It remained in service through 1952.

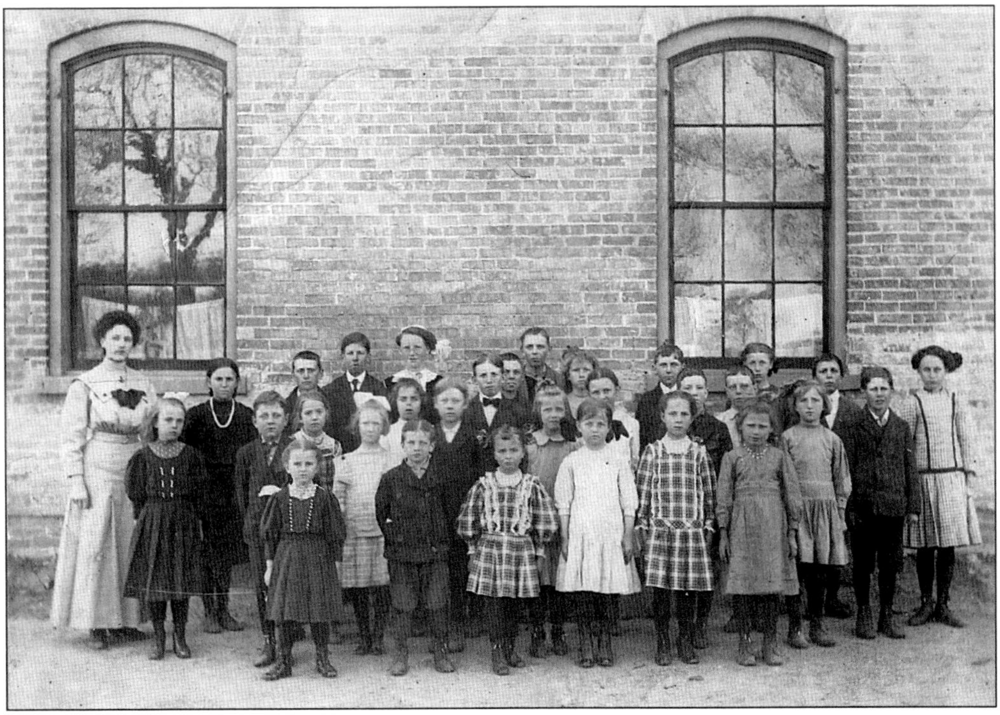

Shown here are Riverside students in grades one through eight with their teacher (far left) in 1912.

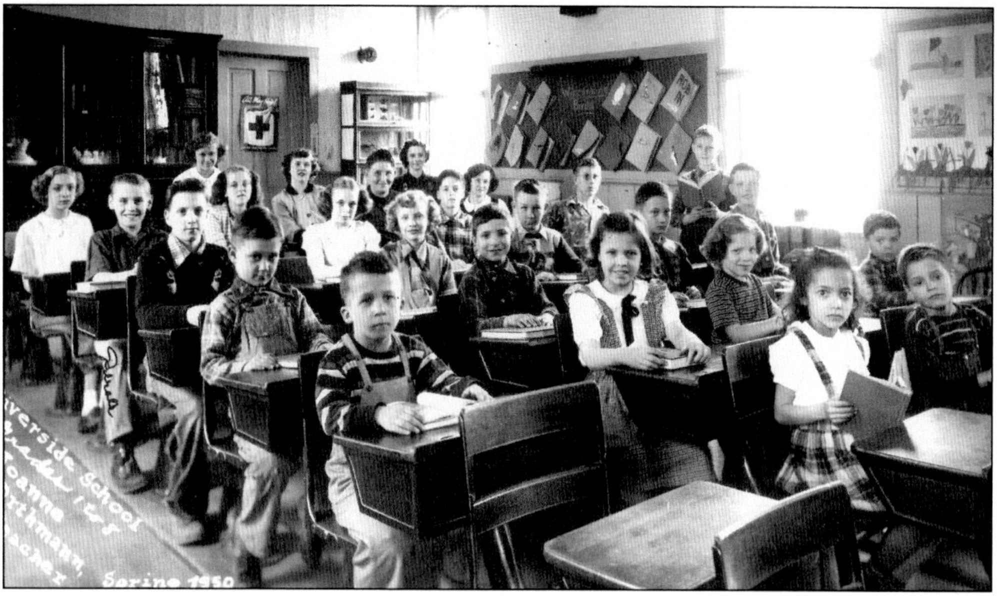

Students at Riverside School smile for the camera in the spring of 1950. They are William Hangartener, Paul Bussiere, John Lecus, Derald Peters, Joyce Klingbeil, Juanita Dujas, Nancy Benning, Russell Keske, June Keske, Faye Scherbarth, Beverly Giese, Nancy Grusnick, Elmer Keske Jr., Joan Houtler, James Acker, Florian Foote Jr., Edwin Lecus, Dennis Paap, Eldon Benning, Gerald Houtler, Paul Keske, Richard Skarie, Joyce Acker, and Edith Keske. Sitting in front of the back door is teacher Joanne Orthmann.

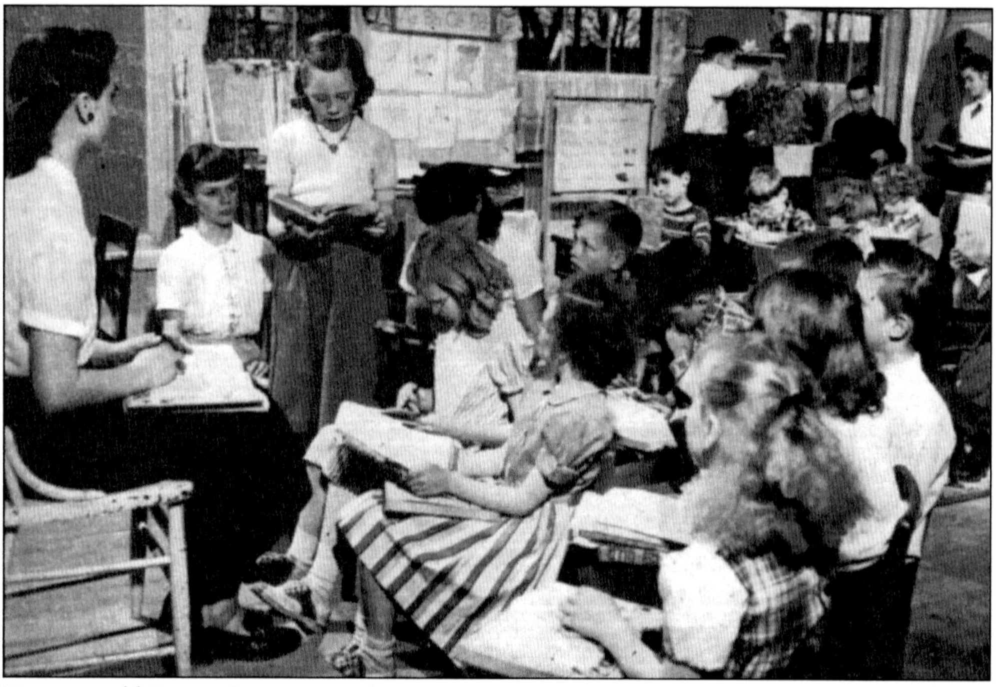

Nine-year-old Bonita Barg recites for a group of third and fourth graders taught by Barbara Koeschner (left) during the final year of operation for Stargard School on South Fifty-first Street in 1952. Koeschner went on teach at the new Ben Franklin School the following year.

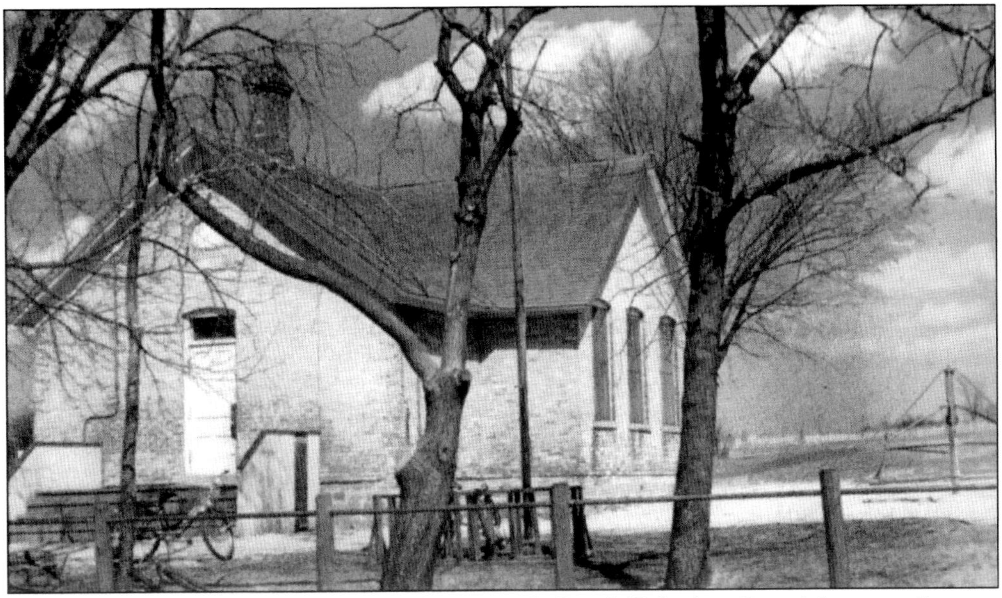

The original Stargard School was built on Smith Road (Fifty-first Street) between Rawson Avenue and Drexel Avenue in 1852. The teacher's salary varied between $24 and $30 for a five-month term. Land was purchased for $100 in 1881 to construct a new building, and the Stargard school shown here was completed in the summer of 1888 for the sum of $700. A new foundation was put under the building in 1900, followed by the addition of a woodshed in 1903 and a 6-by-20-foot addition in 1908.

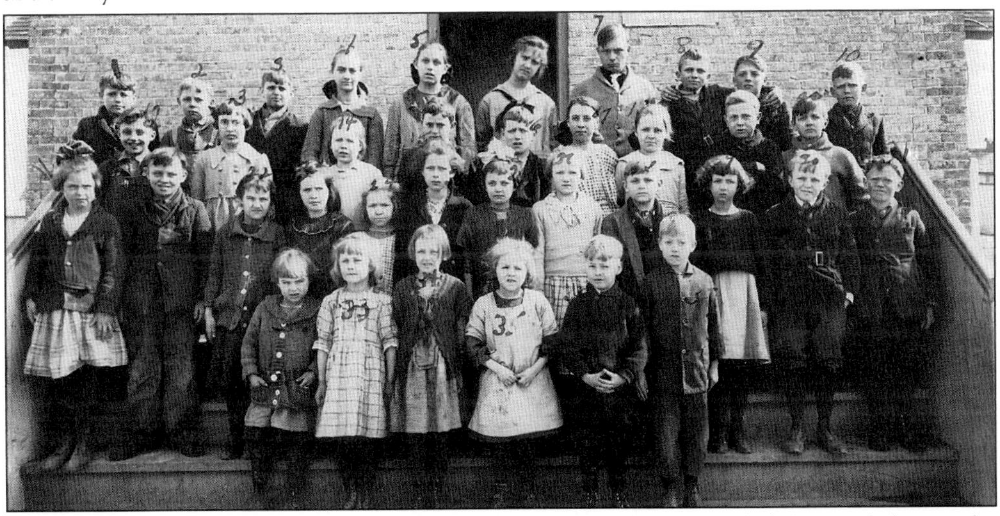

Shown here are the first- through eighth-grade students who attended Stargard during the 1921–1922 term. They are, from left to right, (first row) Esther Guzenda, Anne Darorsak, Evelyn Dietz, Ellen Barg, Sidney Rick, and Clarence Boldt; (second row) Elena Rechinski, Eldon Dietz, Clara Obremski, Clara Wolter, Eunice Barg, Selma Wolter, Mabel Dietz, Ethel Boldt, Eddie Rostankowski, Gladys Farquar, Julian Mueller, and Lawrence Sucharski; (third row) Clarence Dietz, Esther Baumann, Gladys Barg, Edwin Behrendt, Joel Brown, Martha Guzenda, Elaine Barg, Fred Karsten, and Phillip Obremski; (fourth row) Gordon Rieck, Stanley Rechinski, Roy Geilfuss, Regina Obremski, Victoria Rostankowski, teacher Lucille Eilbricht, Edgar Bruss, Thomas Rostankowski, Dillon Wagon, and Larry Sucharski.

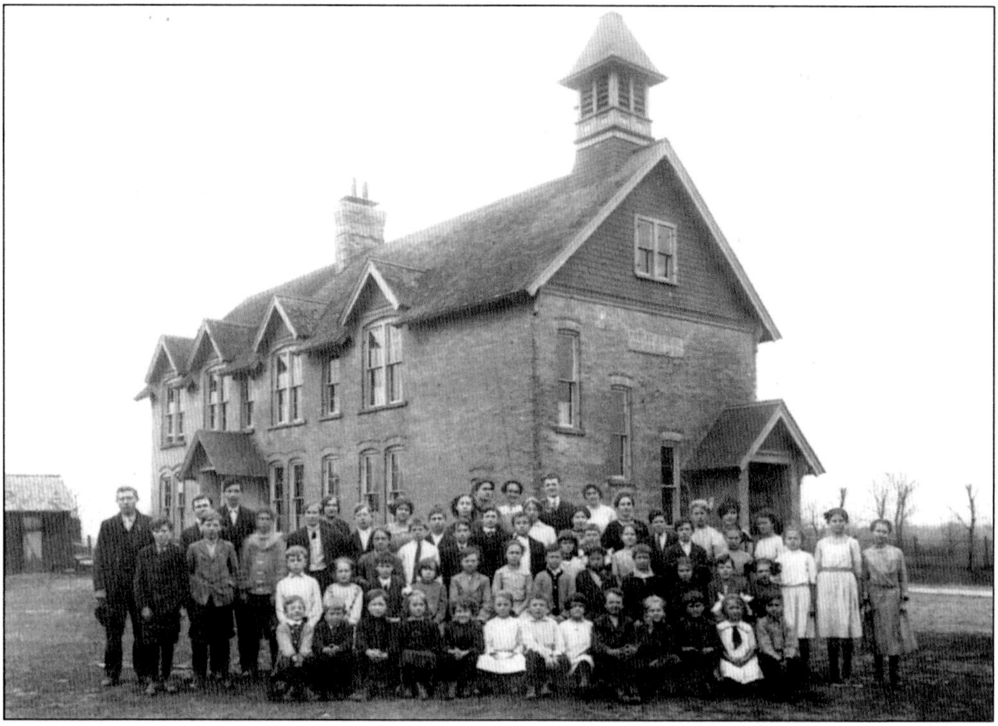

From 1888 to 1918, Oakwood School doubled as the first high school in the Franklin and Oak Creek districts. The first floor was used for elementary grades, and the second floor served youths of high school age. Tuition was 40¢ per week. Today the building serves as a day care center.

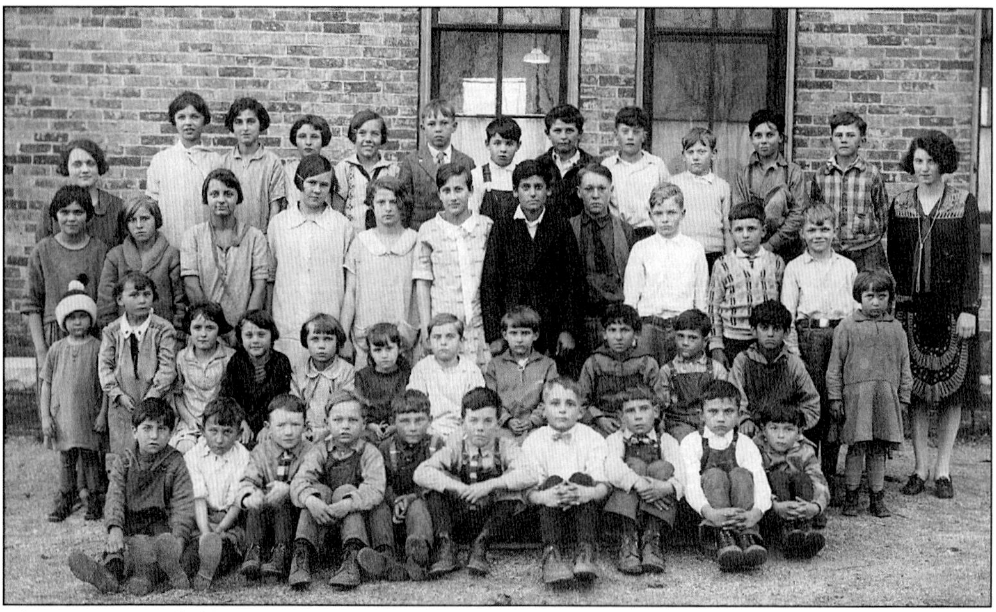

There were 45 children from farm families living in Franklin and Oak Creek who attended grades one through eight at Oakwood School in 1927. The school opened in 1883 along Highway 41 (Twenty-seventh Street) between Ryan Road and Oakwood Road.

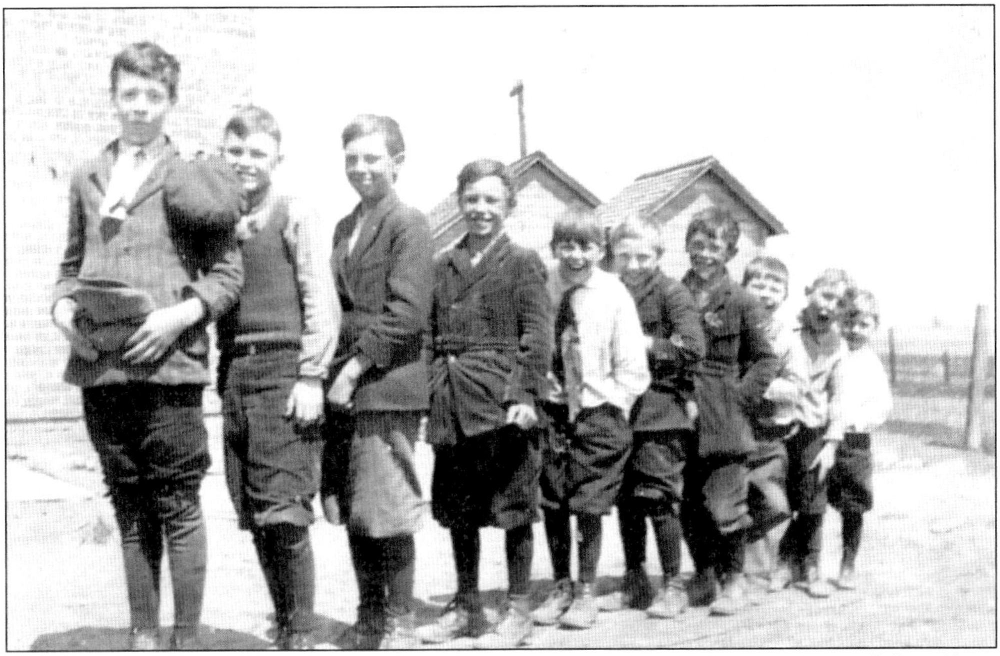

These 10 boys are all smiles at Whelan School in 1925. They are (from left to right) William Brandt, Elmer Delikat, Ed Friebel, Bill Friebel, George Buse, Wilmer Nitz, Otto Friebel, John Yunker, Norman Meyer, and Wilbert Meyer. Delikat was destined to become Franklin's fire chief in the 1950s.

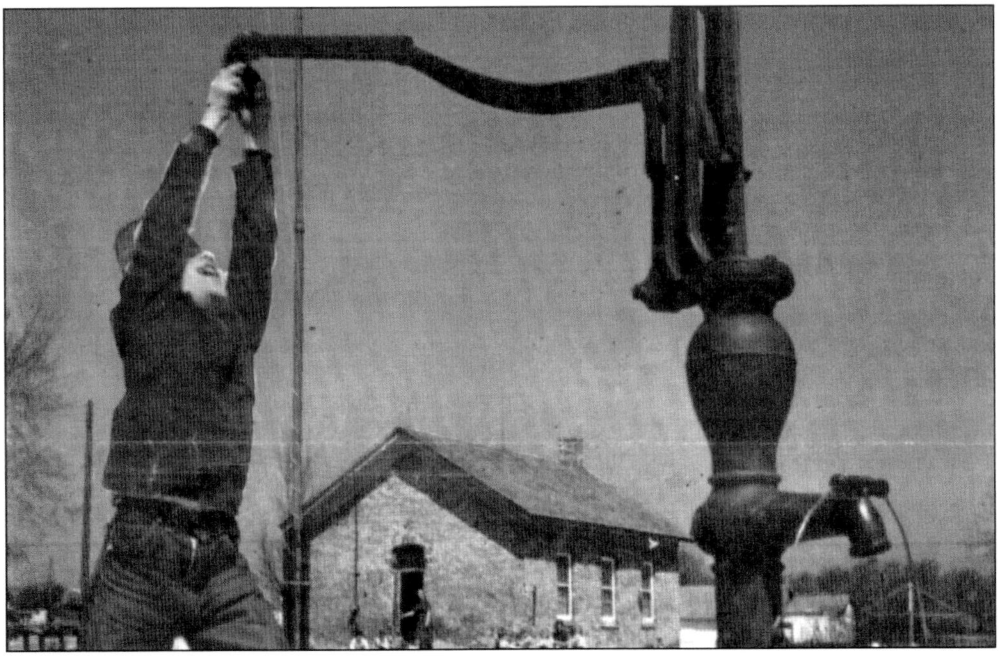

Working the hand pump for well water was a daily task for boys who attended Whelan School. Dennis Schubert, 11, is shown pumping water for the last time in 1953. A week later all the students were transferred to the new Ben Franklin School on South Seventy-sixth Street. (Courtesy of Milwaukee Journal.)

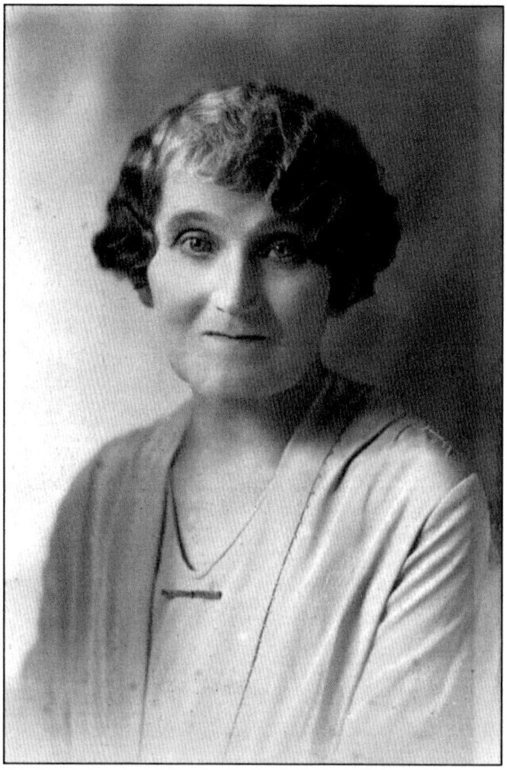

Johannah Whelan, the daughter of Patrick Whelan, donated land at the corner of Puetz Road and Ryan Road for construction of a new school in 1878. The original Whelan School was built on property owned by Patrick Whelan in September 1852 at a cost of $173. Orlando Hill was hired as the teacher and held the position until the district decided on a female teacher in 1868. In 1877, the school property was sold back to Patrick Whelan for $21.75, and a year later, the district secured a loan for $389 to construct a new Whelan school of Milwaukee Cream City brick. It closed in 1953 and was purchased by the Franklin Historical Society in 1969. The historical society then raised funds to move the building to Lions Legend Park in February 1970.

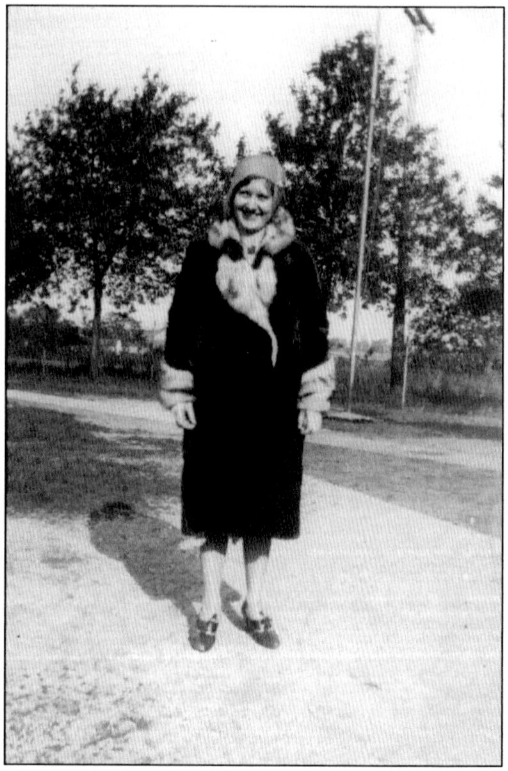

Teaching at Green Valley School during the 1920s and early 1930s was a Miss Garriety. Each year she taught 25 to 35 students in grades one through eight.

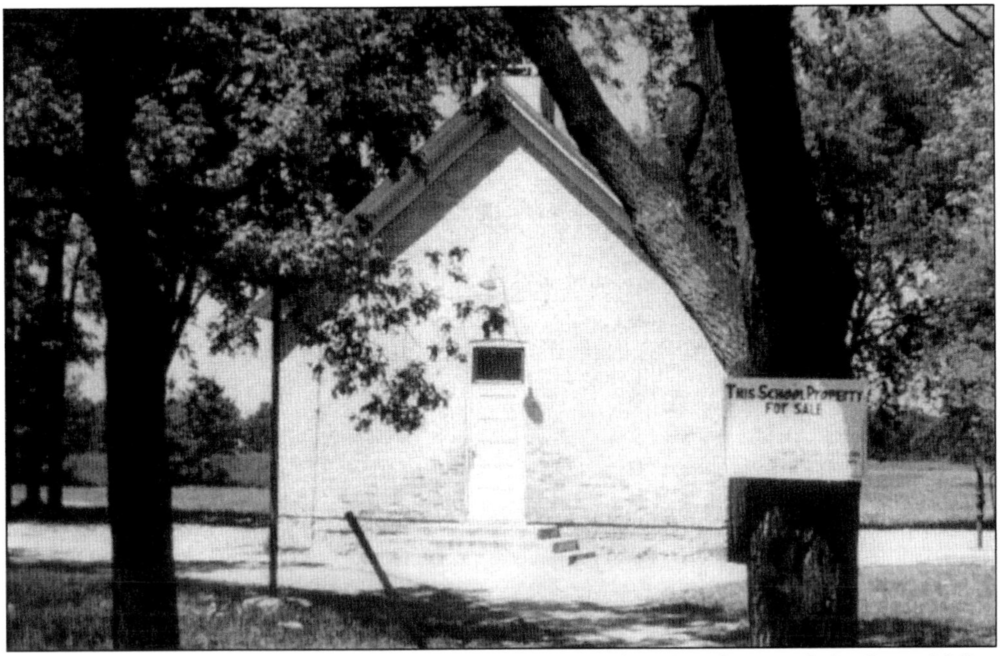

Originally called Thomas White School in recognition of its first district clerk, Green Valley opened in October 1894. It was built at the intersection of Rawson Avenue and Loomis Road. The school term was nine months, and the teacher's salary was $40. The property was put up for sale after the school closed in 1953.

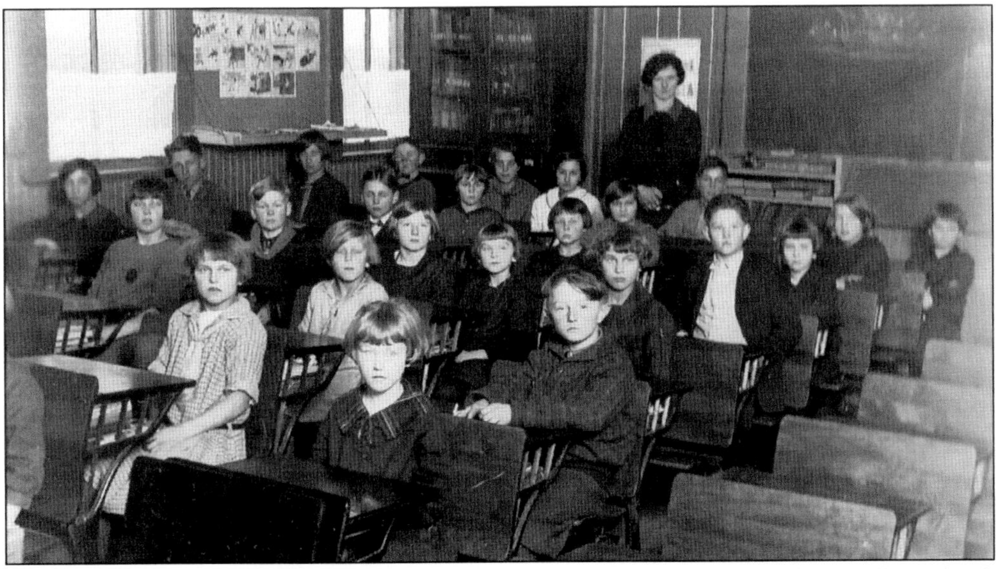

In 1926, there were 26 children from surrounding farm families attending Green Valley School. The students filling out grades one through eight are, from front to back, (first row) Dorothy Kneser, Fred Tess, Esther Folack, John Tretow, Pearl Kneser, Elsie Lehl, and Eunice Fessenbecker; (second row) Frieda Folack, Dorothy Schultz, Esther and Marie Boldt, Marie Ludwig, Gladys Heup, and Robert Jacoby; (third row) Florence Bertram, Orin Wagner, Harvey Kneser, Alice Chezik, Lillian Ludwig, and Harriet Haas; (fourth row) Meta Tess, Lloyd Luck, Lucille Luck, and Clarence Ludwig.

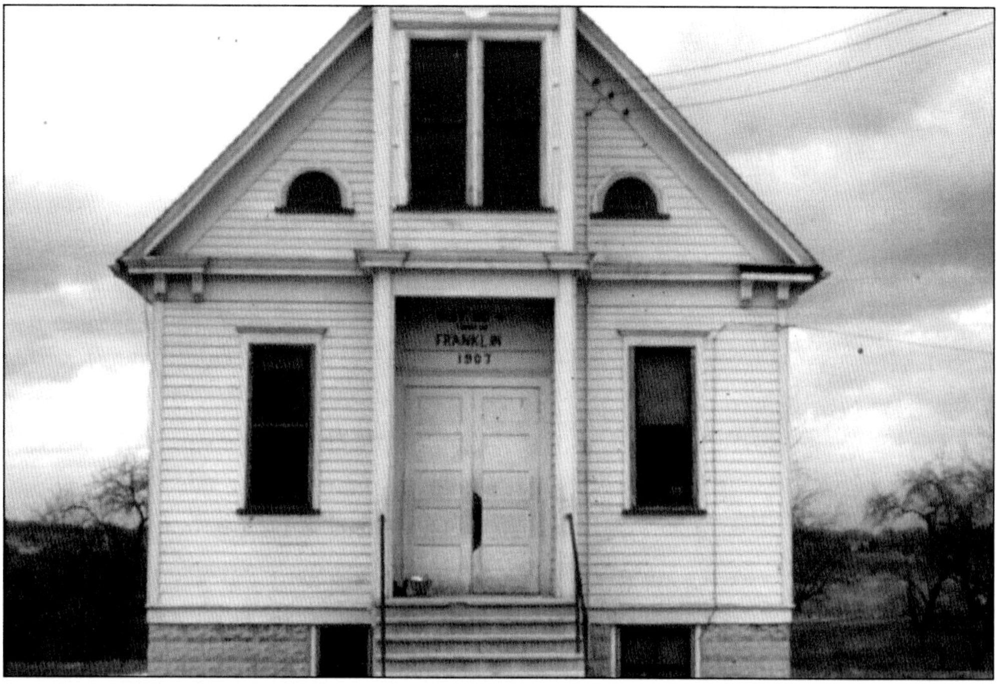

St. Martins School was built along Church Street in 1907 and catered to families living in the St. Martins area. It remained in use as a one-room school until Country Dale School opened in 1955.

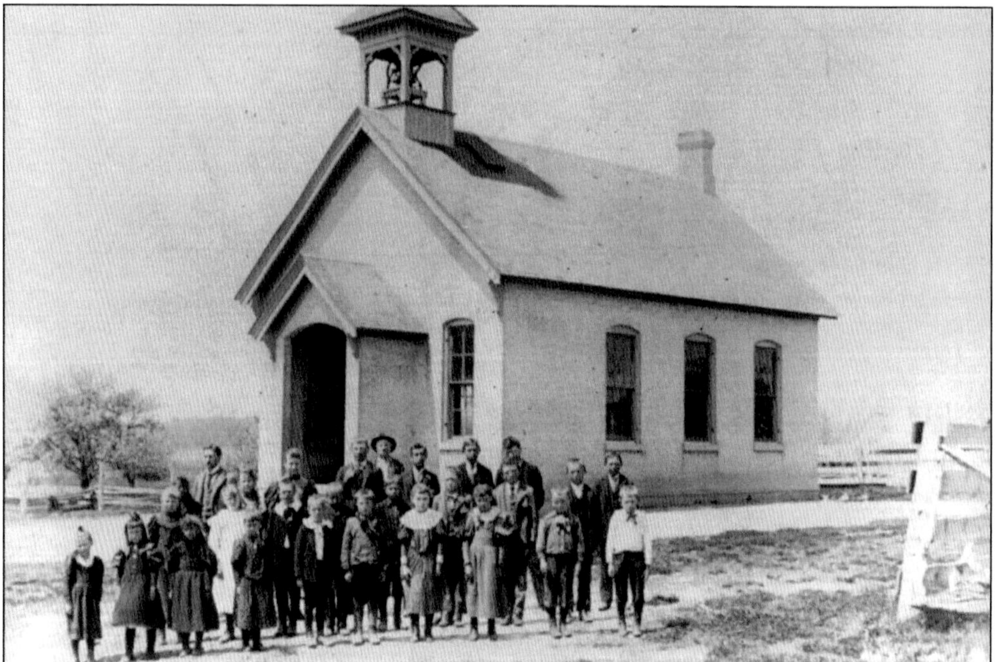

Kilbourn School was one of the newer schools built in Franklin along Twenty-seventh Street (Highway 41) between Rawson Avenue and Drexel Avenue in 1934. It remained open until the late 1950s.

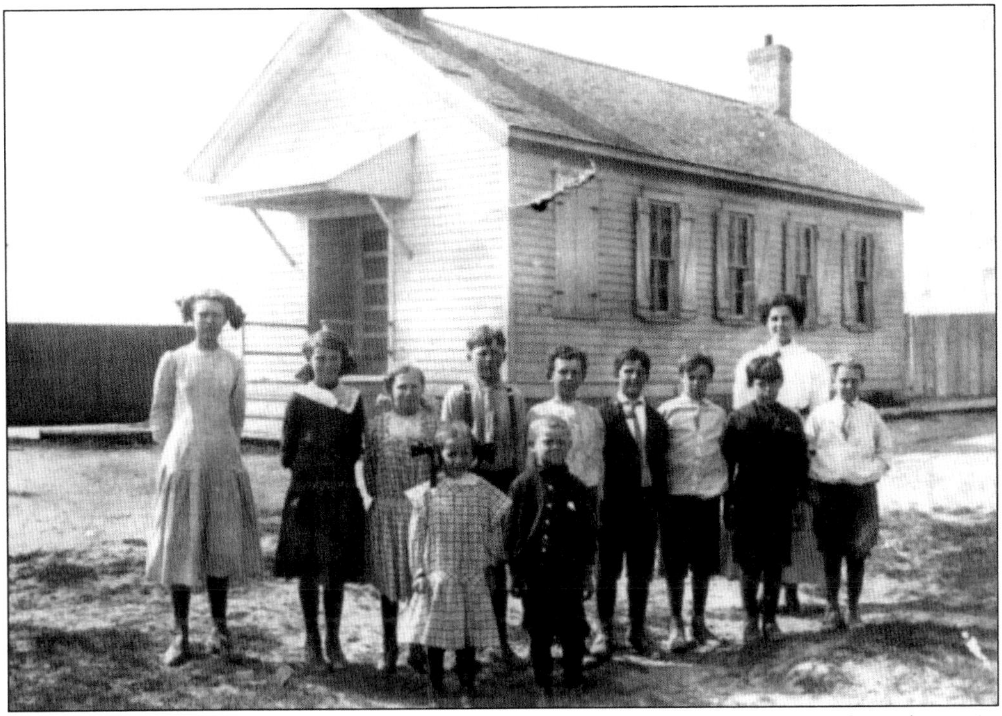

Willow Edge School was established at the corner of 112th Street and Oakwood Road in 1929 and remained in service until a more spacious school was built.

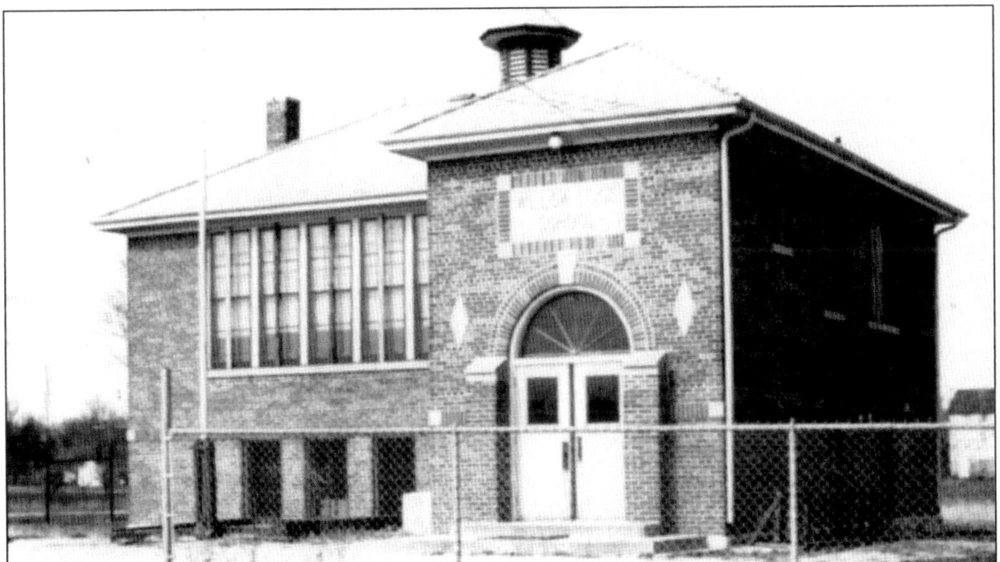

Before Ben Franklin School opened, Franklin's most modern elementary school was Willow Edge. Built in 1950 to replace its wooden one-room predecessor, the two-story brick structure continued to offer education to first and second graders until January 30, 1961, when both its teachers, Vivian Guzniczak and Barbara Wichgers, took maternity leave. Due to the difficulty of finding quality midterm replacements, the school board decided to close the school and transfer the students to Ben Franklin.

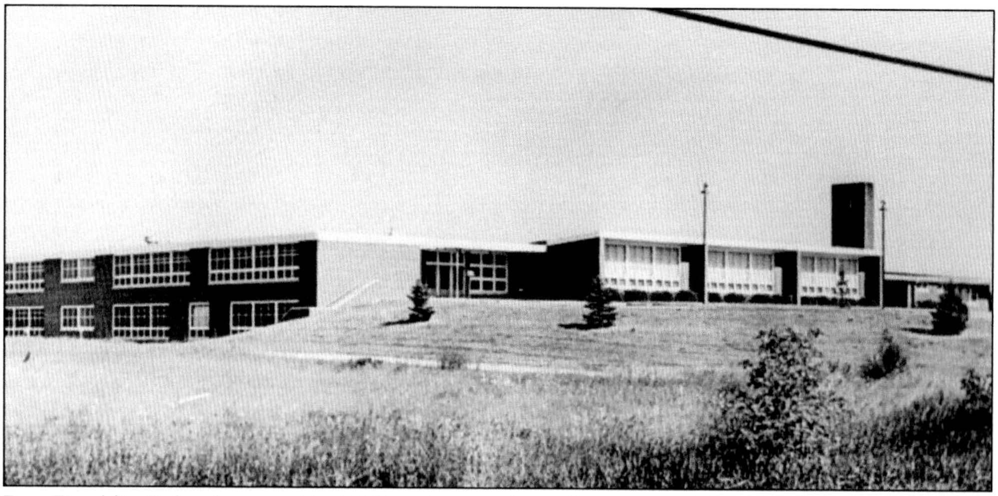

Ben Franklin School opened in 1953 and went through a series of three additions, including a multipurpose room, before it was completed in 1957. The school served the community until it was closed in 1999, razed, and replaced by condominiums in 2001.

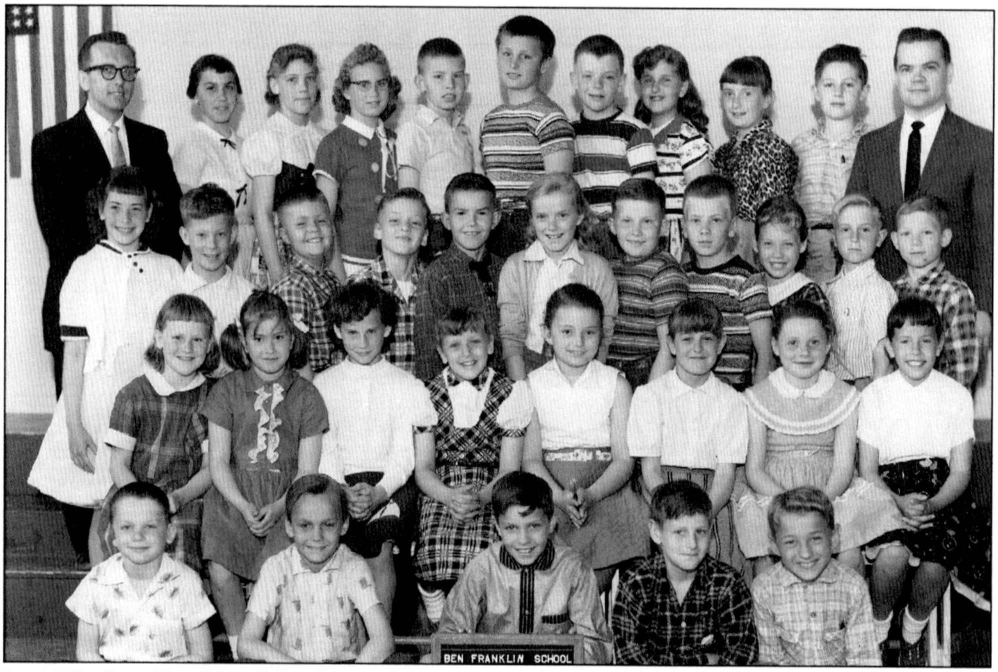

In 1958, Ben Franklin School was five years old with 17 classrooms and an enrollment of 498. This is Ben Franklin's fourth-grade class taught by Gerald Tuchalski (left). The students are, from left to right, (first row) Doug Schmidt, Thomas Seidel, Dennis Schweitzer, Richard Ledzian, and Robert Weber; (second row) Kathy Elliott, Candy Daniels, Virginia Erdmann, Janis Radler, Gayle Mitchell, Sandra Manka, Bonnie Fenner, and Kathy Burckhard; (third row) Theresa Ferrell, Brian Nickolaus, Gary Condon, David Nairn, Ron Rybarczyk, Mildred Bergh, Tony Podriznik, David Spence, Davney Herriges, Peter Lagerman, and Bill Gregor; (fourth row) Pauline Switalski, Sharla Sabroun, Jane McChesney, Delwin Delikat, Kenneth Koplein, Kevin Manske, Judy Farchione, Connie Turner, and David Kuehn. Standing at the top right is principal Harry Guzniczak.

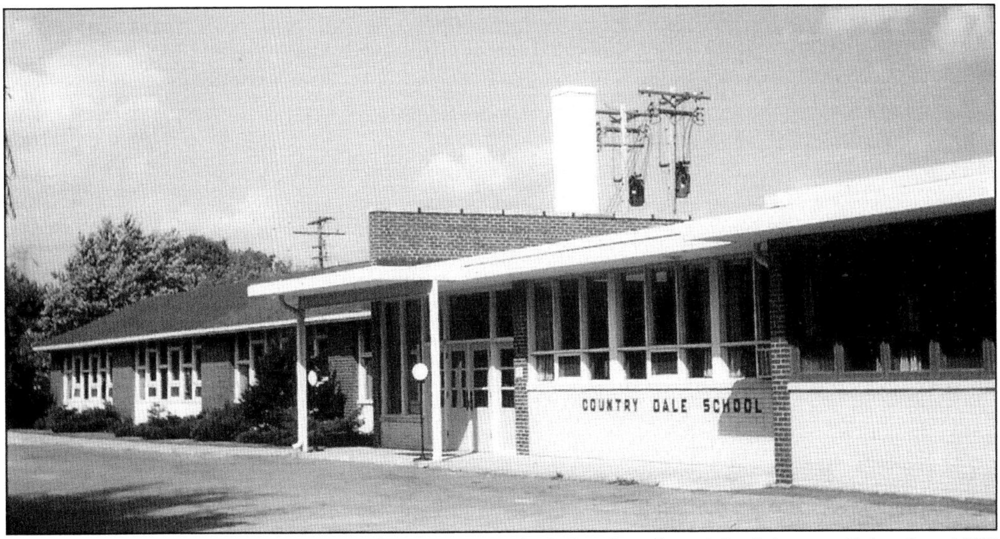

Built along South North Cape Road, Country Dale School replaced St. Martins School in 1957 and merged with Willow Edge School to form Franklin's first modern multiroom elementary school on the west side of Franklin. Country Dale was consolidated with Ben Franklin School to form Franklin School District No. 5 and served as the city's first middle school through the 1960s. .

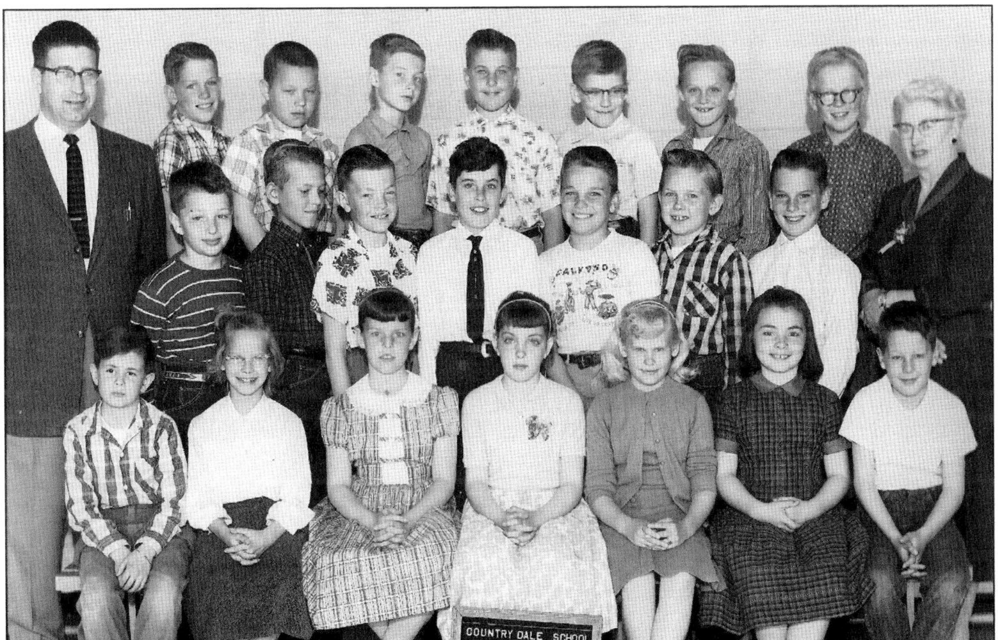

This is the 1958 fourth-grade class at Country Dale School taught by Edward Nickelbine (left). The school had five classrooms with a student population of 130. The fourth graders shown here are, from left to right, (first row) Richard Bristow, Janis Kujawa, Barbara Trojan, Kathy Janiuk, Laurie Thein, Daryl Van Skyhawk, and Bill Bertram; (second row) Walter Amsler, Michael Bruce, John Radtke, Steve Myszewski, Dan Desnica, Monte Swan, and Ted Vahovius; (third row) Bradley McCarthy, Gary Radtke, Robert Schwade, Kerry Smith, Jon Koniecki, unidentified, and Terry Sossaman. Standing to the right is principal Helen Marsh.

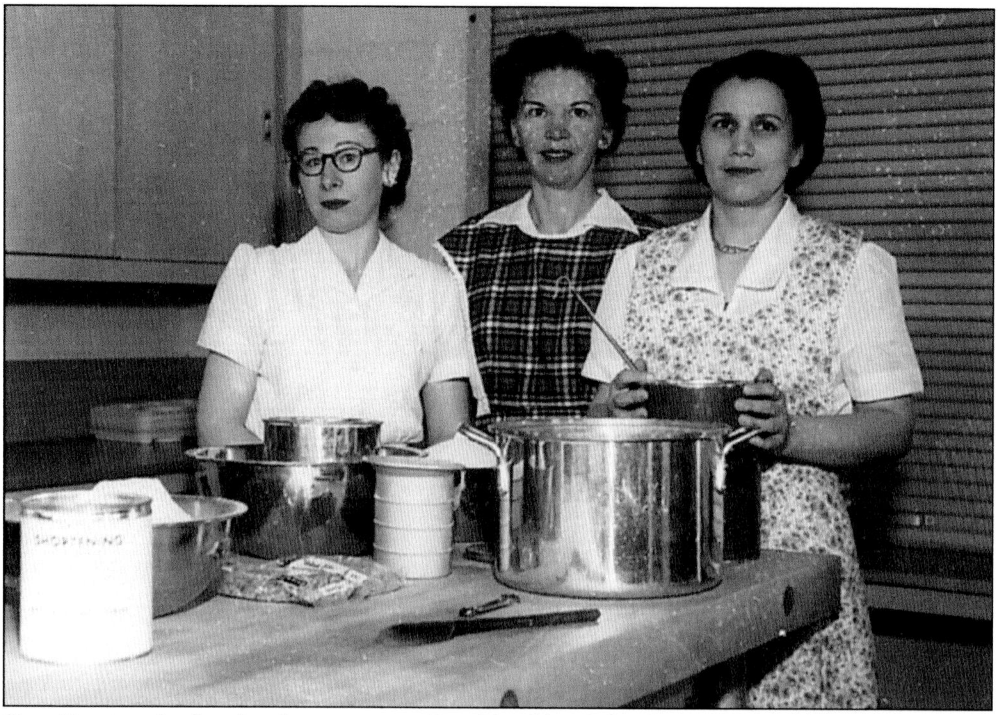

Coordinating the hot lunch program at Ben Franklin School in 1955 are (from left to right) Florence Kuchenbecker, Helen Delikat, and Meta Schmechel, who replaced Lillian Kiefer as head cook. Schmechel went on to direct the kitchen staff at Franklin High School in 1962.

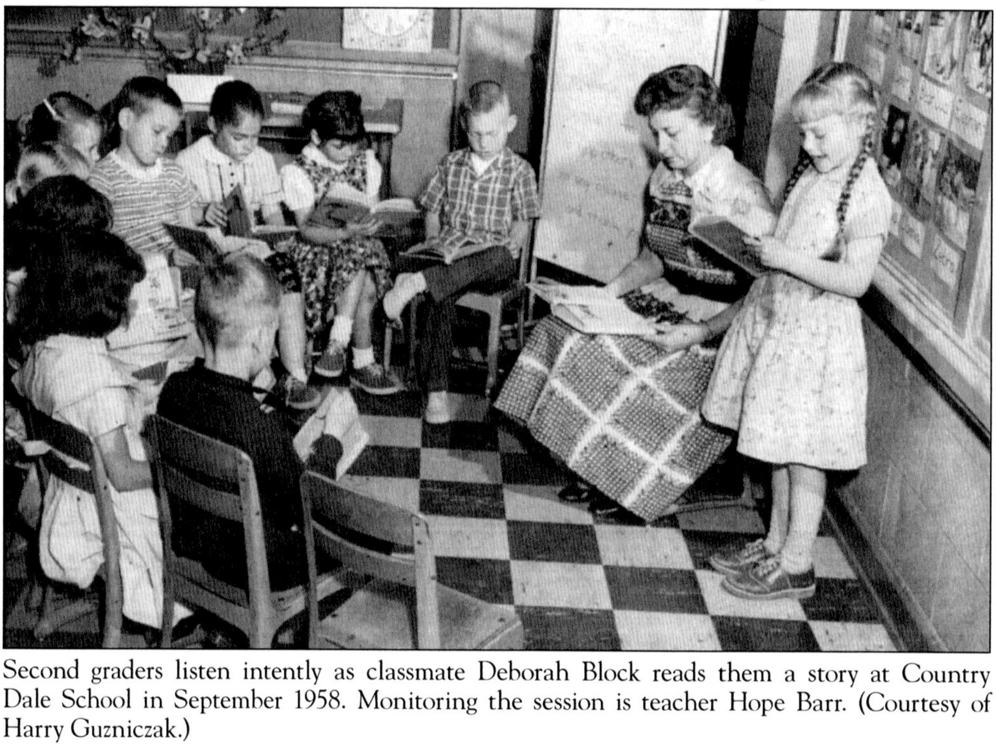

Second graders listen intently as classmate Deborah Block reads them a story at Country Dale School in September 1958. Monitoring the session is teacher Hope Barr. (Courtesy of Harry Guzniczak.)

Bus rides were always adventurous for Franklin youths during the 1950s. Seventh grader Gary Elliott is shown here tugging the scarf of 14-year-old Judy Pares en route to Ben Franklin School in February 1955. (Courtesy of Milwaukee Journal.)

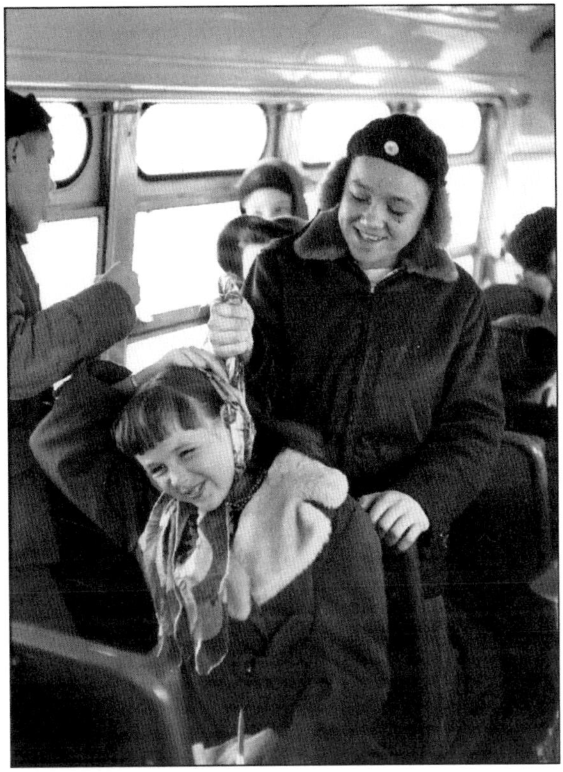

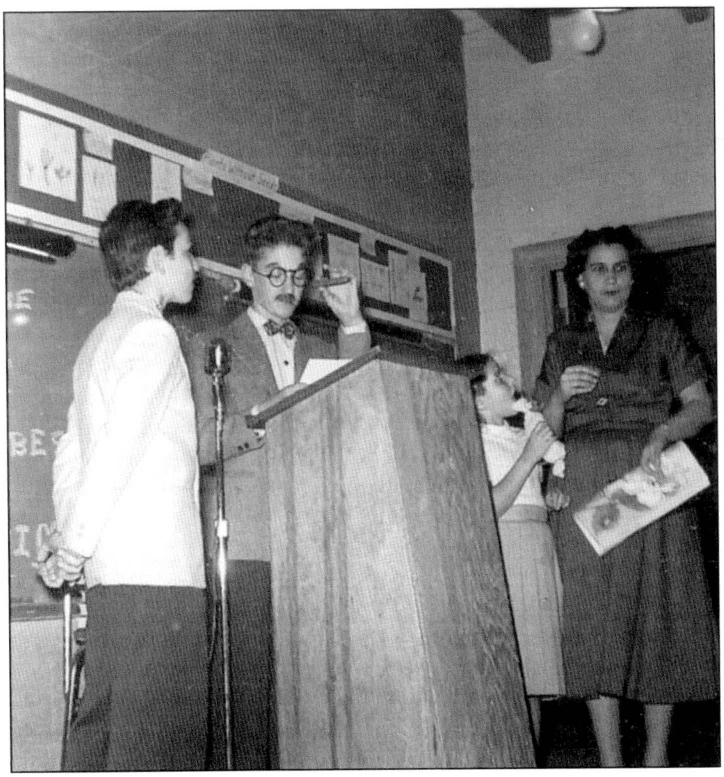

Re-creating the highly rated *You Bet Your Life* television show of 1955 are George Buse (behind podium) as Groucho Marx and Thomas Gibes as his sidekick, George Fenneman. Buse and Gibes were seventh graders at Ben Franklin.

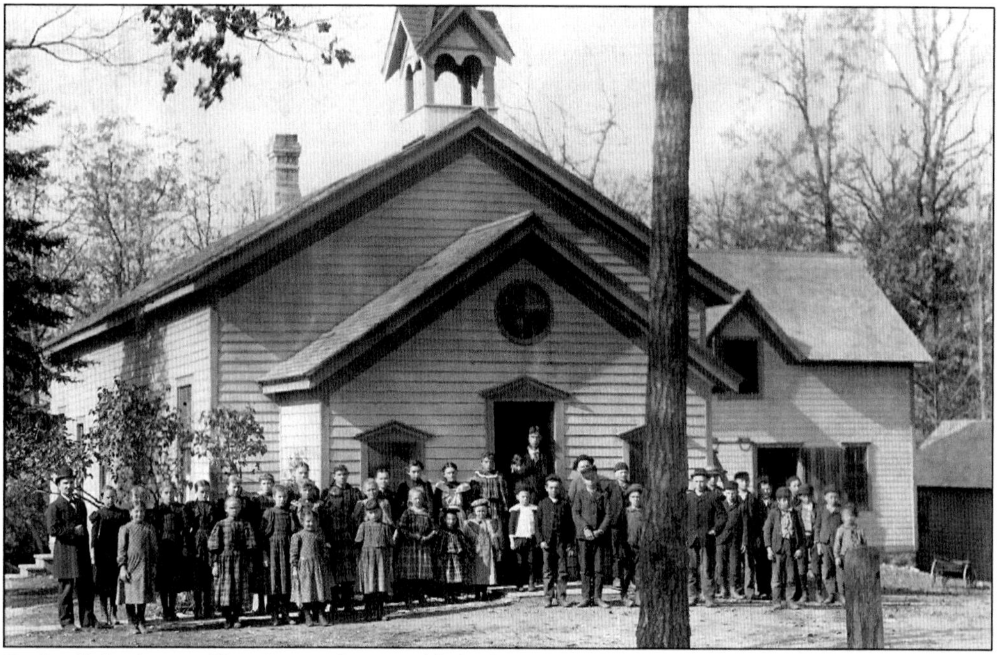

St. Paul's Lutheran Church was first established on Town Line Road (College Avenue) in 1865 and incorporated a German parochial school. A new school was built in 1887 and had 65 pupils enrolled. From 1895 through 1911, Pastor H. Monhardt (shown at far left) taught school at St. Paul's.

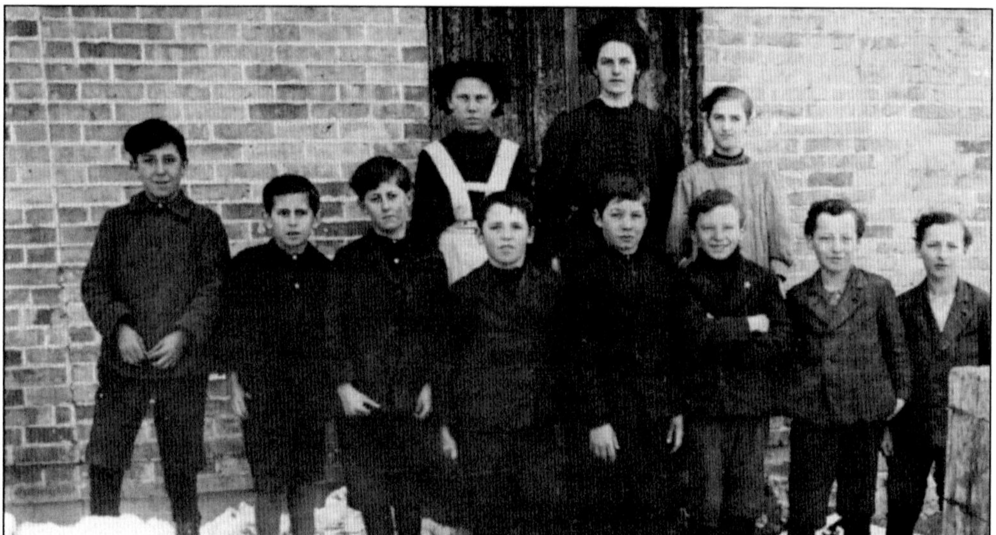

St. James Catholic Church was established by a group of Franklin and Oak Creek farmers on the east side of Kilbourn Road (South Twenty-seventh Street) in 1857. Eight years later the brick school shown here was added with an average enrollment of 15 students. This photograph shows the St. James enrollment in 1909. The students are, from left to right, (first row) Norbert Puetz, Alfred Puetz, Robert Puetz, Roman Puetz, Philip Hauerwas, August Borczykowski, Casper Hagemann, and Hubert Hagemann; (second row) Agnes Prohaska, teacher Anna Puetz, and Louise Puetz.

Seven

Franklin High School

During the 1960s, Franklin began to transition from a rustic farm community to a growing suburb of Milwaukee County. The need for a high school became apparent. When Franklin became incorporated as a city in 1956, there were 320 children in grades one through eight and 95 of high school age. By the time Franklin High School opened in September 1962, the community had 1,025 children in elementary schools and 350 entering high school.

Ground was broken on the hilly Herman Angerstein farm on South Fifty-first Street in December 1961, and the high school opened in September 1962, although the gymnasium was not completed until December, so physical education classes were conducted outdoors as late as November. Guiding Franklin students through those formative years was principal Romuald (Romey) Kucinski.

The school was essentially a junior high that first year, since the student body consisted of 347 8th, 9th, and 10th graders. Franklin students selected the nickname Sabers in tribute to the prehistoric saber-toothed tiger, chose black and gold as their school colors, named their school newspaper the *Saber Slate*, and developed a Gold Shovel football rivalry with St. Francis High School, which opened the same year. Franklin High School students voted to adopt Parkland as the name of a new conference, which would include Greendale, Greenfield, Oak Creek, Whitnall, Muskego, New Berlin, and St. Francis beginning in the fall of 1963.

Competing for two years without a senior class, wins came grudgingly for Franklin's athletic teams, but students never lacked school spirit when it involved bus trips to rival schools to cheer on the Sabers, singing an original fight song coined by band director Al Treske, constructing homecoming floats, attending record hops, or participating in school plays and musicals.

Several major events transpired at the national and international level that also affected students of that time—the Cuban Missile Crisis, the assassination of Pres. John F. Kennedy, the influence of the Beatles on pop culture, and the ever-expanding war in a Southeast Asian country called Vietnam. Such was the environment that shaped Franklin High School's first student body.

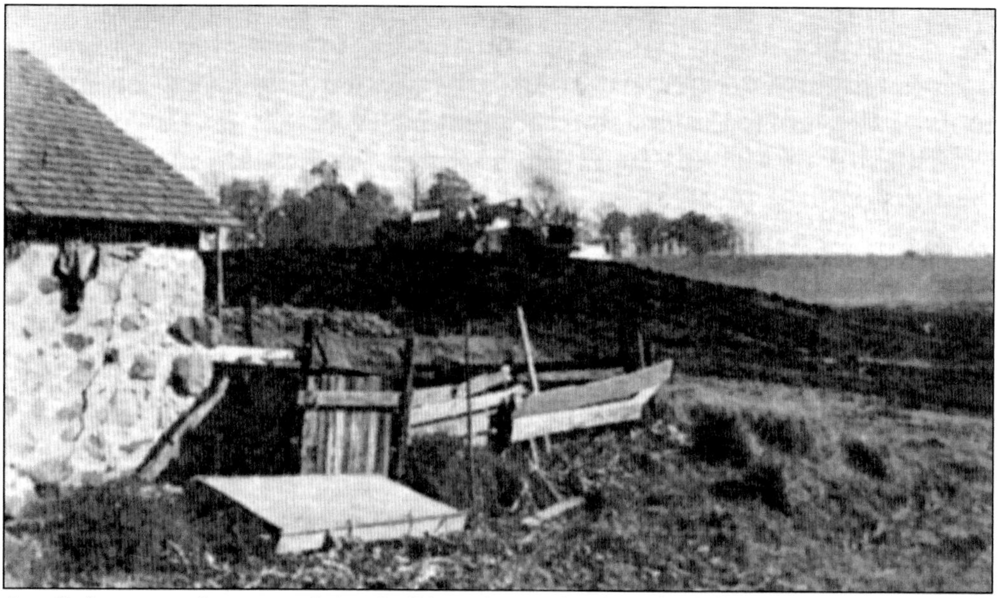

A milk house stands sentry while a bulldozer begins leveling the hilly terrain on the Herman Angerstein farm early in 1962 for construction of Franklin High School along Fifty-first Street just south of Drexel Avenue. A unique feature of the Angerstein farm was that marijuana was grown there during World War II to provide hemp (ropes) for U.S. warships. (Courtesy of Saber Slate.)

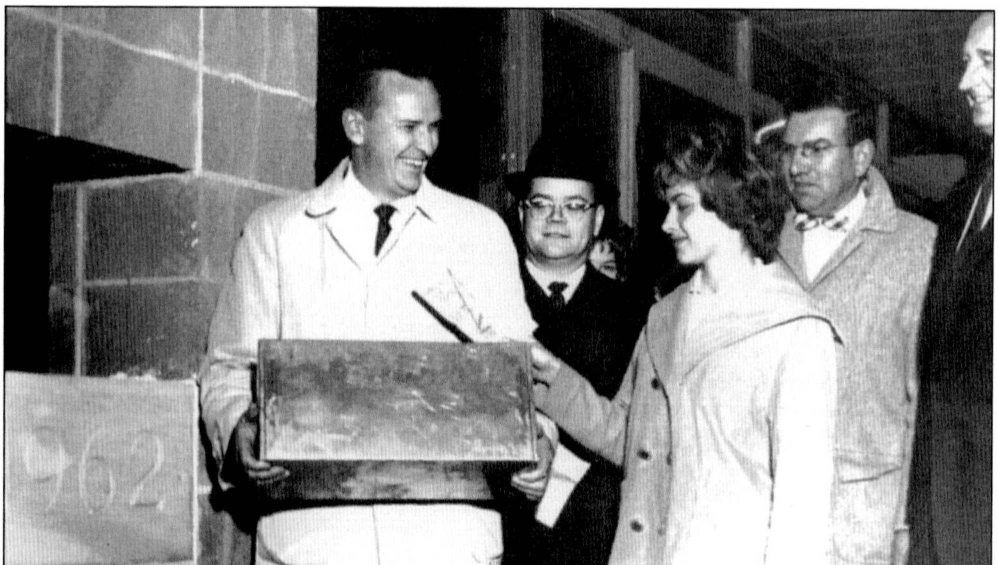

A month after Franklin High School opened, cornerstone ceremonies were held on October 28, 1962. Franklin school board chairman Herman Diedrich holds a metal box into which student council president Pat Metz places documents and photographs. Others participating in the ceremonies are, from left to right, superintendent of schools Harry Guzniczak, school board member Lester Erdman, and Franklin High School principal Romauld (Romey) Kucinski. Contents of the box are scheduled to be revealed on the school's 50th anniversary in 2012. (Courtesy of Franklin High Yearbook.)

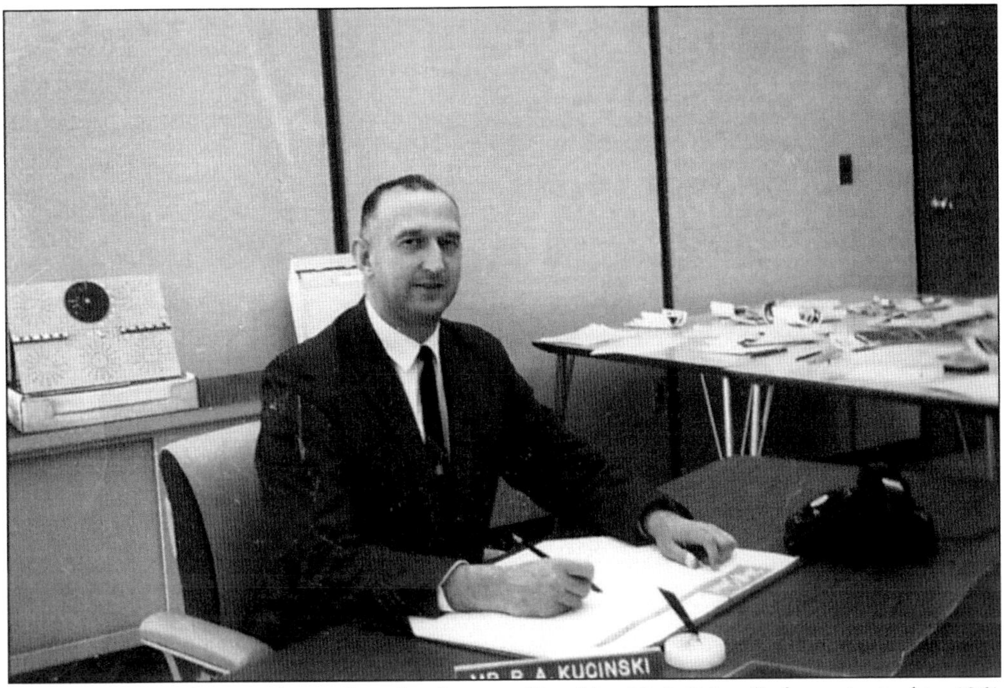

Romuald (Romey) Kucinski was hired to become Franklin High School's first principal in 1961 and held that role for 29 years. After retiring as principal in 1990, he served as Franklin High's transportation coordinator until 1999. (Courtesy of Franklin High Yearbook.)

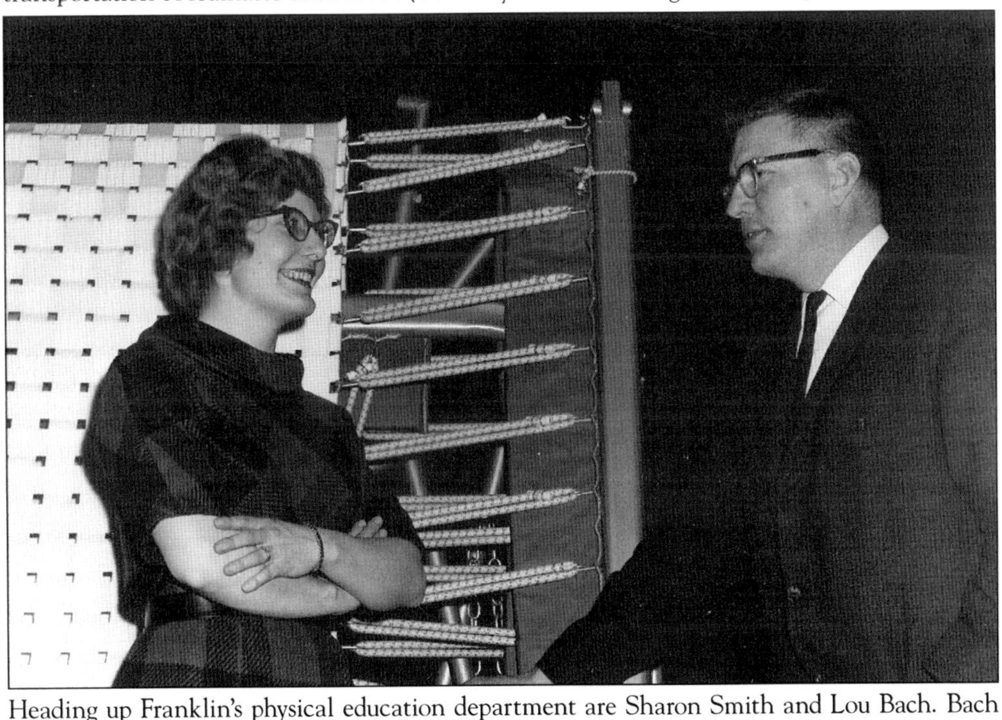

Heading up Franklin's physical education department are Sharon Smith and Lou Bach. Bach wore many hats during the 1960s, serving as athletic director, head football coach, and golf coach. (Courtesy of Franklin High Yearbook.)

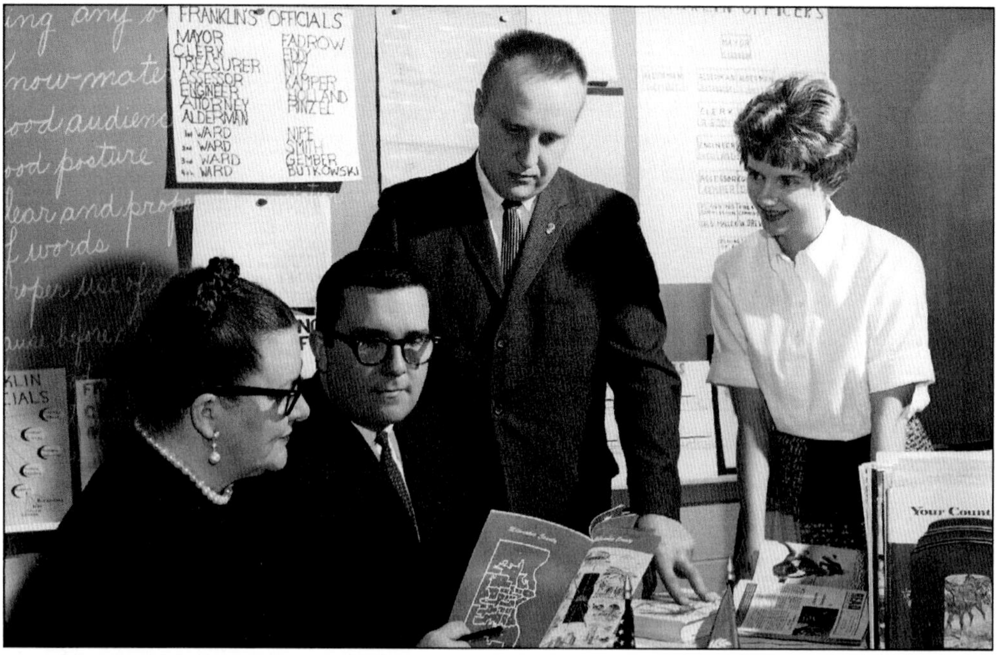

Because Franklin High School opened without a senior or junior class, the school provided education for eighth-grade students during its first two years, 1962–1963 and 1963–1964. Directing the eighth-grade classes are (from left to right) Viola Prokupek, David Thomson, Karl Wegerbauer, and Lynn Patzer. (Courtesy of Franklin High Yearbook.)

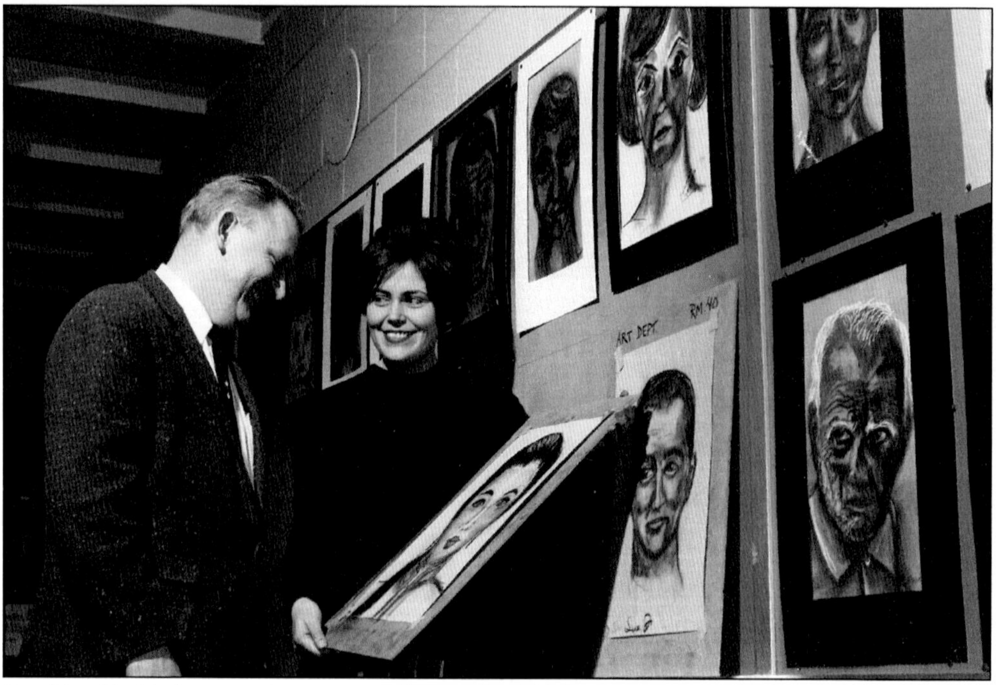

Franklin High's fine arts departments during the 1960s were directed by Al Treske (band) and Pat Seramur (art). Treske, who wrote the school's fight song and alma mater theme, remained band director until his retirement in June 1988. (Courtesy of Franklin High Yearbook.)

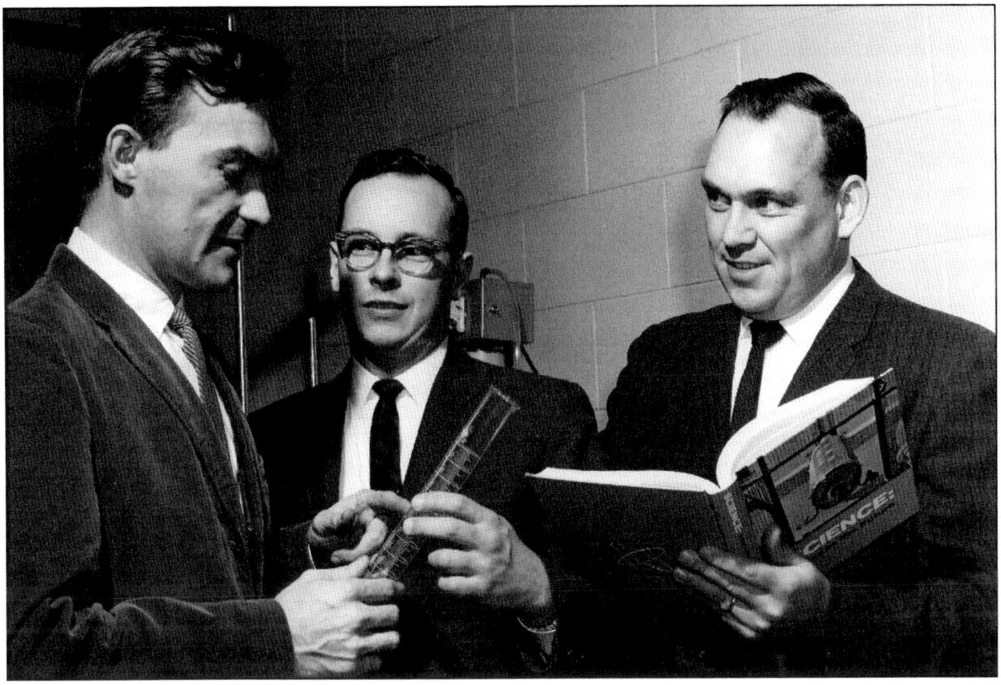

Directing science and math classes at Franklin High during the 1960s are (from left to right) Fran Sand, John Stannard, and David Engleson. Stannard taught algebra and geometry, Sand taught chemistry and general science, and Engleson headed the science and conservation fields. (Courtesy of Franklin High Yearbook.)

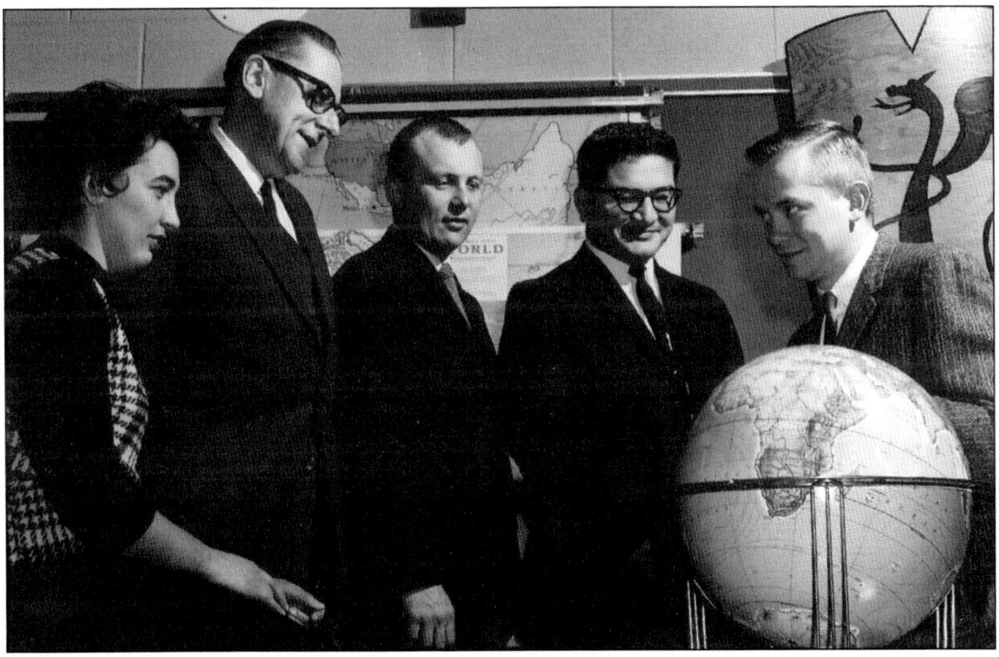

Language arts and social studies at Franklin High in 1962 were directed by (from left to right) Theolinde Deitche (German), Paul Musolf (English), Al Block (social studies), Martin Moreno (Spanish), and Lowell Seider (English and Latin). (Courtesy of Franklin High Yearbook.)

SABER SLATE

VOL. 1, NO. 1 FRANKLIN HIGH SCHOOL NOVEMBER 21, 1962

A STAR IS BORN

CORNERSTONE CEREMONY

On Sunday, October 28, 1962, the cornerstone for the new Franklin High School was laid. The documents, including work of students and pictures of the new school, were placed in the box by Miss Patricia Metz.

The program consisted of selections played by the band under the direction of Mr. Treske, and the pledge of allegiance and the Star Spangled Banner led by James Gyuro. Greetings and remarks were made by Mr. H. E. Guzniczak, Superintendent of Schools, Mr. Herman Diedrech, director of the school board, Lester Erdman, school board member, Mr. R. A. Kucinski, principal and Miss Patricia Metz, student council president. An open house followed the ceremony.

Fifty years from now, in the year 2012 A. D., another important event will be held. It will be the opening of the box con-

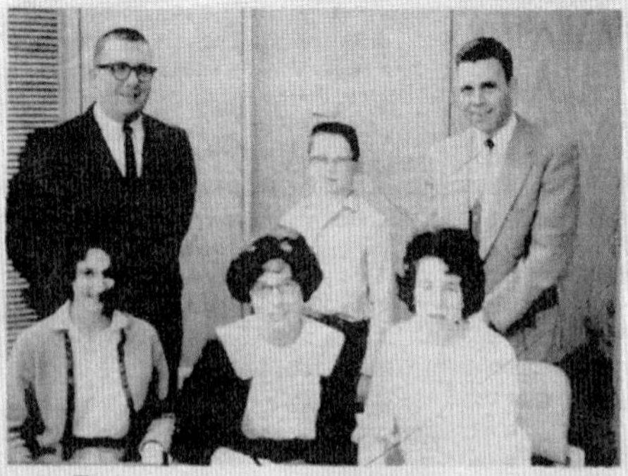

SABER SLATE advisors and editors are, standing from left to right, Mr. Thomson, Douglas Schmidt and Mr. Puffer. Seated are Joyce Ebben, Carlyn Albrecht and Sandra Webster.

This first year at the new high school brings forth many new and interesting experiences. One of the new creations is destined to be a star. Yes, here, a star has been born. And who is it? Why, the Franklin High School's newspaper, "The Saber Slate".

The students on this staff chose this club voluntarily from a list of clubs given to all the students.

(Cont'd from col. 1) taining the documents placed in the cornerstone. We cannot predict the future but let's hope all of us can say, "Yes, I was there at that memora-

There are 22 members and four advisors including Mr. Puffer, Mr. Thomson, Mrs. Ruedinger, and Miss Seramur.

The name was chosen by the school students by a majority vote. They were given a list of names, and room to write their own suggestions.

Many problems came along with the struggling new star, but these are being solved as we go along.

We are planning five more issues to be published this year, so be on the lookout for them. S. Webster

WATCH FOR THE NEXT ISSUE

A tradition was born with the first issue of Franklin High School's student newspaper, the *Saber Slate*, published in November 1962. The editors were all sophomores and freshmen since the school had no upperclassmen. One story notes that the contents of a metal box placed in a cornerstone will be revealed on the school's 50th anniversary in September 2012. (Author's collection.)

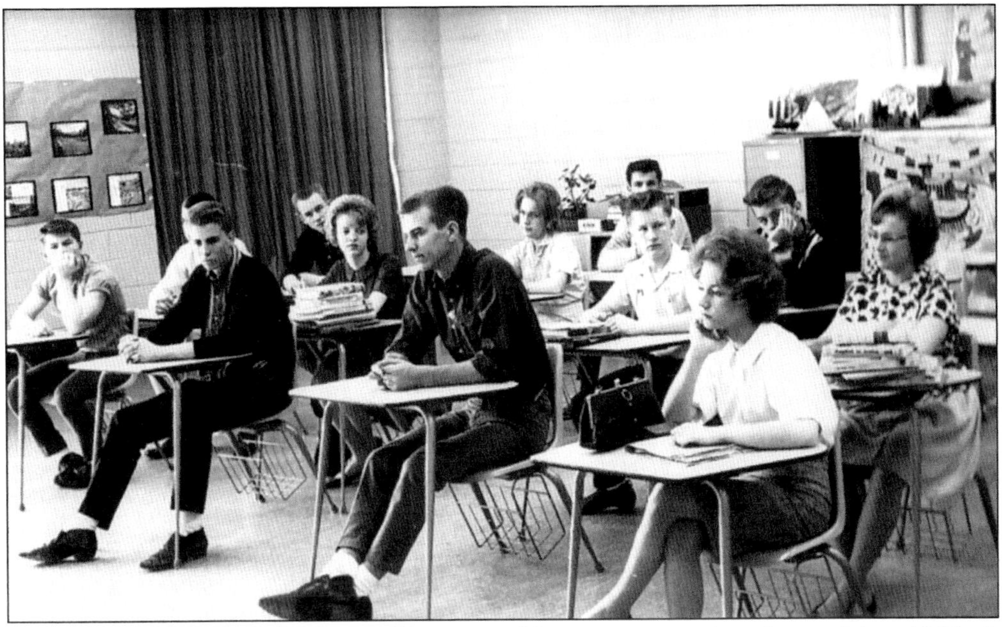

Members of Franklin High's first student council listen to instructions from advisor Al Block in 1962. Shown are, from left to right, (first row) Rich Fontenot, Frank Brugger, Mike Bruce, and Barbi King; (second row) John Appleyard (hidden), Geanine Barg, Rusty Sem, and Jane McChesney; (third row) Tom Hareng, Melody Elliott, and Robert Werner; (fourth row) Jim Gyuro.

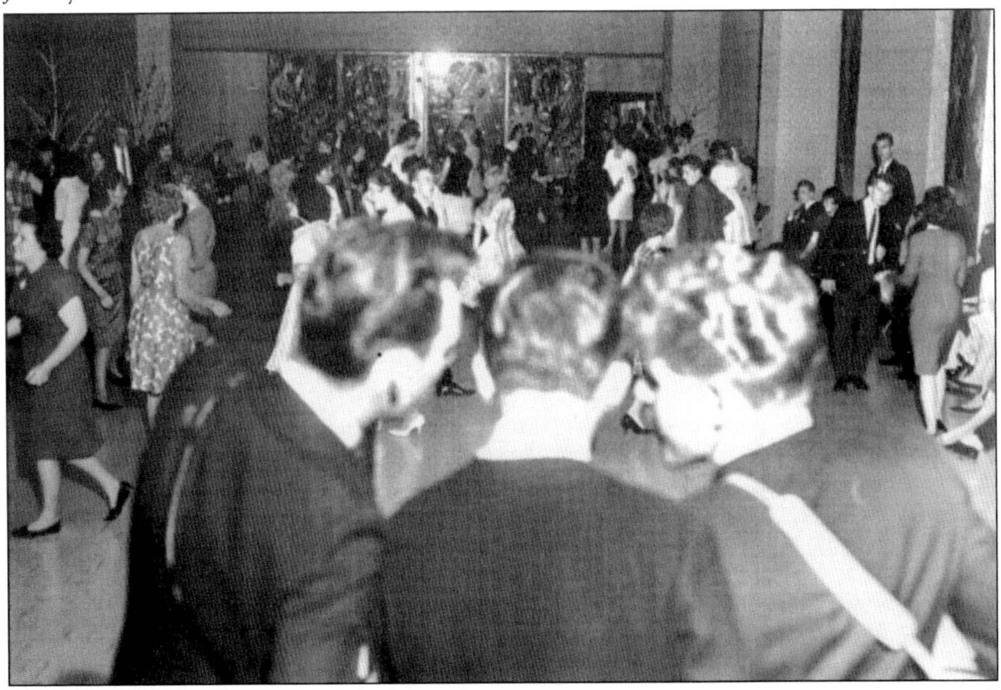

Students dance to the music of the Midnighters (foreground) at Franklin High's first Snowball dance in December 1962. The dance was held in the high school cafeteria. (Courtesy of Franklin High Yearbook.)

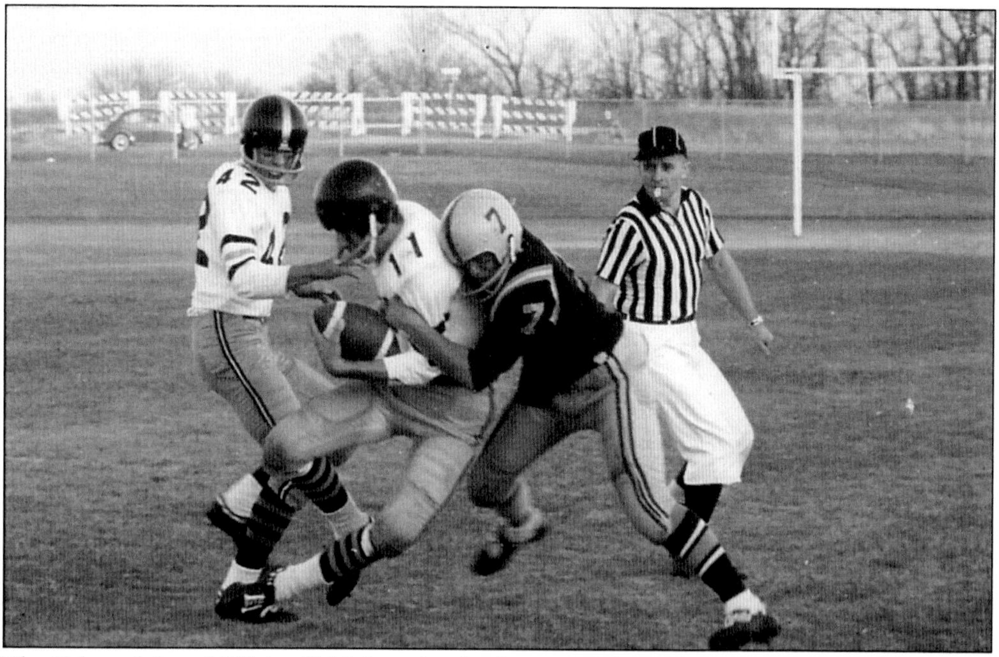

The Sabers defeated Whitnall 19-6 in the final game of the 1964 season to compile a record of 3-3-1. Here Franklin senior quarterback Mike Zolecki (11) is tackled as junior Ken Rieland (42) looks on. The previous year the Sabers made their debut in the new Parkland Conference without a senior class and scored just 13 points the entire season. (Courtesy of Franklin Hub.)

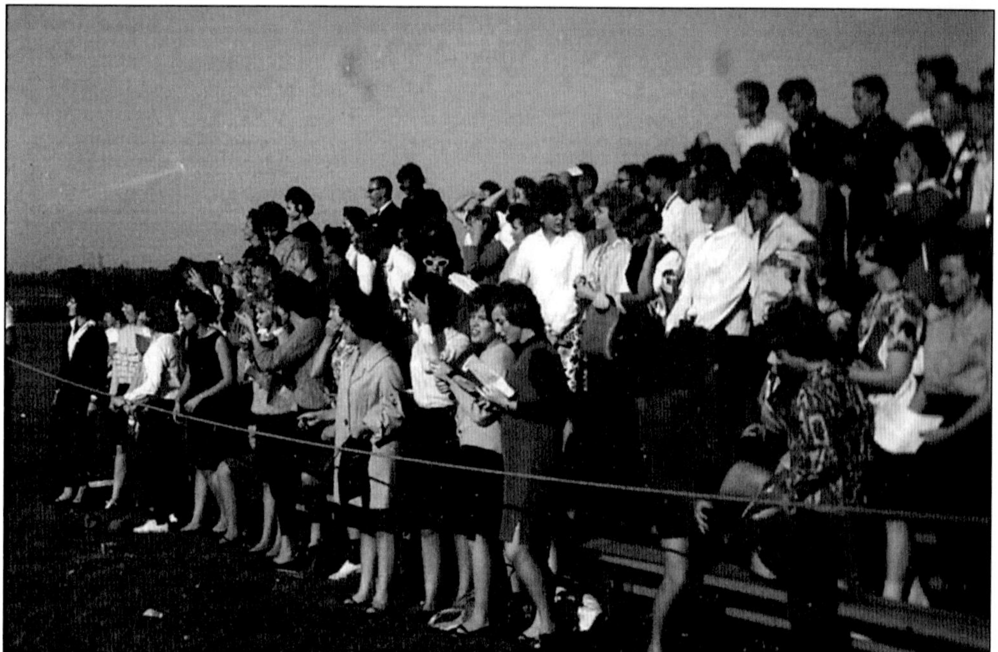

Franklin High School students cheer on the Fighting Sabers during the school's first season of varsity football competition in 1963. Lacking a senior class, Franklin's student population was 483. (Courtesy of Franklin High Yearbook.)

Franklin's Gold Shovel football rivalry with St. Francis High School began with a 20-13 junior varsity victory over the Mariners in 1962. The shovel signified that both high schools broke ground and opened the same year. Proudly displaying the trophy is the Franklin coaching staff of (from left to right) David Thomson, Jim Keepers, Lou Bach, and Martin Moreno. (Courtesy of Franklin High Yearbook.)

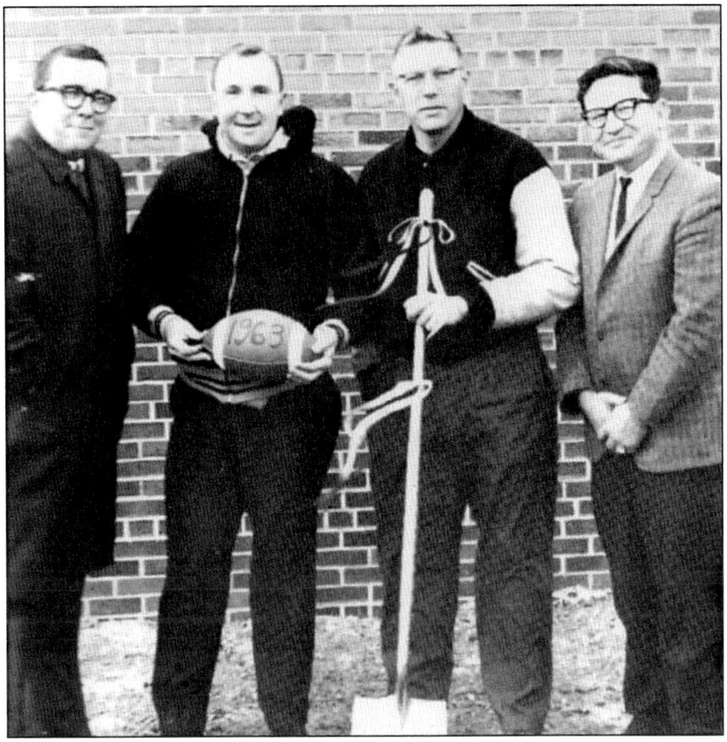

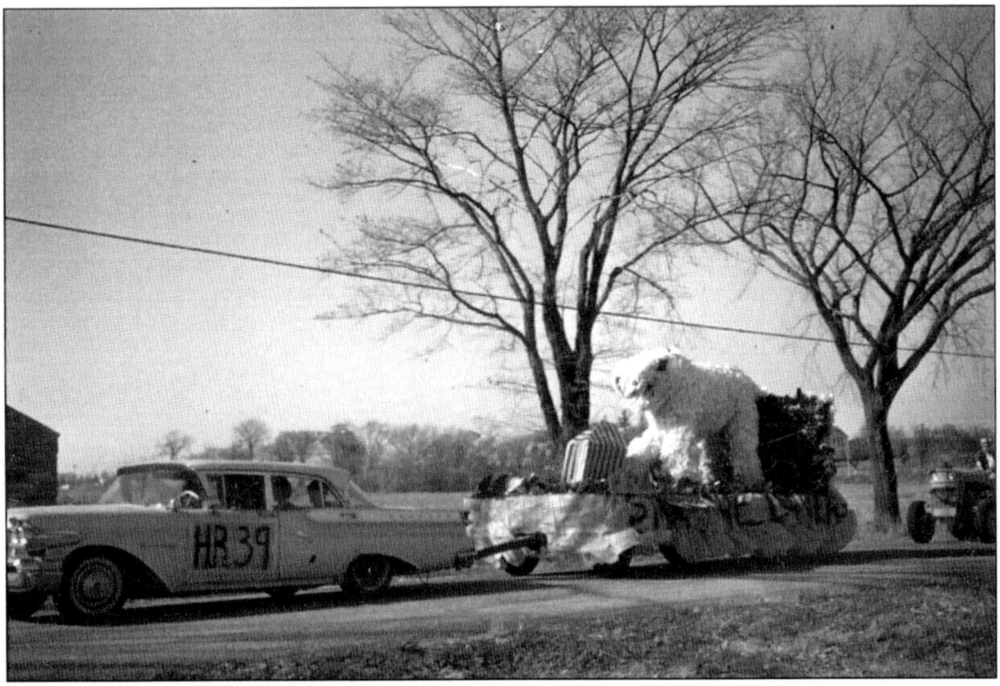

Franklin High held its first homecoming parade on October 24, 1964. With a student body of just 555, each Franklin High School homeroom produced a float that was paraded down Fifty-first Street from Pleasant View elementary school to the high school. (Courtesy of Bonnie Fenner-Homan.)

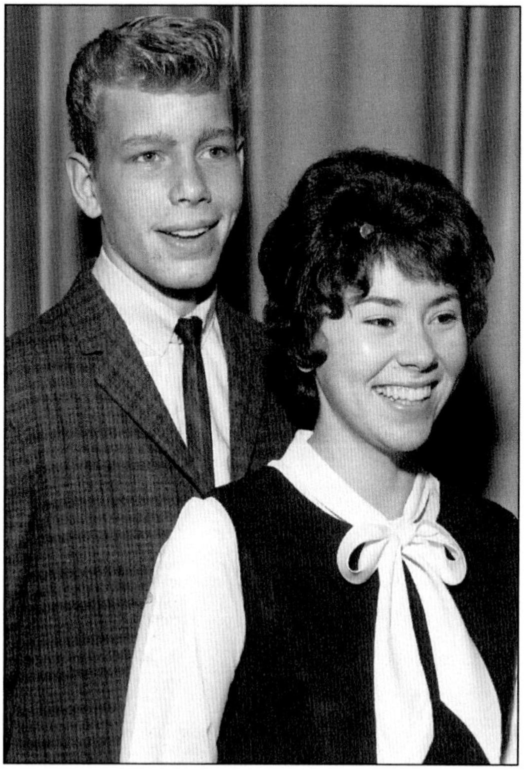

Reigning over Franklin High School's first homecoming court in October 1964 were seniors Steve Boyd and Geri Perea. Members of their court were Linda Schneiger, Sue Hisey, Mary Thurow, Sandy Schultz, Dennis Higgins, Loren Keske, John Bowitz, and Roy Kainz. It was a unique event since the school still had no alumni returning home that fall. (Courtesy of Franklin Hub.)

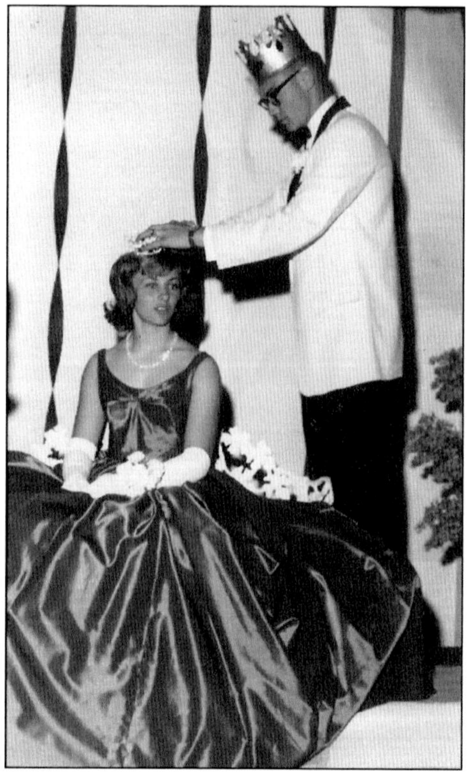

The first prom at Franklin High featured Mark Crnkovich as king and Pat Metz as queen. The prom was held in the Franklin High gymnasium in May 1964. Crnkovich and Metz were members of the junior class. (Courtesy of Franklin Hub.)

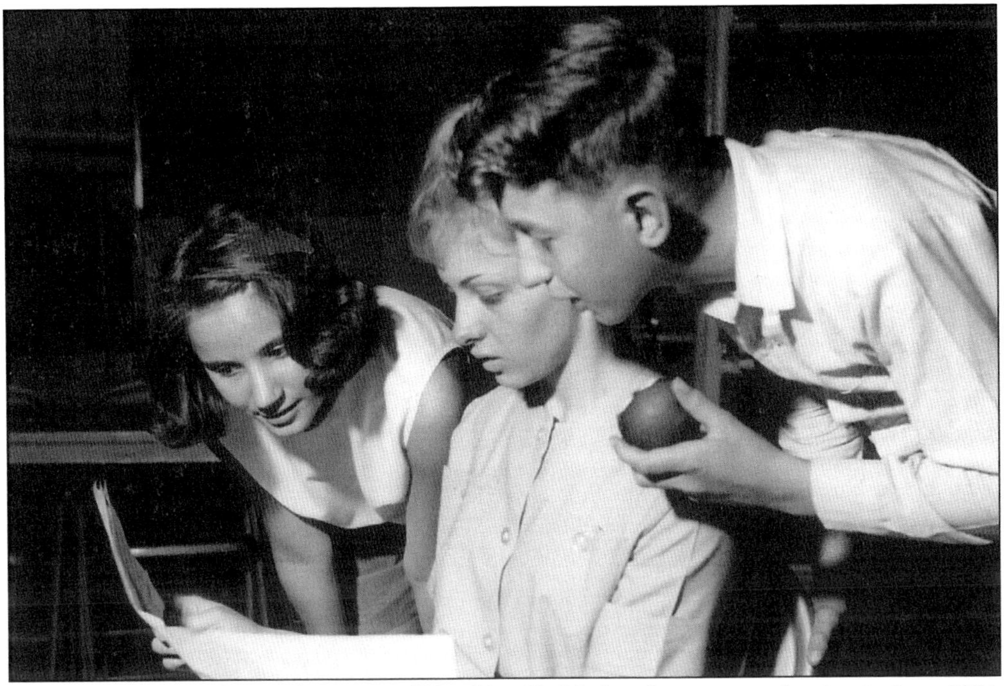

Home Sweet Homicide was the name of Franklin High's first dramatic production in June 1964. Rehearsing their lead roles are (from left to right) Sandi Spies as April, Pat Metz as Dinah, and Bob Weber as Archie. (Courtesy of Franklin Hub.)

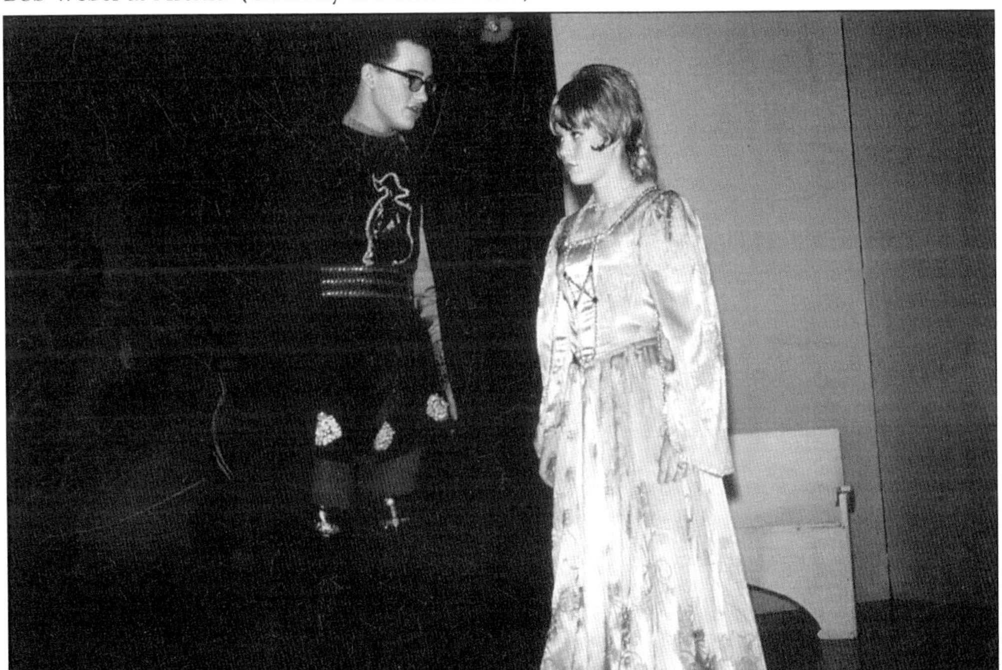

Reprising the roles of Sir Galahad and Evelyn are seniors Dave Ross and Davney Herriges in the musical *A Connecticut Yankee* staged at Franklin High in 1965. (Courtesy of Bonnie Fenner-Homan)

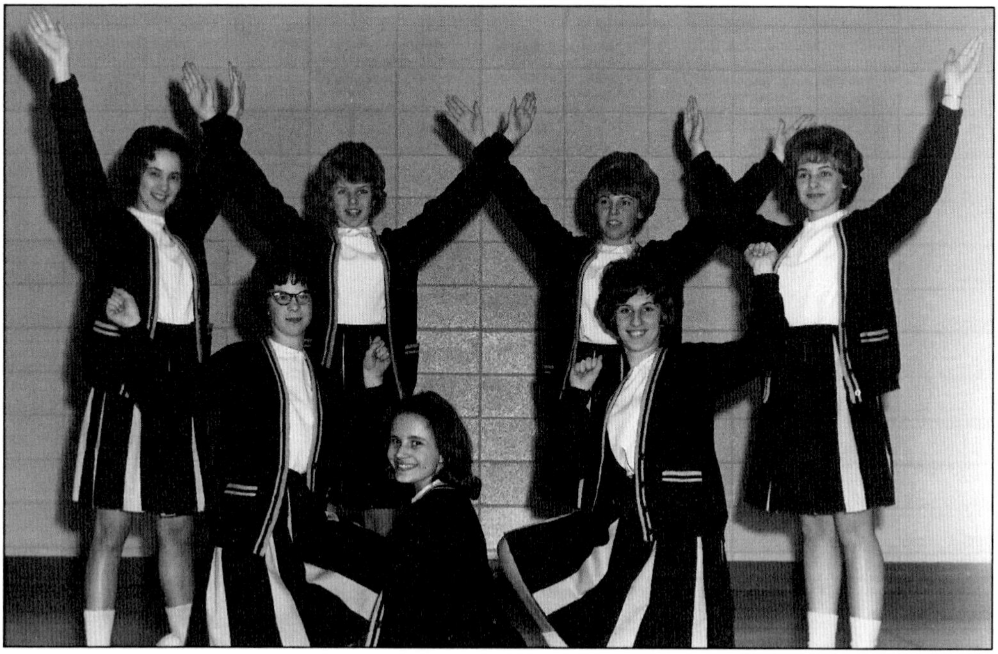

Leading the cheers for the Franklin Sabers in 1962–1963 are the following sophomores: from left to right, (first row) Sandi Spies; (second row) Sandy Schultz and Kathy Sell; (third row) Joyce Ebben, Christine Pugh, Sharon Szczesniakiewicz, and Pat Metz. (Courtesy of Franklin High Yearbook.)

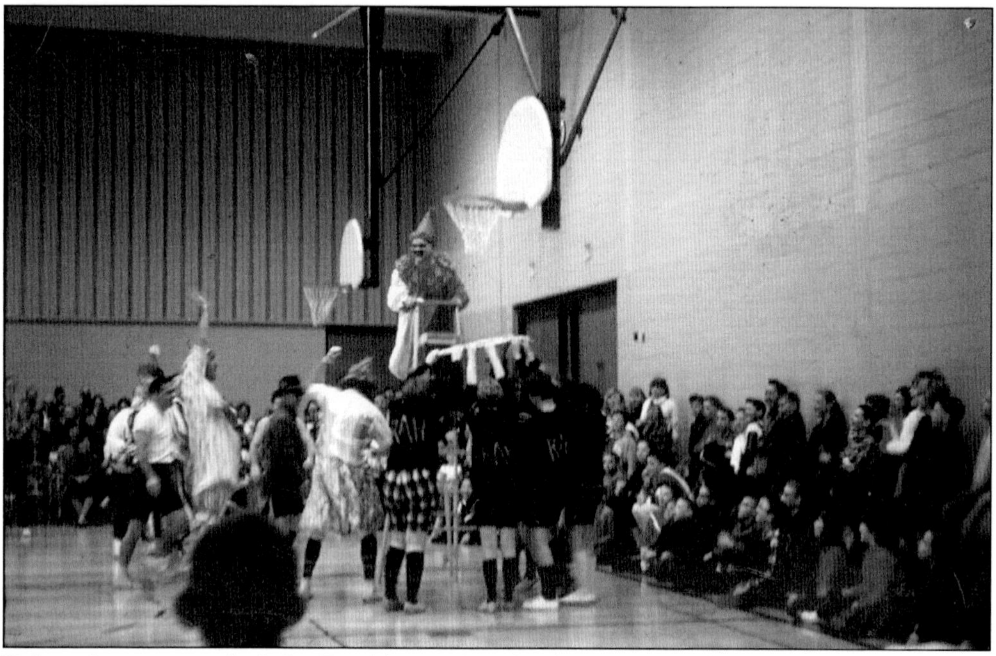

Kids and parents packed the Franklin High School gymnasium for a zany basketball game between school board members and city administrators in 1964. It was followed by a game between the high school varsity and faculty. Proceeds from the event went toward purchasing band uniforms. (Courtesy of Bonnie Fenner-Homan.)

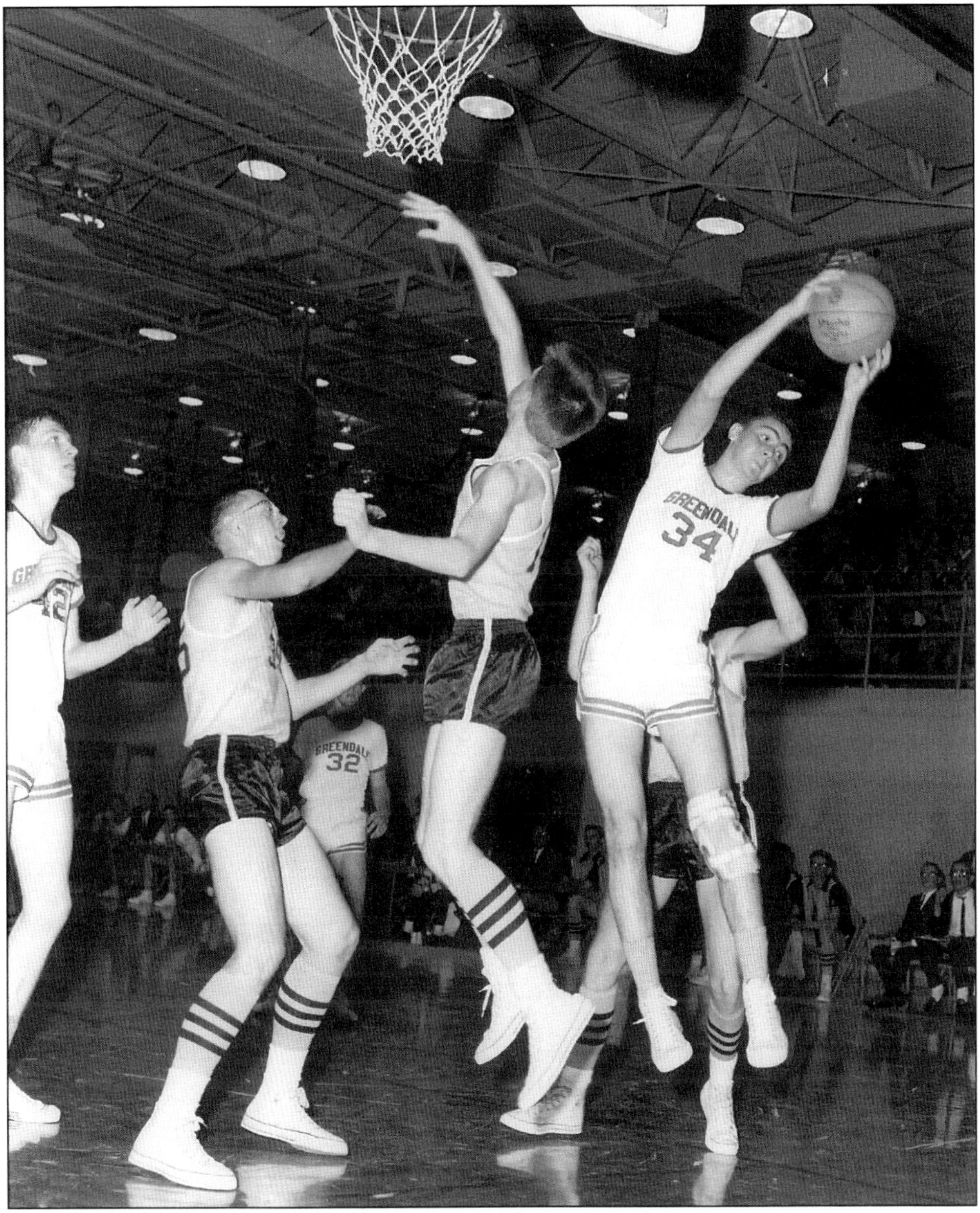

Sophomores Hartley Dus (left) and Monte Swan (center) battle Parkland rival Greendale for a rebound during Franklin's first varsity basketball season in 1963–1964. The Sabers posted 1-13 records their first two seasons before finishing 9-5 in 1966. Swan became Franklin's first player voted to the Parkland all-conference team as a senior. (Courtesy of Franklin Hub.)

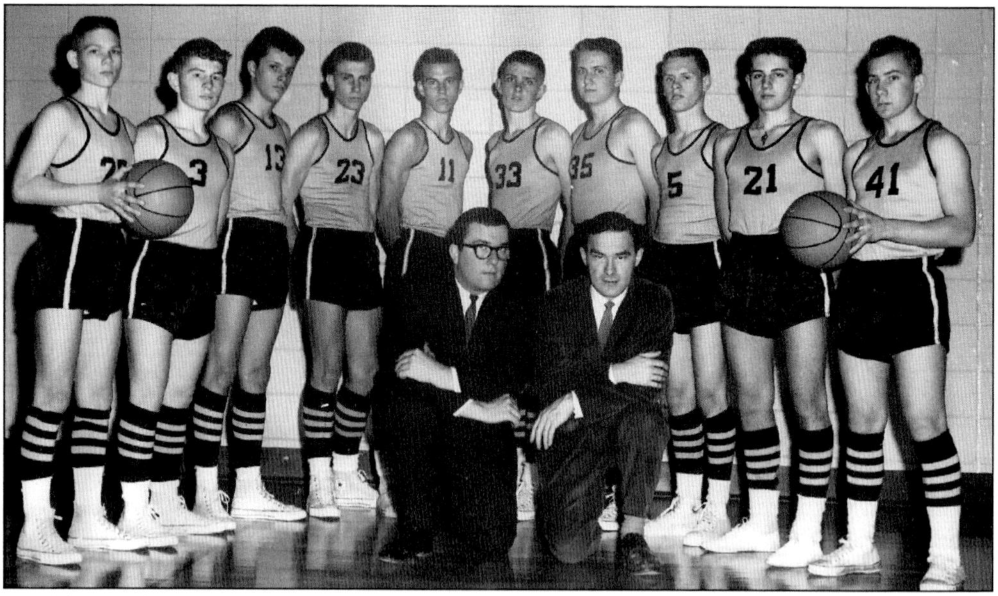

Franklin High School's first basketball team was made up of freshmen and sophomores who played a junior varsity schedule during the 1962–1963 season and finished with a record 3-11. The players are (from left to right) Bill Gregor, Rich Fontenot, Dale Reissing, Frank Brugger, Mike Bruce, Tim Kirchner, Lloyd Martin, Walter Natynski, David Kuehn, and Dan Schreiner. The Sabers were coached by Dave Thomson (left) and Fran Sand. (Courtesy of Franklin High Yearbook.)

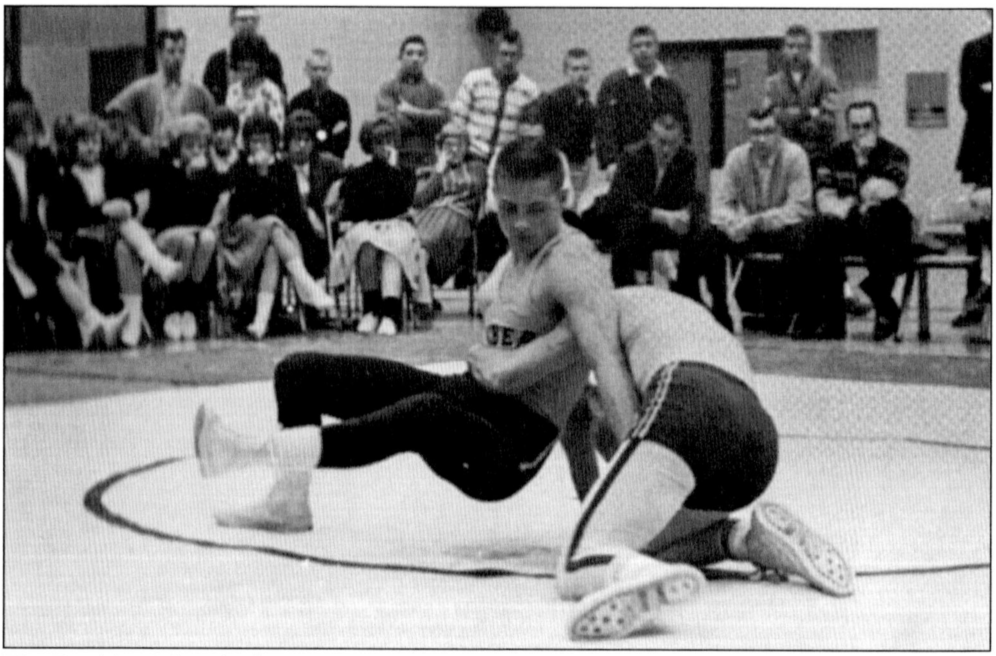

The Franklin Sabers had a more successful start in wrestling than they did in basketball during the 1962–1963 season, winning six dual meets while losing eight. Here Loren Keske makes a reverse move on an opponent during a meet in the Franklin High gymnasium. (Courtesy of Franklin High Yearbook.)

Loren Keske, Franklin's star athlete in football, wrestling, and track, confers with Mike Walden, a WTMJ TV sportscaster who spoke at the school's sports banquet in 1964. (Courtesy of Franklin Hub.)

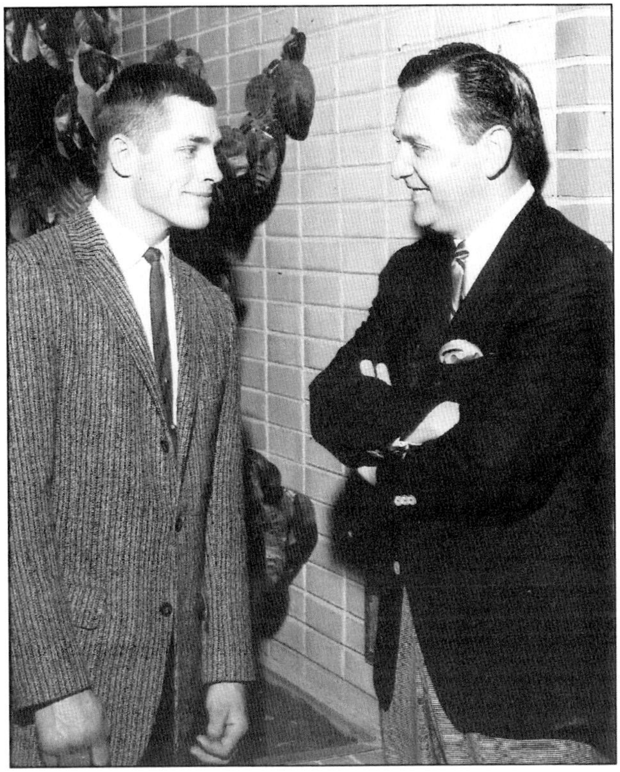

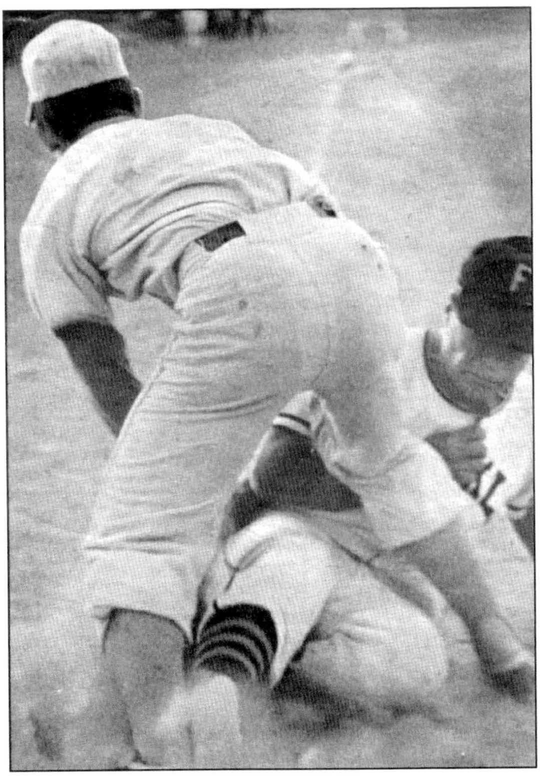

Sliding into home with the tying run is Franklin's John Horvath underneath the tag of New Berlin's George Zuniga. Horvath scored on a wild pitch after hitting a triple in the seventh inning. The game went 10 innings before New Berlin secured a 2-1 victory to capture the 1965 Parkland Senior League championship. New Berlin finished with an 11-3 record, one win better than Franklin. (Courtesy of Franklin Hub.)

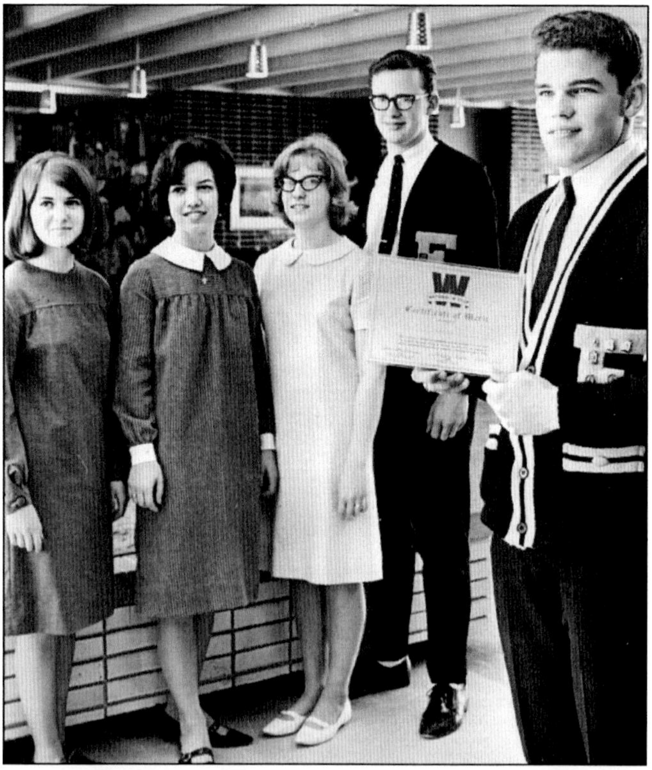

Shown here are members of Franklin High School's class of 1966 who earned college scholarships. They include (from left to right) Betty Marshall, Christine Weinert, Sandra Leiteritz, David Ross, and Robert Mayer, who received a certificate of merit from the National W Club at the University of Wisconsin. (Courtesy of Franklin Hub.)

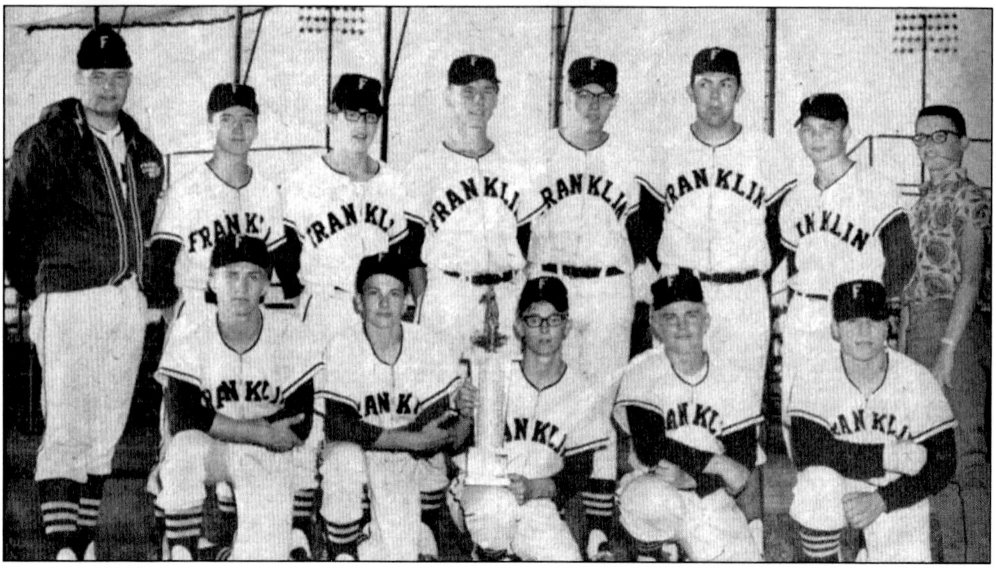

Franklin High's first sports championship came during the summer of 1966 when the Sabers won the Parkland Senior League baseball crown by posting a 10-4 record. The team includes, from left to right, (first row) Gary Greene, Jim Burac, Tom Bowitz, Terry Wilbur, and John Horvath; (second row) coach Len VandenBoom, Craig Leinonen, Keith Kneser, Keith Glaser, Hartley Dus, Randy Goede, Bill Gregor, and Doug Schmidt, statistician. The Sabers capped the season with a 3-2 victory over Suburban Conference champion West Allis Central at McCarthy Park. (Courtesy of Tri-Town News.)

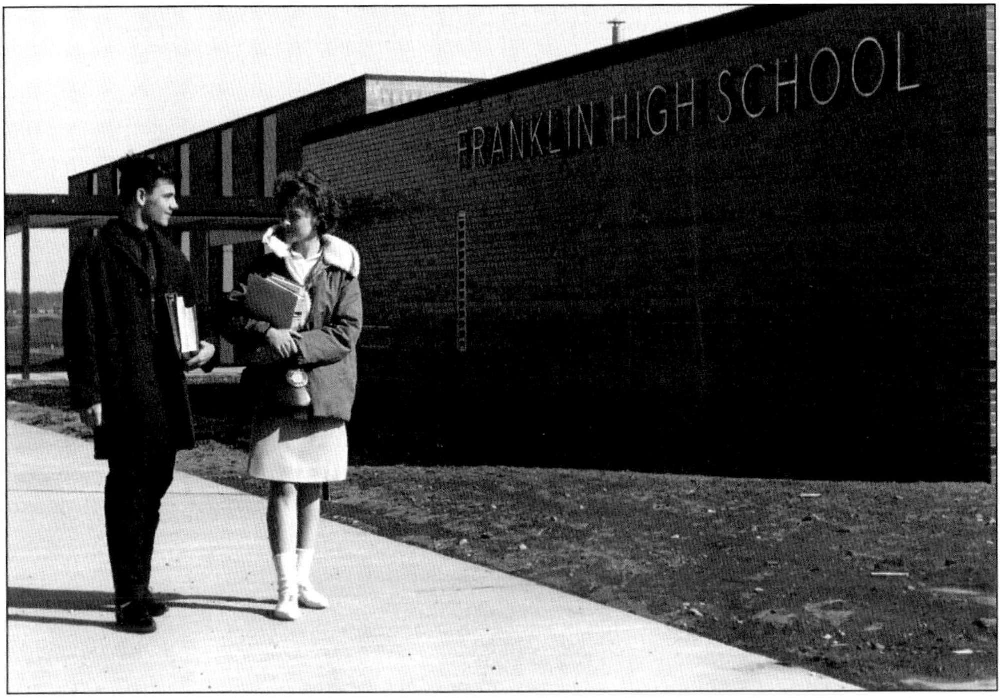

Strolling down the sidewalk in front of Franklin High School as it existed in 1963 are sophomores Jim Gyuro and Pat Metz. Metz served as school president for 1962–1963, and Gyuro was elected to succeed her. (Courtesy of Franklin High Yearbook.)

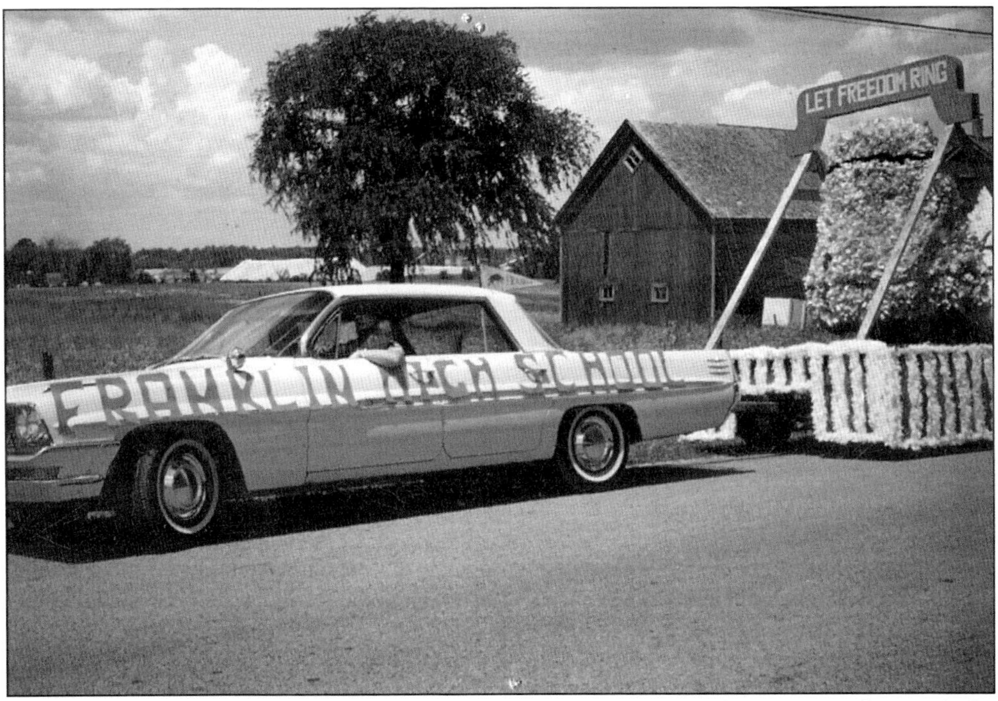

Franklin High students got into the Independence Day spirit in 1964 by creating a float with the theme "Let Freedom Ring" for the city's July 4 parade. (Courtesy of Bonnie Fenner-Homan.)

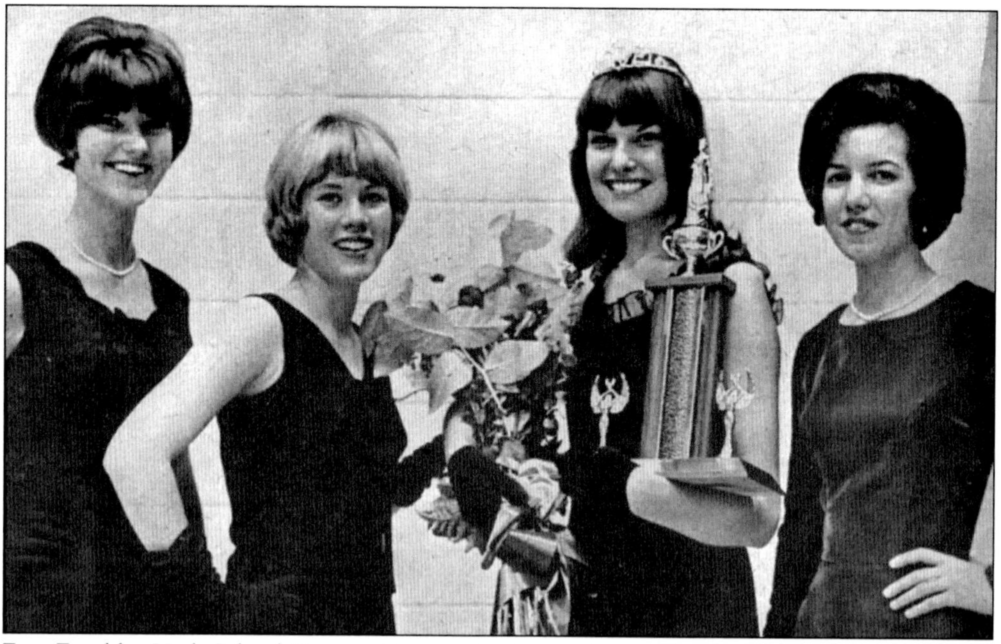

Four Franklin High School 17-year-olds were finalists in the 1965 Franklin Junior Miss pageant. The winner was Bonnie Reeves (second from right). The other finalists are (from left to right) Mary Lyman, Davney Herriges, and Christine Weinert. (Courtesy of Franklin Hub.)

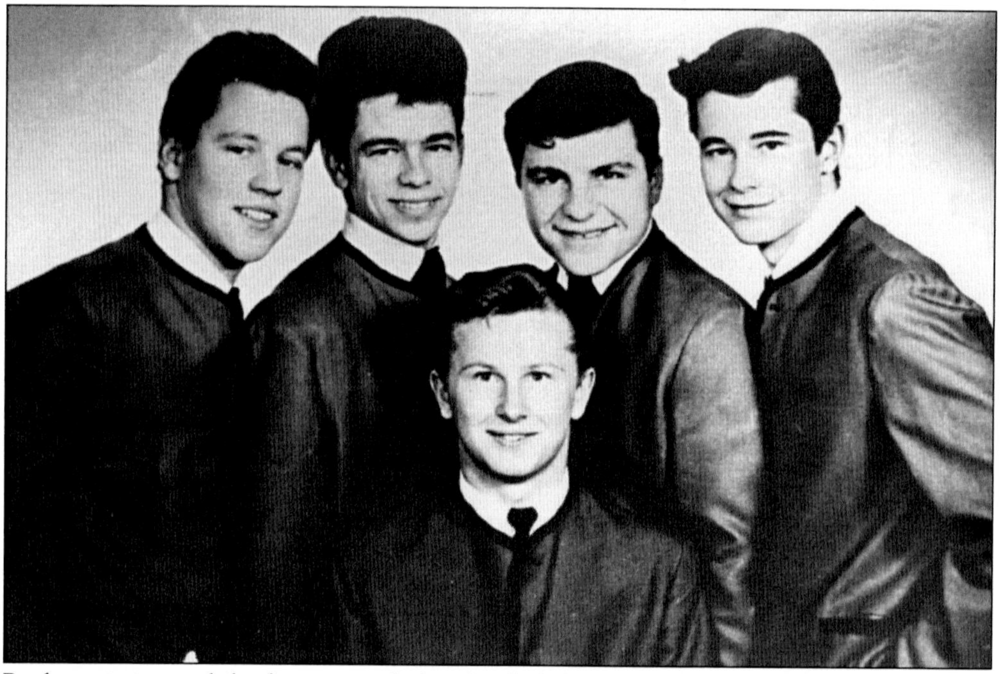

Rock music inspired the formation of a band called the Mar-Vells who fashioned Beatles-style lapelless blazers in 1964. The band includes (from left to right) Paul Holicek, Ed Schulz, Rusty Sem, John Horvath, and Mike Ralston. All were Franklin High students except Holicek. After playing area high school dances, the Mar-Vells continued to perform at Milwaukee nightclubs into the 1970s. (Courtesy of John Horvath.)

Eight

Franklin Historical Society

The Franklin Historical Society evolved from an adult education class taught by Al Block, director of instruction at Franklin High School, who recognized that the city was beginning to undergo rapid change and sought to preserve its history. Dennis Horvath served as acting chairman when the historical society was organized in February 1969. The society was incorporated as a nonprofit organization in July 1969 and became an affiliate of the Wisconsin State Historical Society the following year.

Through the leadership of individuals such as Al Block, Vernon Barg, Vivian Guzniczak, James York, James Kamper, Carl and Pearl Schultz, Lillian Boldt, Matt Englert, Doug Schmidt, and Barbara Pforr, the Franklin Historical Society has developed a strong working relationship with the local government to restore and maintain historic buildings, provide living museums, and offer educational programs that ensure the community's rural history will be preserved.

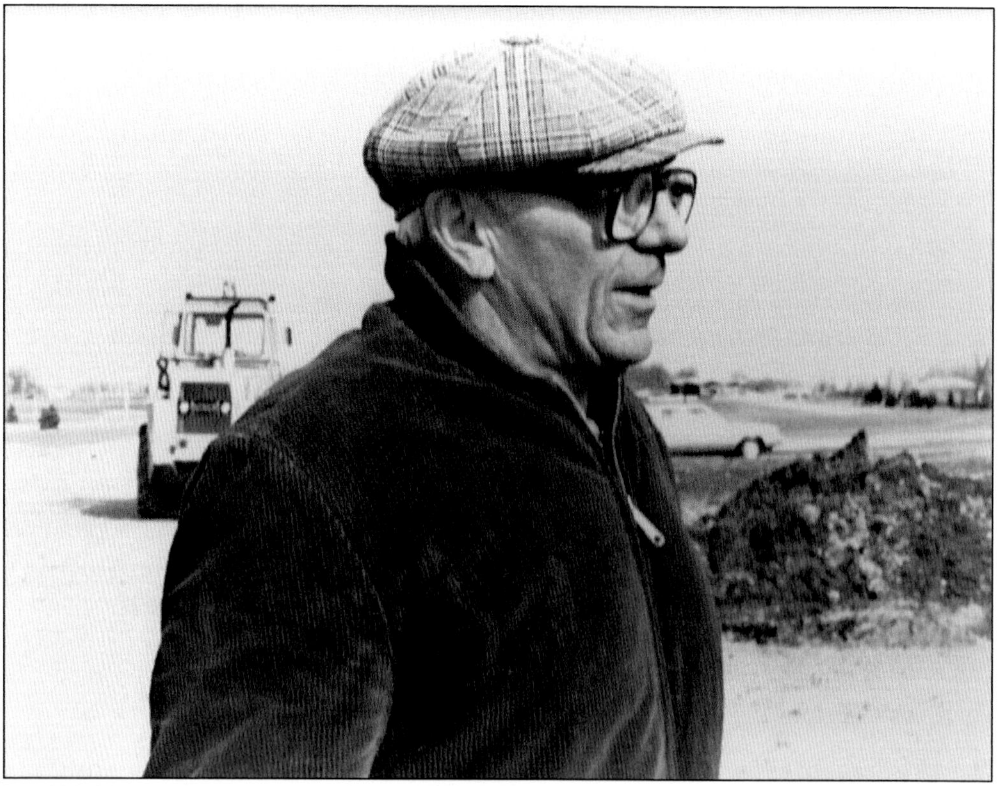

In 1983, Vernon Barg was named Man of the Year by the Franklin Historical Society. Shown here supervising the move of St. Peters Chapel to Lions Legend Park, Vernon was the grandson of John Barg, who began farming on Smith Road (South Fifty-first Street) during the late 1880s. Vernon followed in the footsteps of his father, Edward, who served as Franklin's town clerk for 32 years. Vernon was city clerk from 1954 to 1960, served on several city commissions, and spearheaded efforts to move and renovate four historic buildings after the Franklin Historical Society was formed in 1969. Vernon Barg died on October 26, 2006, and the city of Franklin named a Lions Legend Park pavilion in his honor a year later.

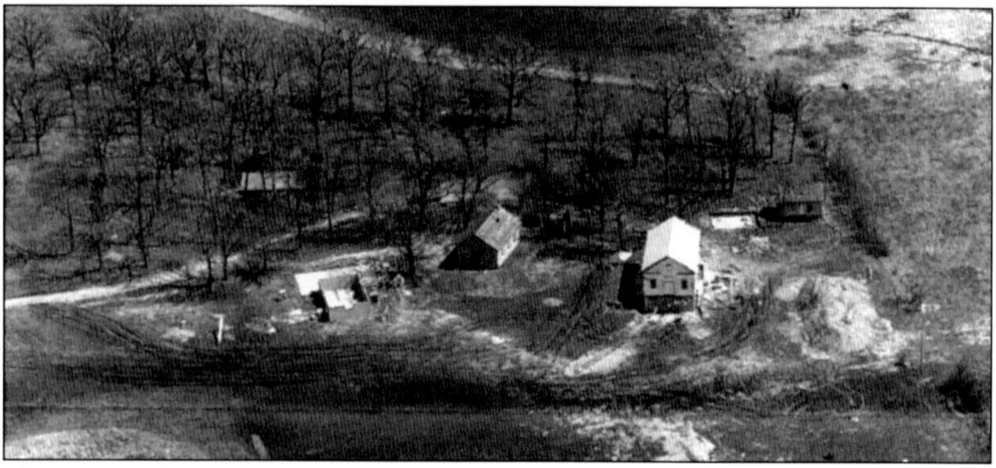

This is an aerial view of Franklin's Lions Legend Park in its early stages of development in 1976. (Courtesy of Franklin Hub.)

Whelan School celebrated its opening as the Franklin Historical Society's first living museum in the summer of 1970. The last of Franklin's one-room schools, Whelan closed in 1953 and was moved to Lions Legend Park in 1969. It was stripped down to its wood infrastructure and awaited restoration with a Cream City brick exterior.

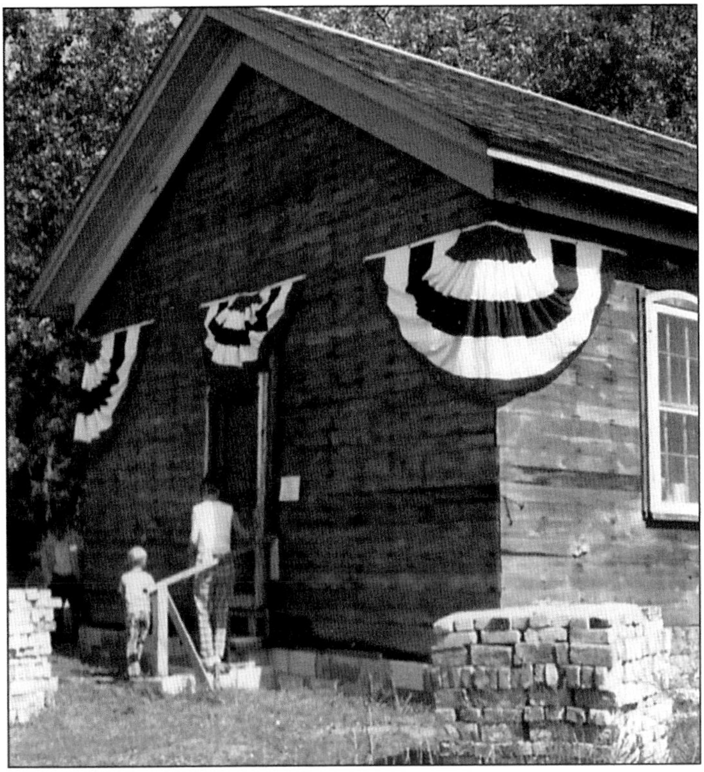

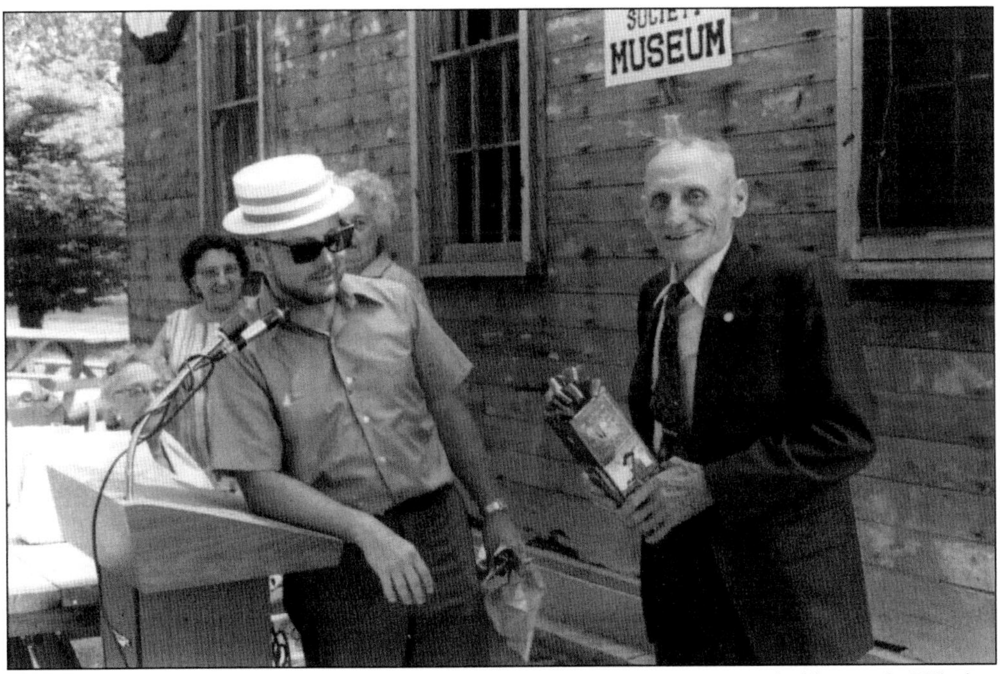

Tom Godsell is shown here accepting the item he won in an auction held outside Whelan School during the summer of 1970. The Franklin Historical Society began fund-raising efforts to restore historic buildings moved to Lions Legend Park.

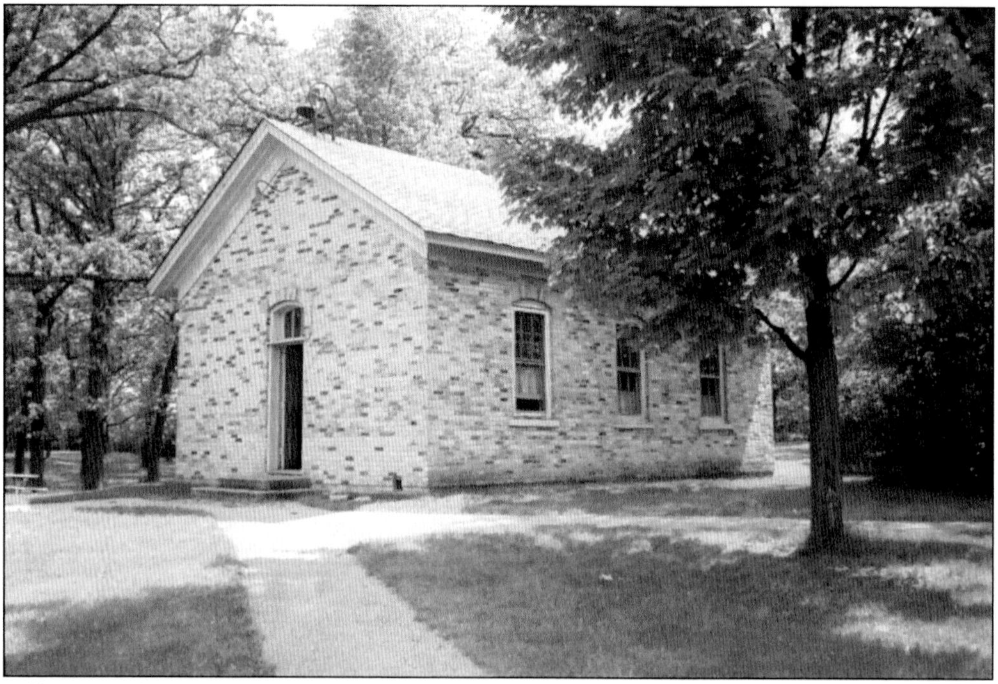

Fully restored, Whelan School has been one of Franklin's most utilized historic buildings in Lions Legend Park over the past 30 years. Elementary school classes are invited to sign up for a day of lessons in a one-room school.

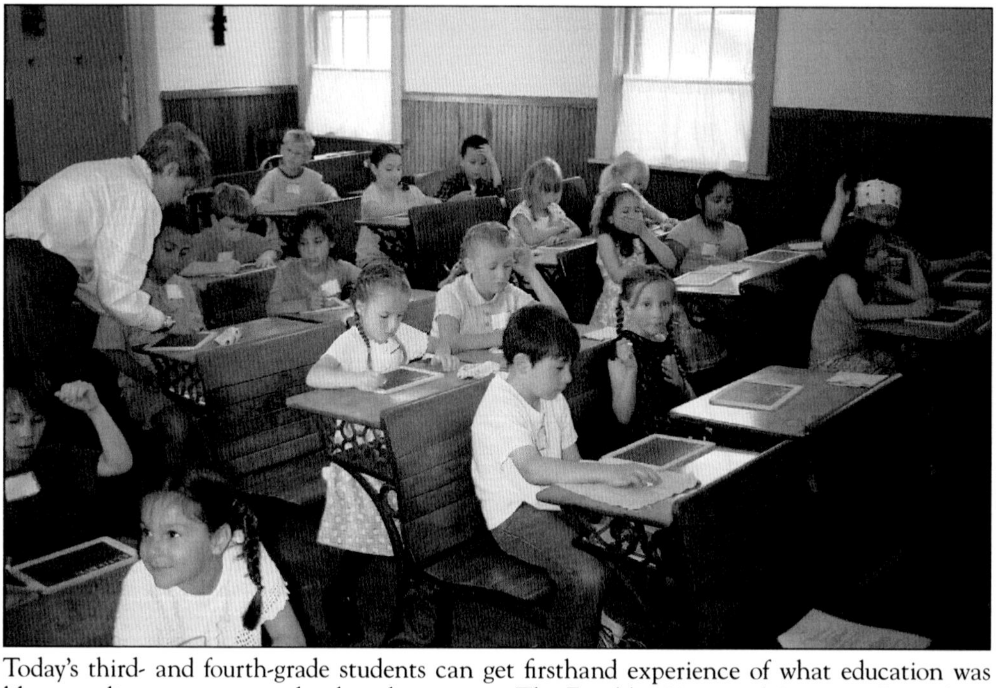

Today's third- and fourth-grade students can get firsthand experience of what education was like attending a one-room school in the country. The Franklin Historical Society offers school for a day in the restored Whelan School. Here students receive hands-on instruction from the teacher, Luanne Burdick.

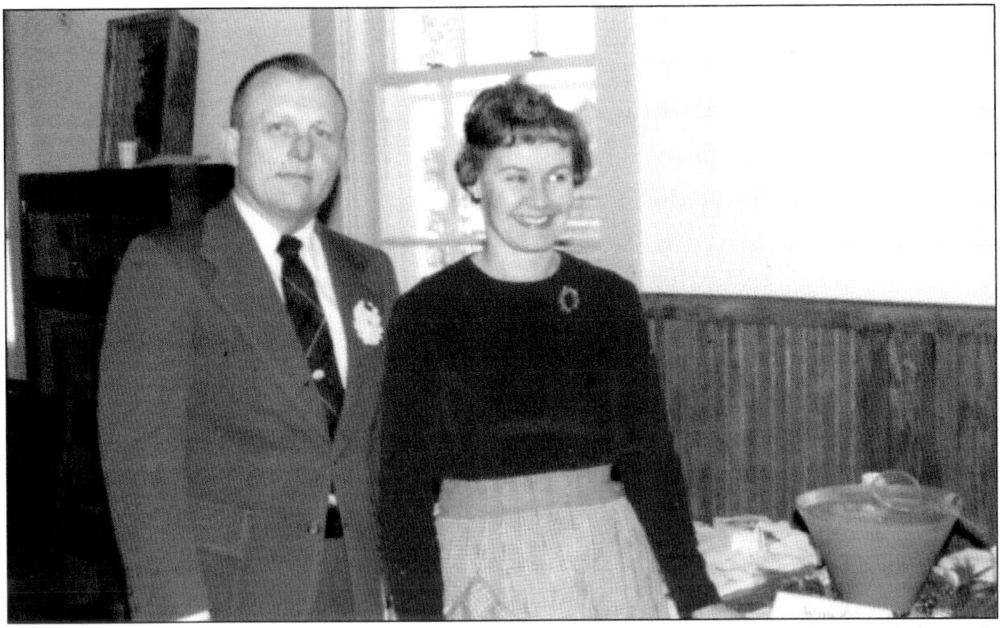

The architect behind the Franklin Historical Society was Al Block, who along with his wife Carol began efforts to preserve Franklin history in 1969. As a director in public education, Al Block recognized Franklin's rapidly changing identity and dedicated his efforts to preserving the community's rural roots through an adult history class he taught at Franklin High School. Carol Block worked diligently as a volunteer for the society until her death in April 2008.

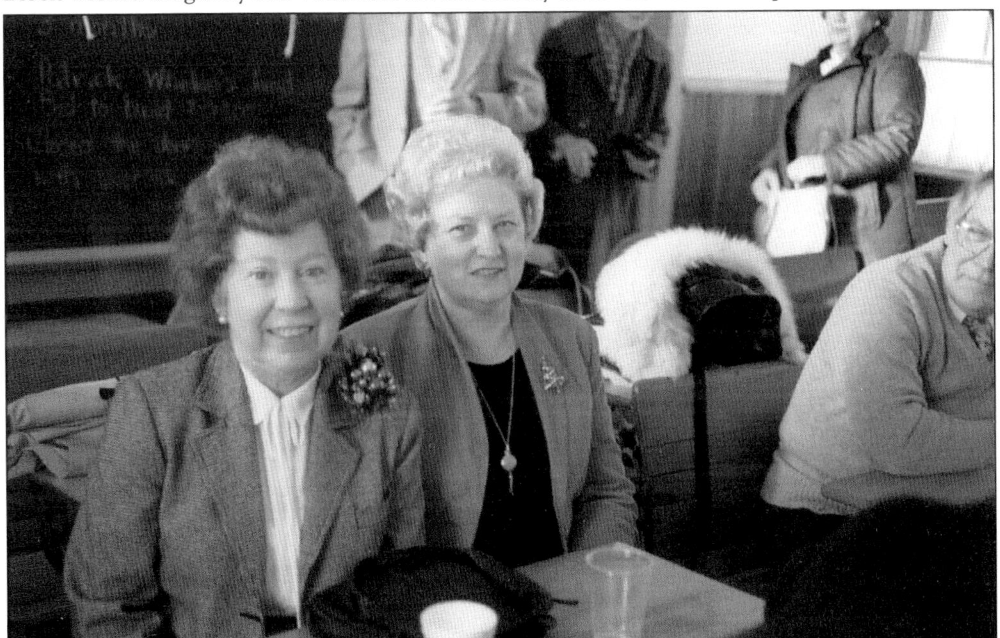

Sharing a desk during a Christmas open house at the Whelan School are two of Franklin's longest-serving elementary teachers, Florence Burns (left) and Hope Barr. They began teaching in Franklin's one-room schools and finished their careers at Ben Franklin School and Country Dale School, respectively. Looking on from the next desk is Hope's husband, Jack Barr.

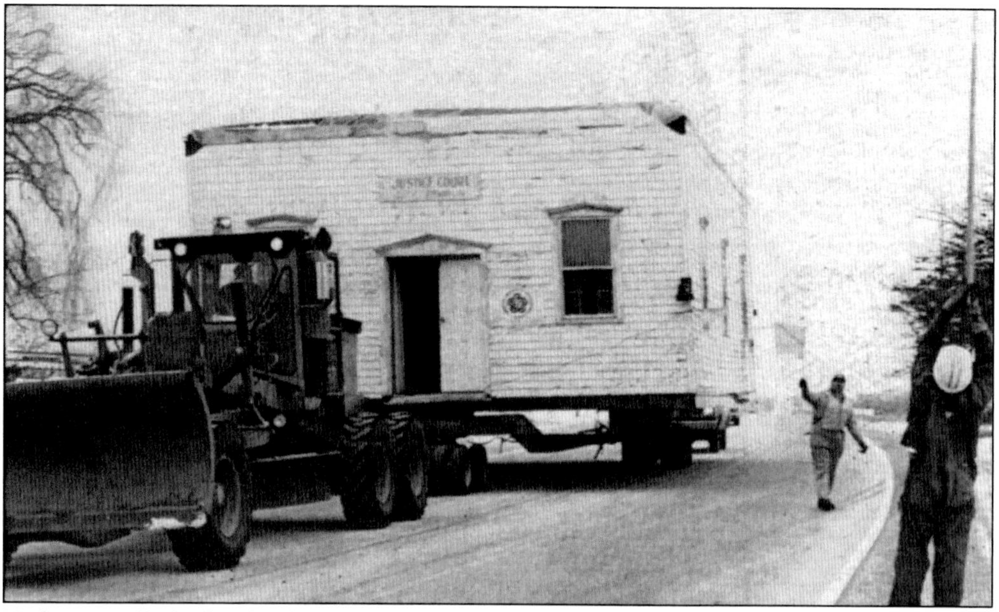

Highway traffic had to be directed in January 1976 as Franklin's old town hall was relocated from Ryan Road to a new home in Lions Legend Park. A basement foundation was built by a construction skills class at Franklin High School. In 1980, the town hall was turned over to the Franklin Historical Society and converted into a museum. (Courtesy of Franklin Hub.)

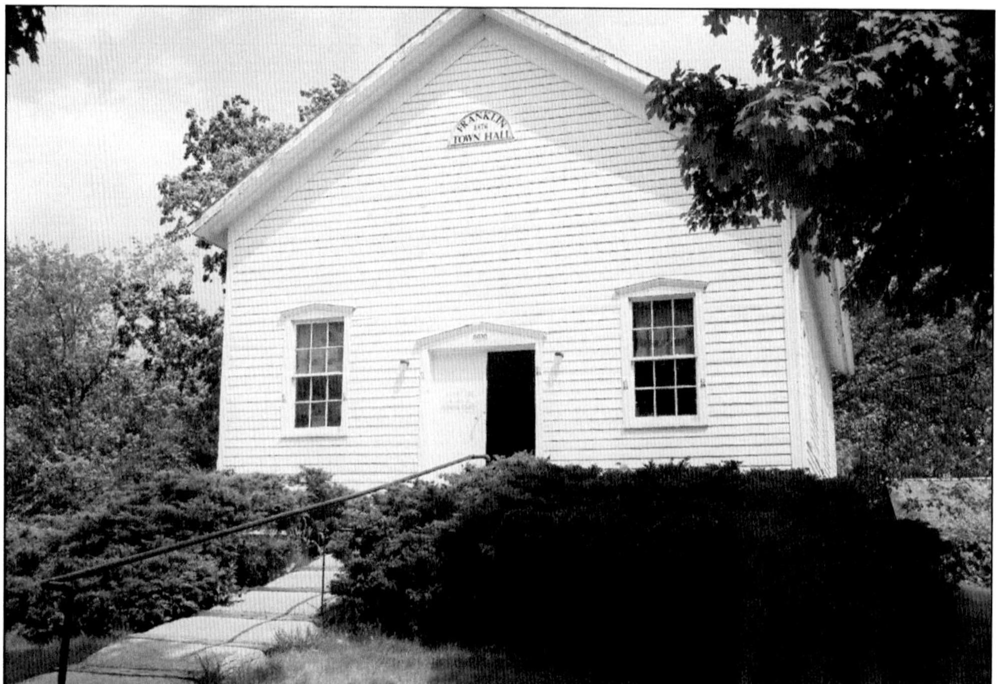

This is Franklin's old town hall where it has stood atop an incline in Lions Legend Park since 1976. A year later, volunteers scraped paint, replaced old boards, and painted the exterior. The town hall now serves as an office and museum for the historical society.

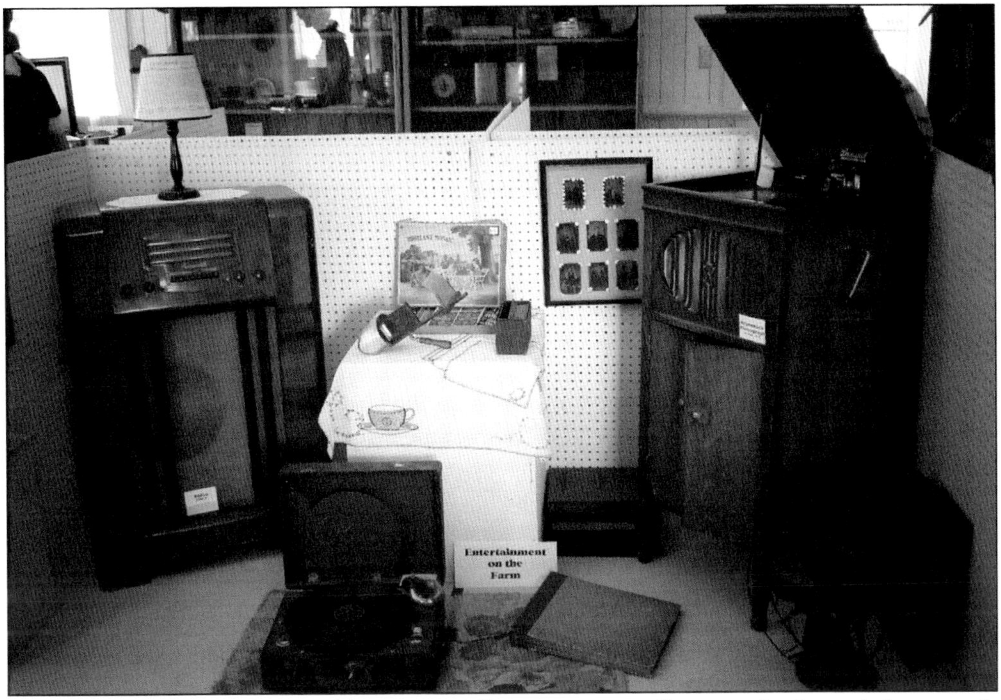

One of the exhibits in the Franklin Town Hall museum is a collection of radio and phonograph items that provided home entertainment during the 1920s and 1930s.

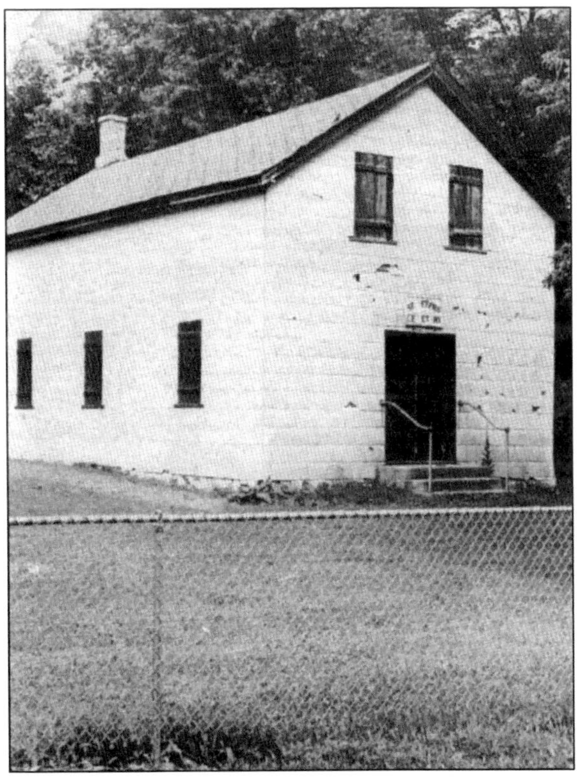

Built in 1868, St. Peters Chapel stood as a silent sentinel on the northern edge of the cemetery until it was moved in 1983. The cemetery was established on two acres purchased for $140 along Colby Road (Sixty-eighth Street), between Rawson Avenue and Loomis Road. St. Peters Chapel served a small Lutheran congregation and was where funeral services were held and school was taught in German by Rev. Gottleib Blankenheim during the late 1800s. (Courtesy of Franklin Hub.)

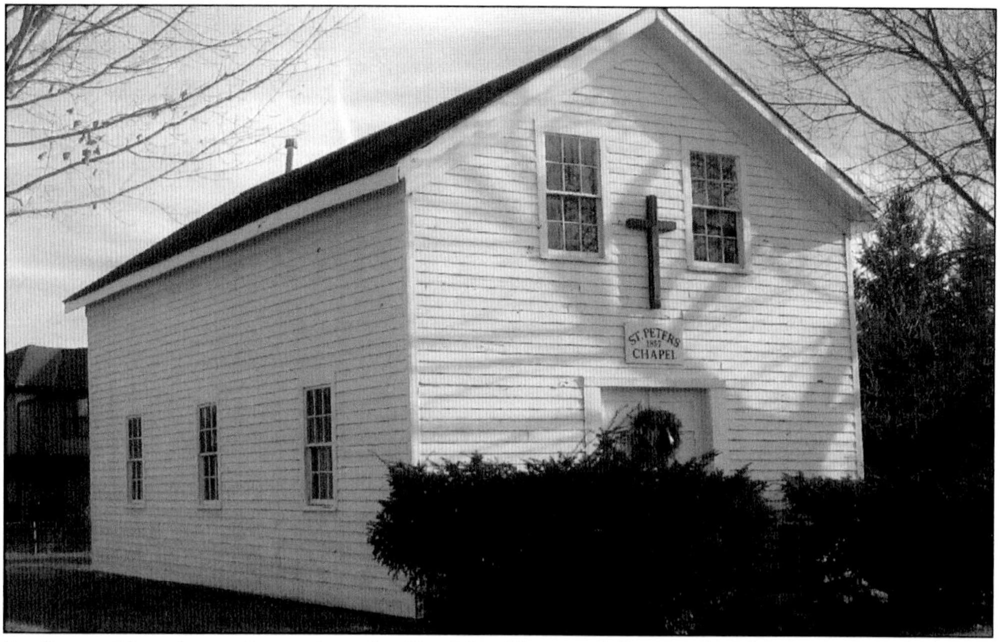

St. Peters Chapel was donated to the Franklin Historical Society by the St. Peters Cemetery Association and transported to Lions Legend Park in February 1983. Vernon Barg, a member of the historical society board, undertook the project of refurbishing the interior of the building. Today the chapel is used for nondenominational Christmas services and is rented out for quaint wedding ceremonies.

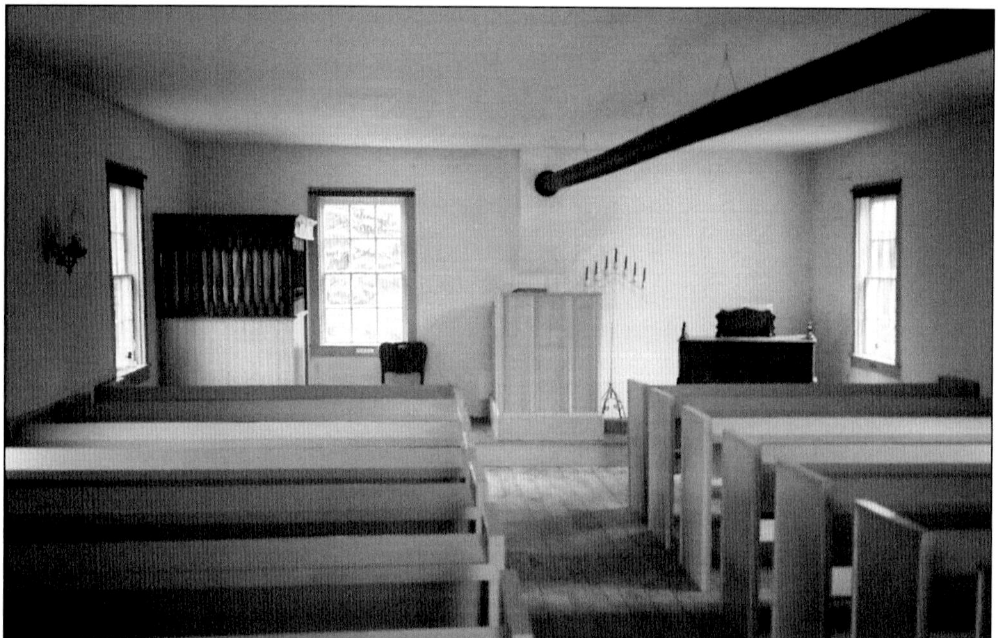

The 40-foot-by-26-foot interior of the St. Peters Chapel features a vestibule for the pastor and 15 wooden pews for churchgoers. After sitting dormant for many years in St. Peters Cemetery on South Sixty-eighth Street, the chapel was moved to Lions Legend Park and renovated in 1983.

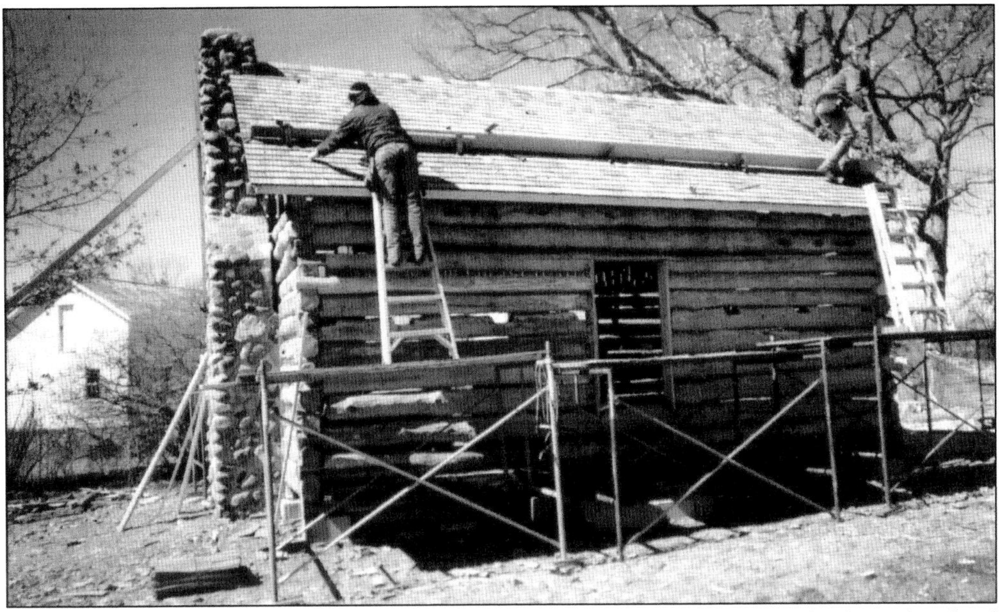

This log cabin built by Michael Sheehan in 1836 is generally regarded as the first of its kind in Franklin. The property was sold to Michael Godsell in 1911, and the cabin remained in the Godsell family until 1967 when the homestead was sold to G. J. Contractors, developers of the Mission Hills subdivision in St. Martins. The contractor allowed the Franklin Historical Society to detach the cabin from the farmhouse that was built around it and move it to Lions Legend Park in 1975. The Sheehan-Godsell cabin is shown here being restored by Eagle Restorations in 2003. The project was completed in June 2004.

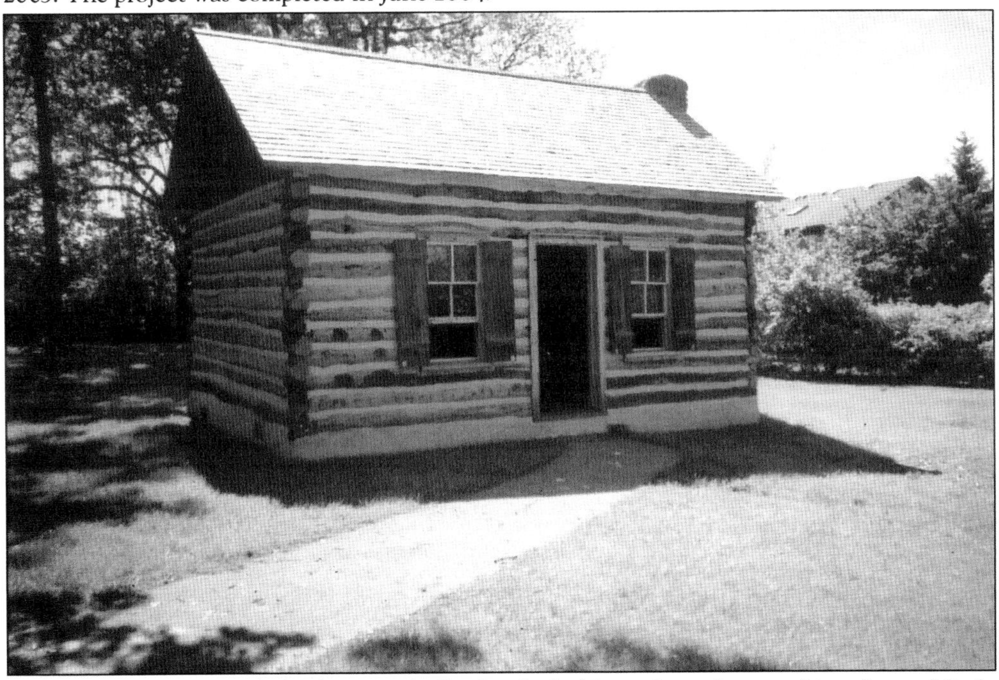

This is what the restored Sheehan-Godsell cabin looks like today in historic Lions Legend Park. The restoration process included a new fireplace and sleeping loft.

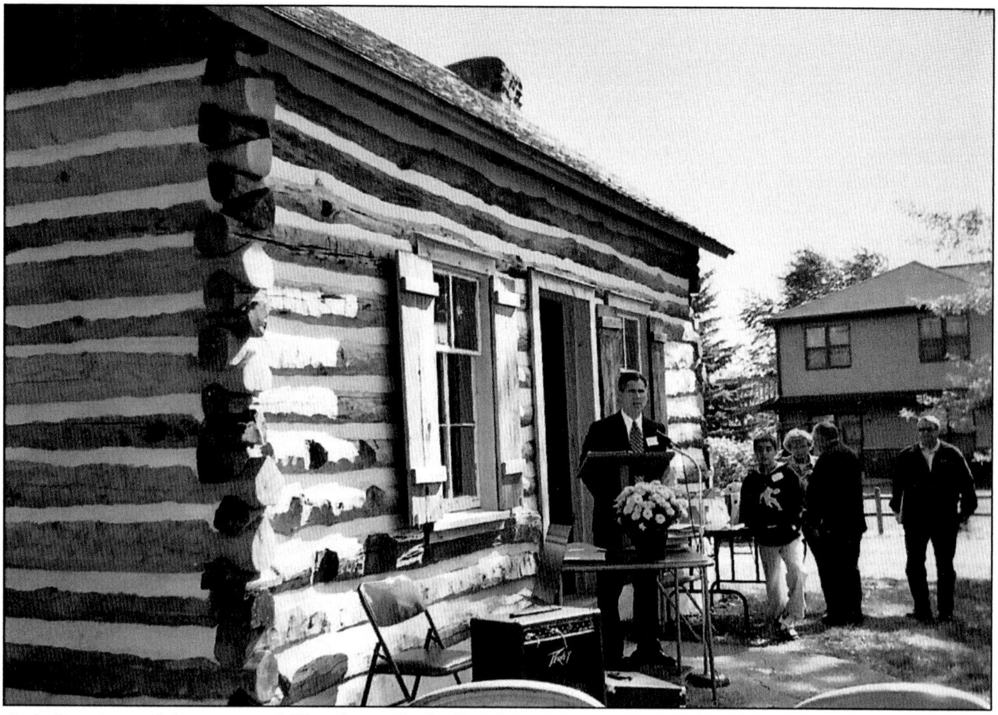

A dedication of the restored Sheehan-Godsell cabin in Lions Legend Park was held on October 3, 2004. Among the dignitaries who spoke at the function was Franklin mayor Fred Klimetz.

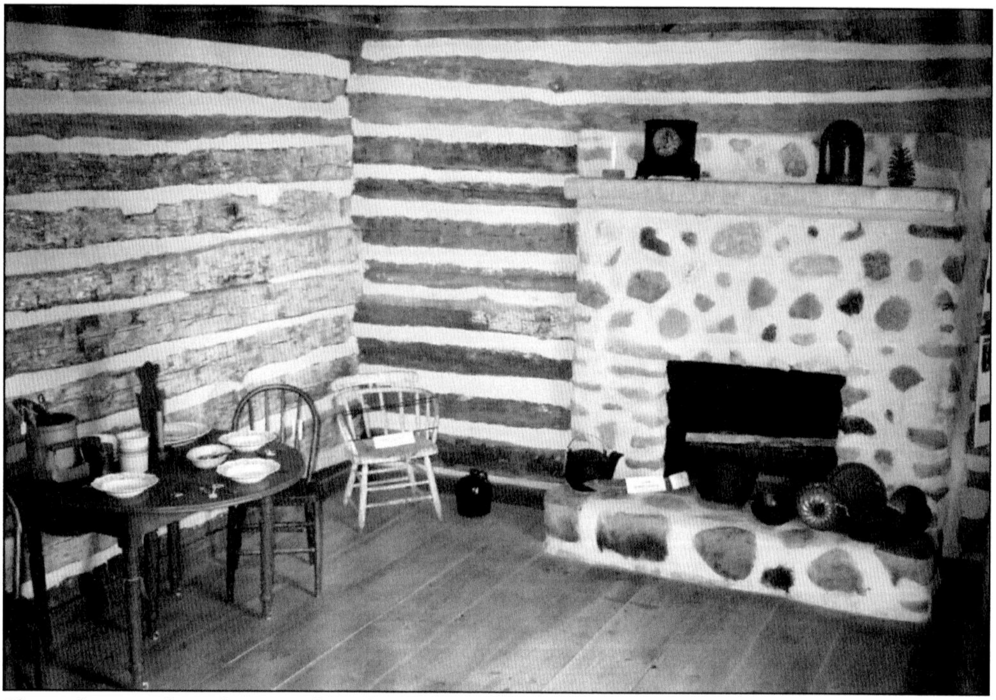

Shown here are furnishings and artifacts that depict cabin life in the 1800s. The Sheehan-Godsell cabin is opened for tours during summer months. (Courtesy of Franklin Hub.)

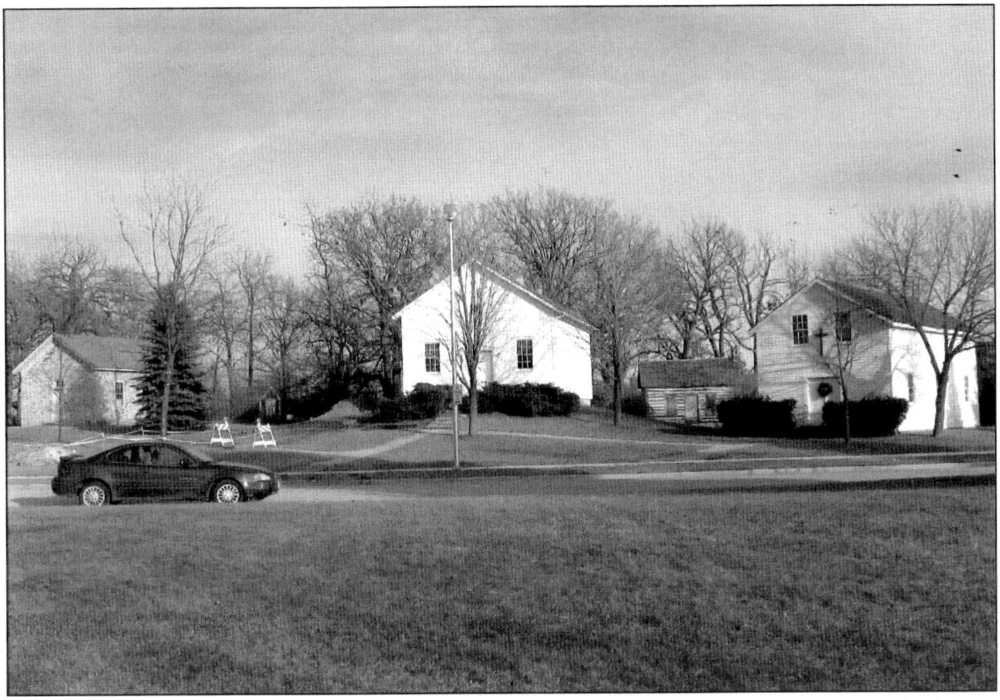

This is how Franklin's historic area in Lions Legend Park appeared in 2006. The buildings are (from left to right) Whelan School, town hall, Sheehan-Godsell cabin (background), and St. Peters Chapel.

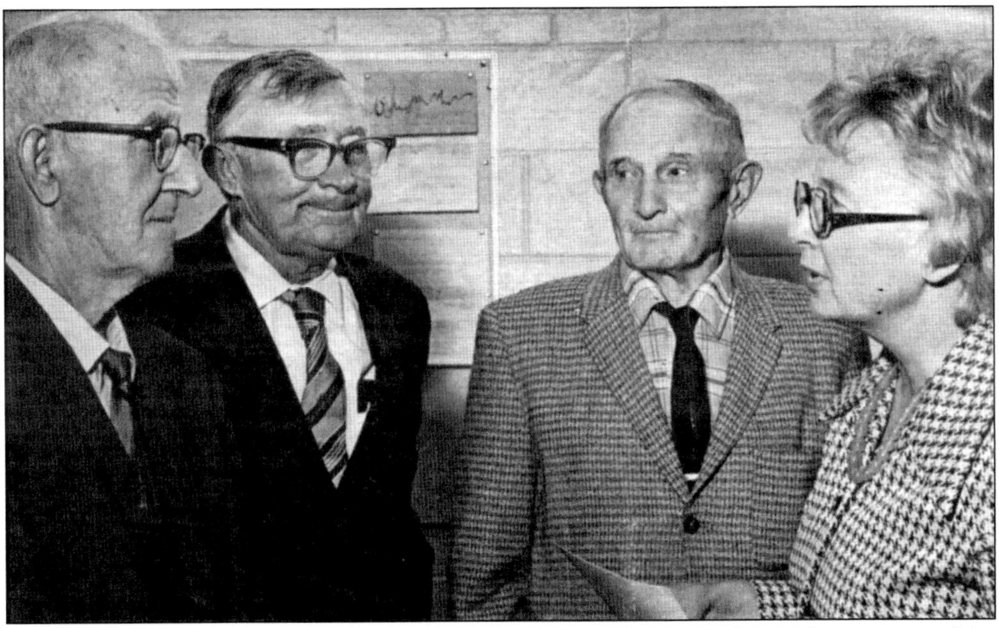

The Franklin Historical Society began a Founder's Day celebration to honor descendants of the community's earliest families. Honored in 1973 by historical society president Vivian Guzniczak are (from left to right) Norbert Puetz, William Boldt, and Charles Schweitzer.

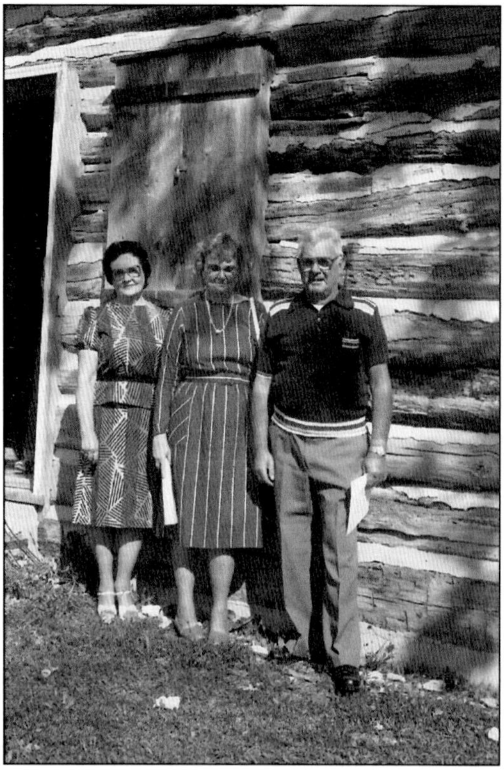

Founder's Day in 1985 included recognition of the Ludwig family by the Franklin Historical Society. From left to right, Marie Schumacher, Grace Hareng, and Fred "Fritz" Ludwig were grandchildren of Fred and Mary Ludwig, who began farming on Sixty-eighth Street in 1886. (Author's collection.)

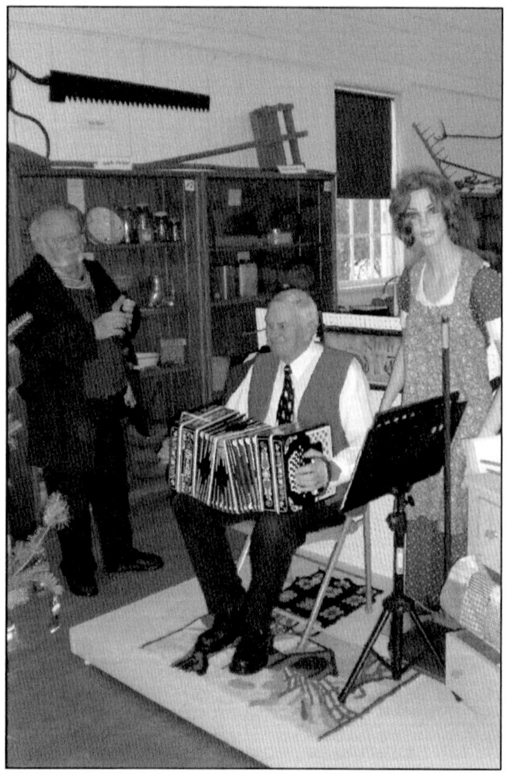

Lifelong Franklin resident Vernin Tretow can usually be found supplying accordion music at functions sponsored by the Franklin Historical Society. He is shown playing at the Christmas open house in the old town hall in 2008. Listening intently is Dale Pforr.

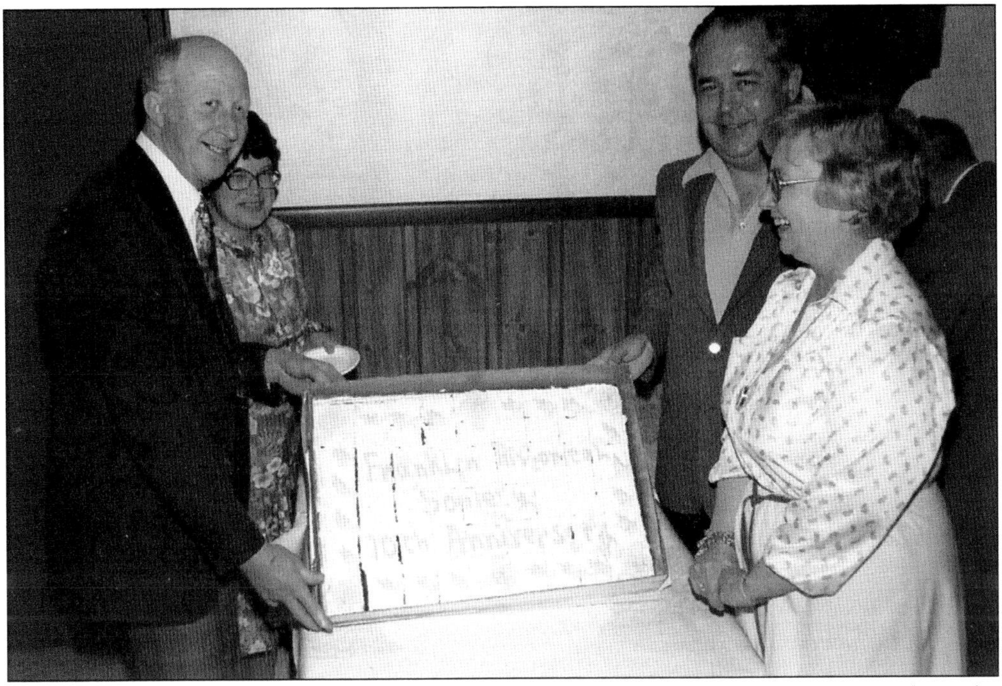

A cake commemorated the Franklin Historical Society's 10th anniversary in 1979. Making the presentation to Vivian Guzniczak, president of the historical society, are (from left to right) Carl Schultz, Theresa Sweeney, and John Camper.

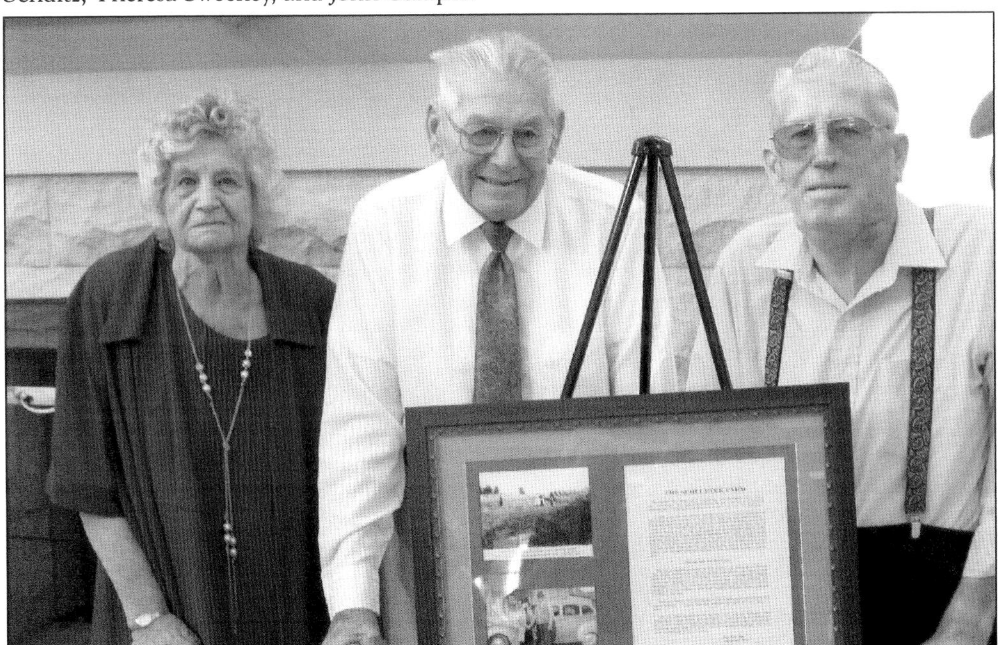

In September 2007, the Franklin Historical Society honored the Schleuter family for donating the farmland on which the Franklin Public Library and Lions Legend Park were built south of Drexel Avenue. Participating in the dedication at the library are (from left to right) Laura Schneiger, Ed Schleuter, and Ray Schleuter.

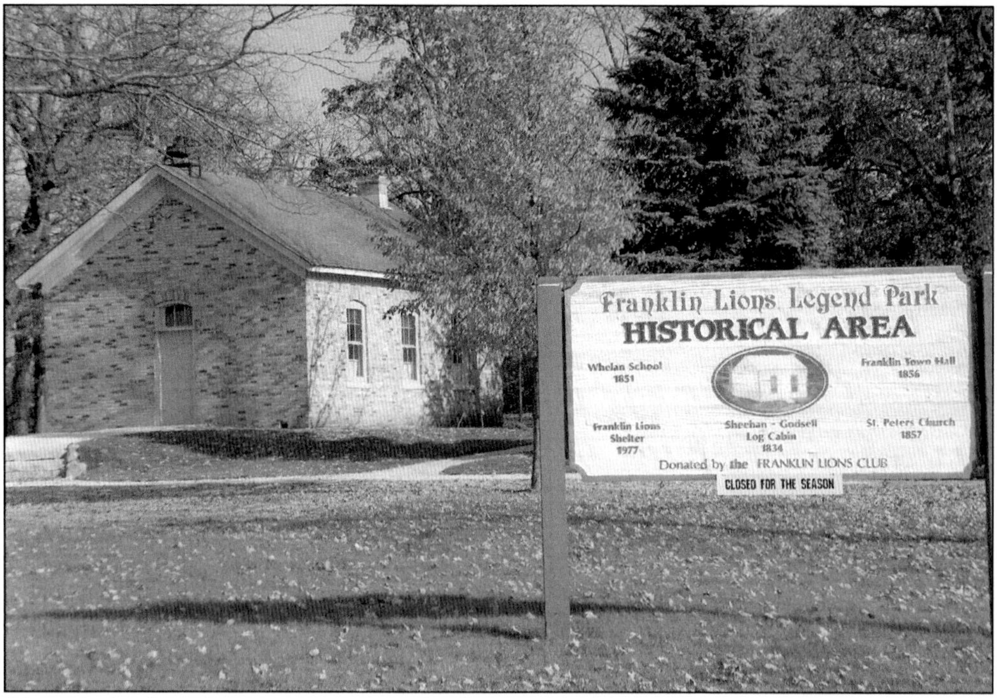

Through funding from a community development building grant, Titan Construction was hired in 2008 to build a handicap access ramp to the old town hall, along with new pathways connecting the historic buildings in Lions Legend Park. A new concrete stoop was poured, and the pathway was leveled in front of Whelan School for easier access to Franklin's other historic buildings.

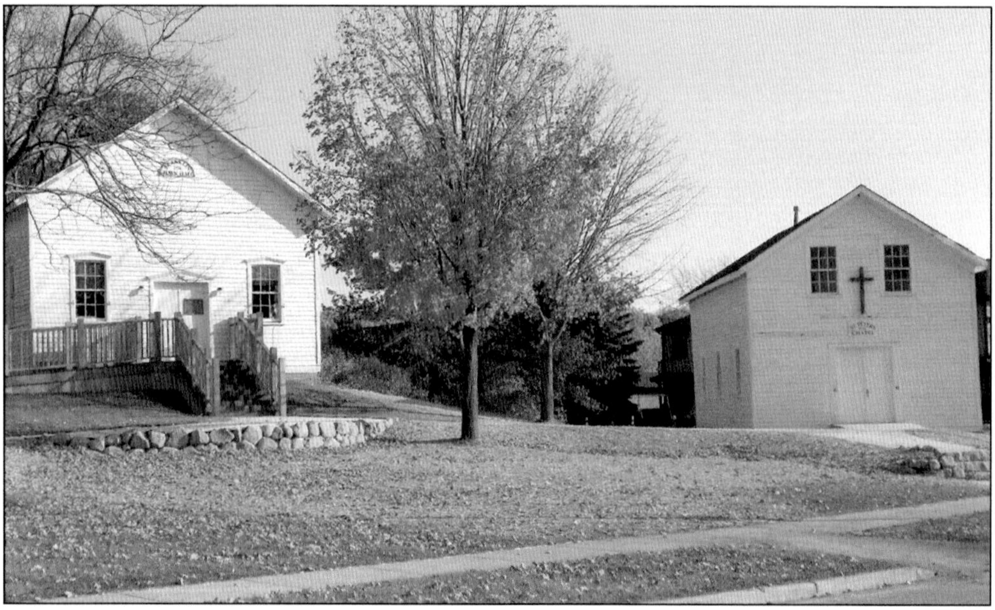

This is the end result of the grading and landscaping projects undertaken by Titan Construction in October 2008. The project was designed through the combined efforts of Franklin's engineering department, Quorum Architects, and the Franklin Historical Society.

Nine

The Building Boom

There was little change to Franklin's rural landscape until the 1950s when two housing developments, Security Acres and Towne, triggered the community's first spurt of nonfarming growth. The Mission Hills subdivision followed in the 1960s and Root River Heights in the 1970s.

With the influx of nonfarming families, Franklin suffered growing pains. The community needed to attract more commercial development to offset the costs of more schools, fire and police protection, highway improvements, and other city services. During the 1960s, Franklin began developing an industrial park off Sixtieth Street south of Ryan Road. This had been the location of a federal government Nike missile defense system during the 1950s.

By the year 2001, Franklin bore little resemblance to the agricultural community of a century earlier. The rudimentary industrial park had been transformed into a shiny new business park, the economical housing developments of the 1950s were dwarfed by expansive single-family dwellings, and the city had a spacious new library, a post office, a law enforcement facility, and multiple fire stations. A Milwaukee County sports complex and a $3.6 million Polish cultural center added to the mix.

Meanwhile, popular haunts such as the Hales Corners Speedway and 41 Twin Outdoor Theater had been replaced by a Menards superstore and Northwestern Mutual Insurance office high-rise.

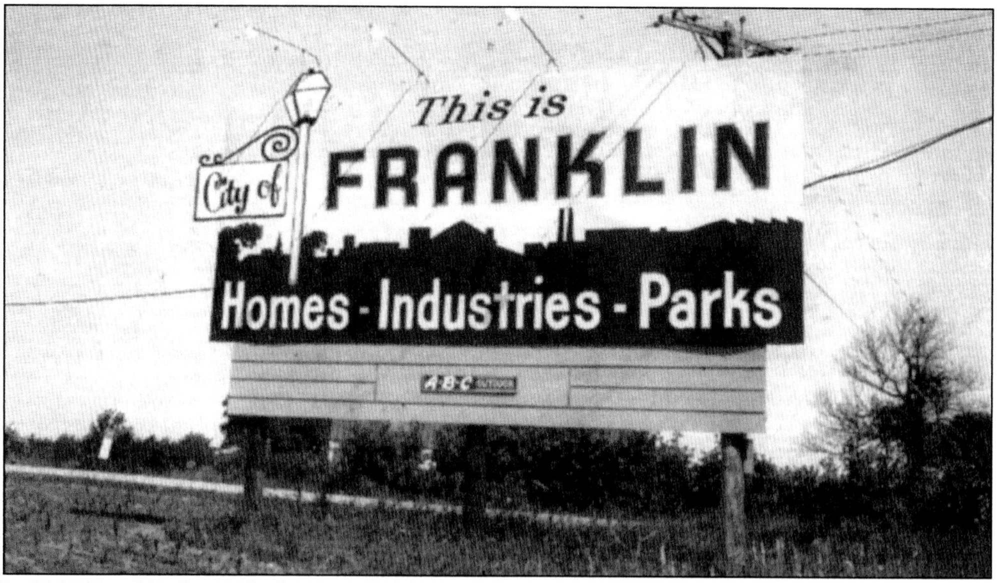

In 1964, Franklin began looking toward future development. The Franklin Industrial Commission erected billboards along main highways to promote the city as a place to live, work, and play. (Courtesy of Franklin Hub.)

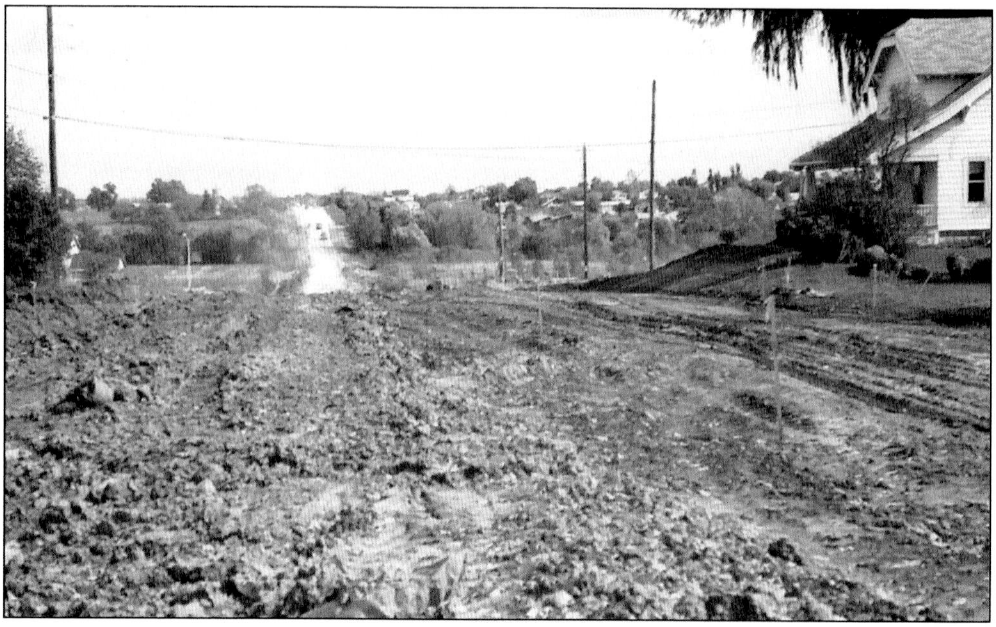

One of Franklin's first major street renovation projects was the widening of Drexel Avenue from Fifty-first Street west to Seventy-sixth Street in the summer of 1983. This view is of the Drexel excavation east from Sixty-eighth Street toward the Root River. (Author's collection.)

Franklin's first condominium development broke ground in 1971 on Tuckaway Country Club property at the corner of Sixty-eighth Street and Drexel Avenue. Participating in the ceremonies are (from left to right) Norman Hintz, Franklin mayor John Hyde, city engineer Jack Bennett, and Ray Stemper. (Courtesy of Franklin Hub.)

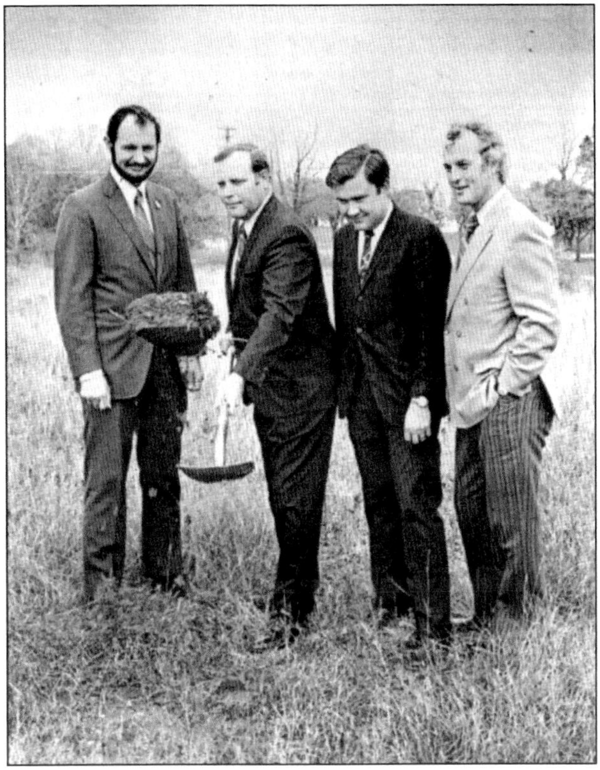

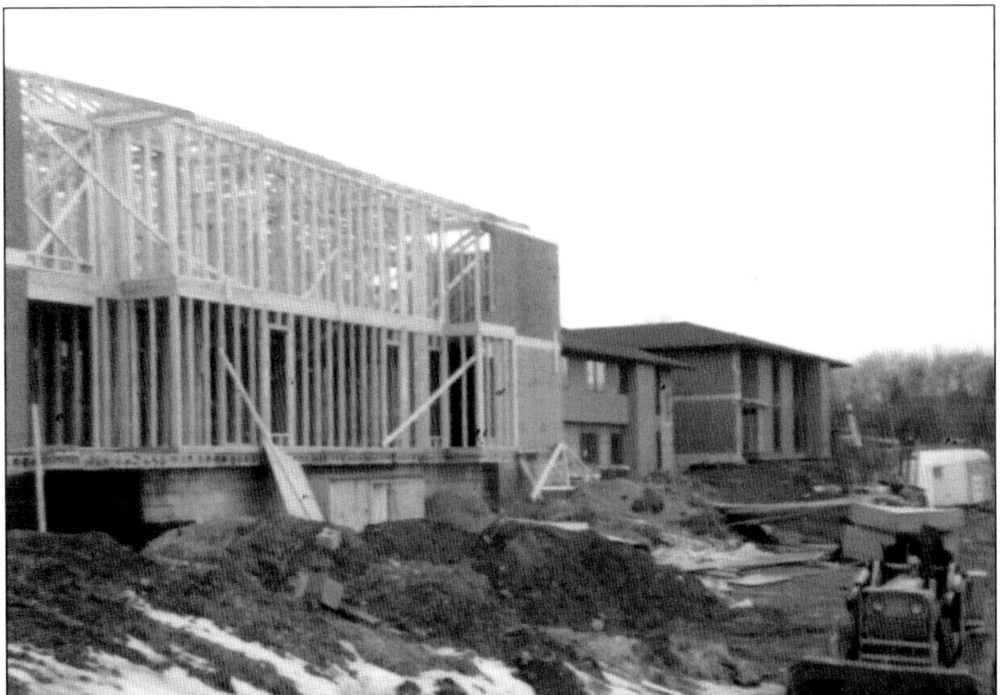

Construction of Franklin's first retirement condominium complex got underway on Tuckaway Country Club property in 1971. Units went up for sale the following year. (Author's collection.)

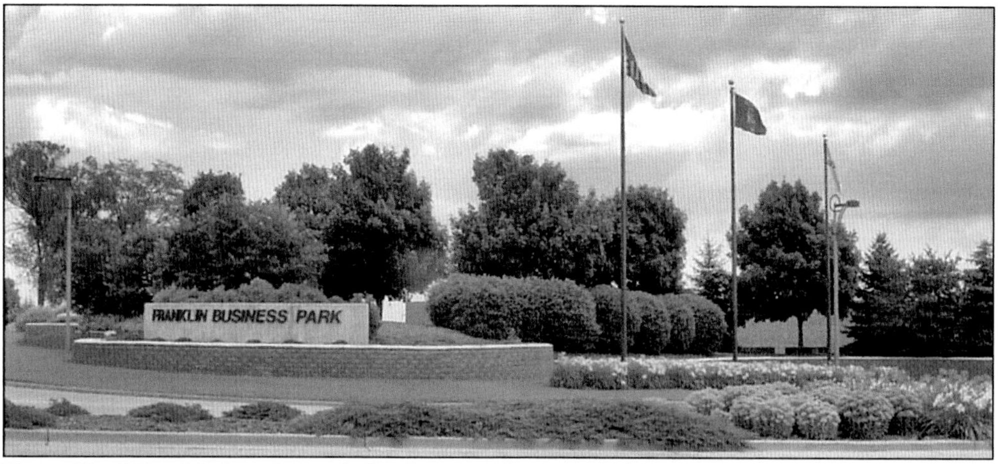

Phase II of Franklin's industrial development began in the mid-1990s when approximately 370 acres went for sale at Fifty-first Street south of Ryan Road. The new Franklin Business Park adjoined the Phase I industrial park located to the east.

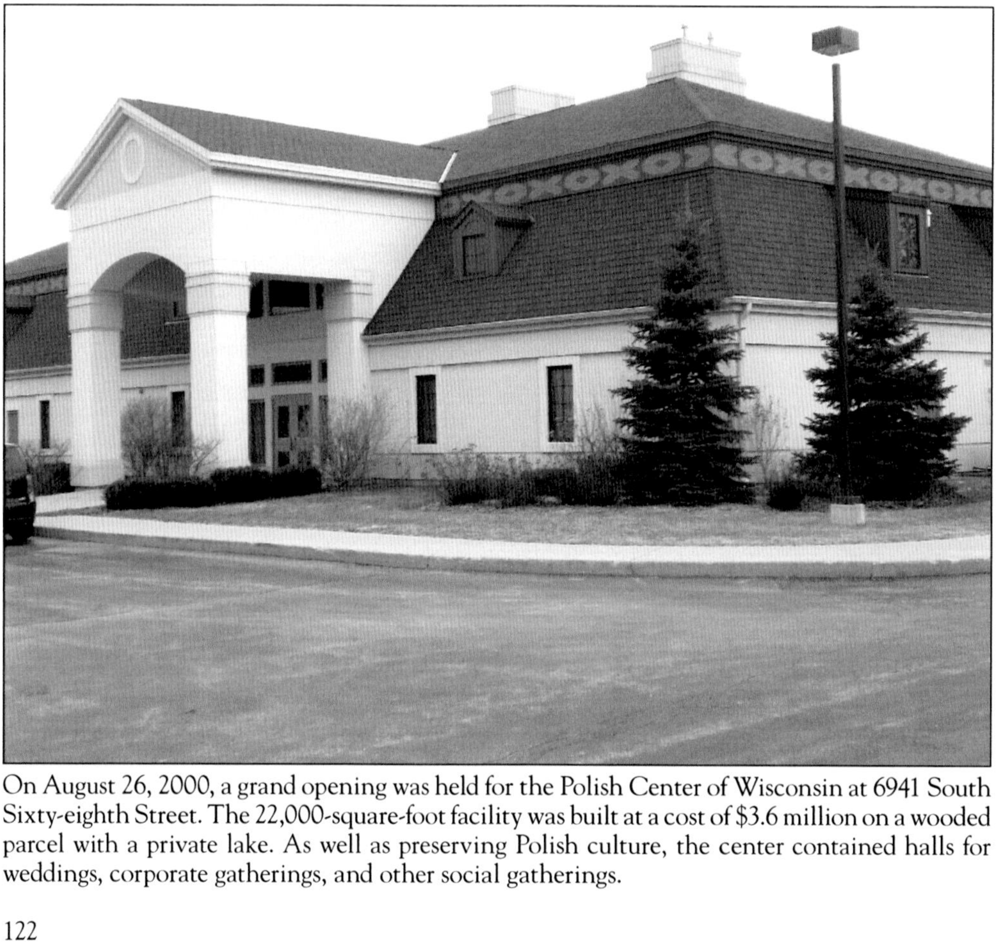

On August 26, 2000, a grand opening was held for the Polish Center of Wisconsin at 6941 South Sixty-eighth Street. The 22,000-square-foot facility was built at a cost of $3.6 million on a wooded parcel with a private lake. As well as preserving Polish culture, the center contained halls for weddings, corporate gatherings, and other social gatherings.

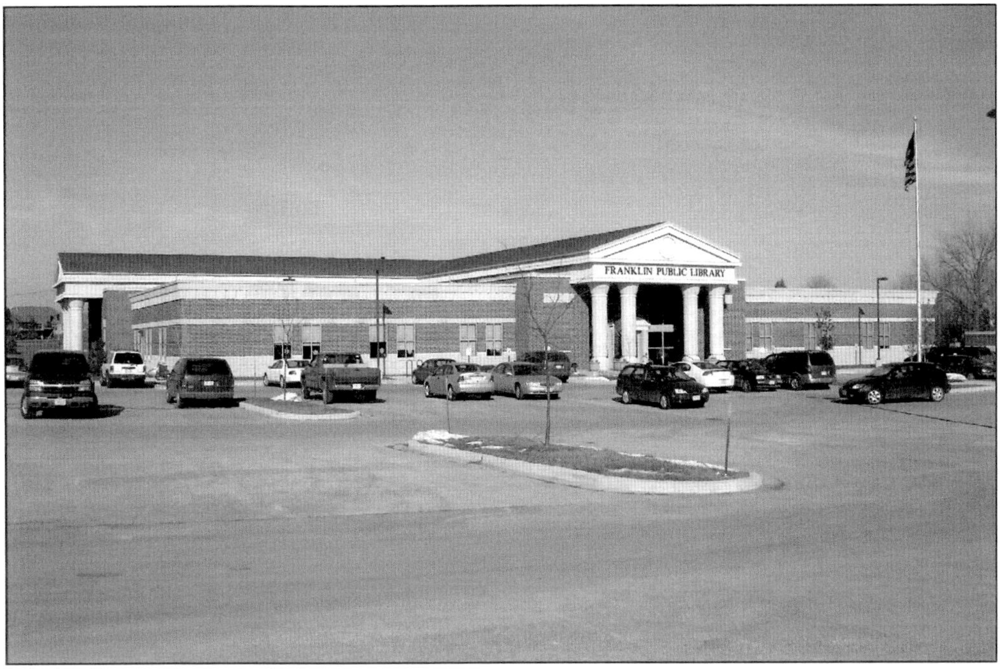

The Franklin Public Library, which had operated out of city hall since 1980, moved into this spacious new home in May 2002. It was built at the corner of Drexel Avenue and Loomis Road on a section of the former Schleuter farm.

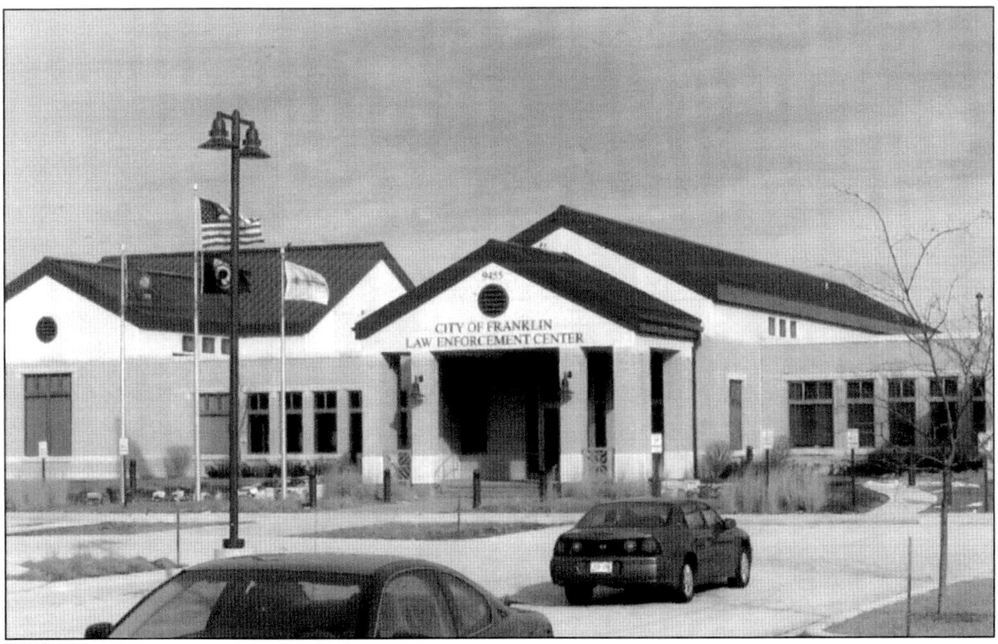

The Franklin Police Department, which for a time operated out of a farmhouse during the 1960s, moved into a state-of-the-art law enforcement center in 2001. Located at 9455 West Loomis Road, the new station occupies 68,000 square feet, which is four times the size of its previous headquarters. In addition to overseeing all police operations, the facility includes a municipal court.

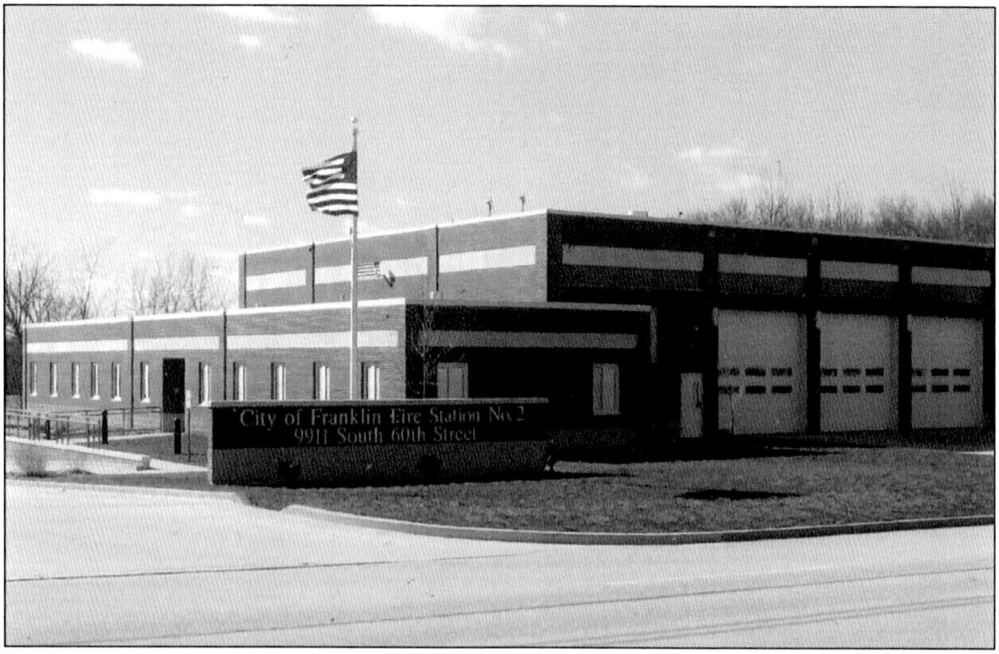

In a break from the traditional split-face block exterior, the Franklin common council approved construction of fire station No. 2 at 9911 South Sixtieth Street in 2001. The fire station cost $1.3 million using brick, which the city plan commission recommended to set a quality standard for future public buildings.

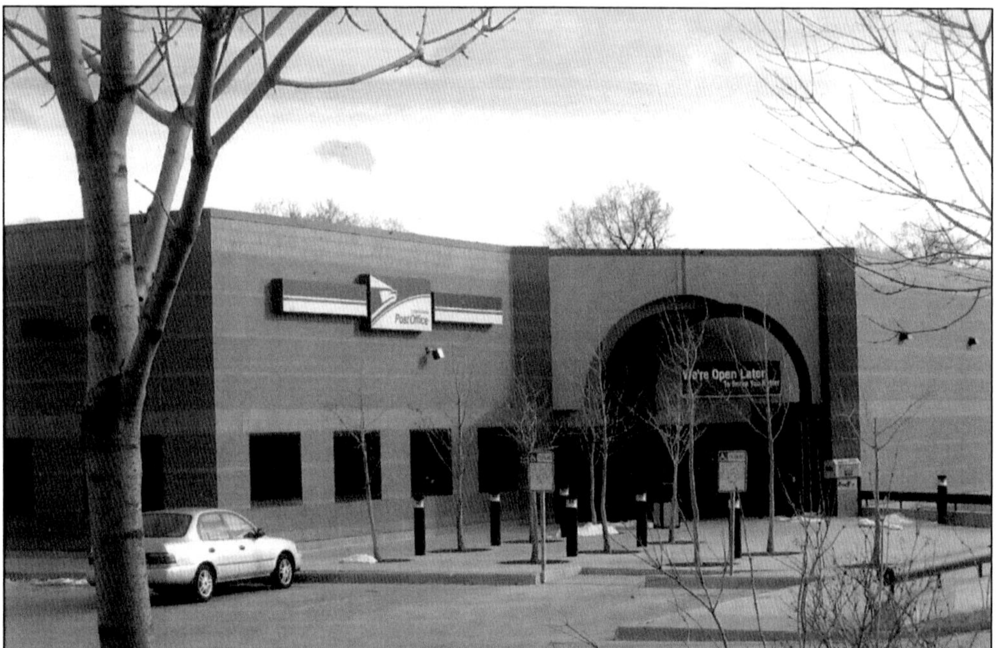

By 2001, Franklin had outgrown its ability to share the neighboring Hales Corners post office as its central station, and the spacious new branch shown here was opened along Loomis Road, a half mile south of Franklin's city hall.

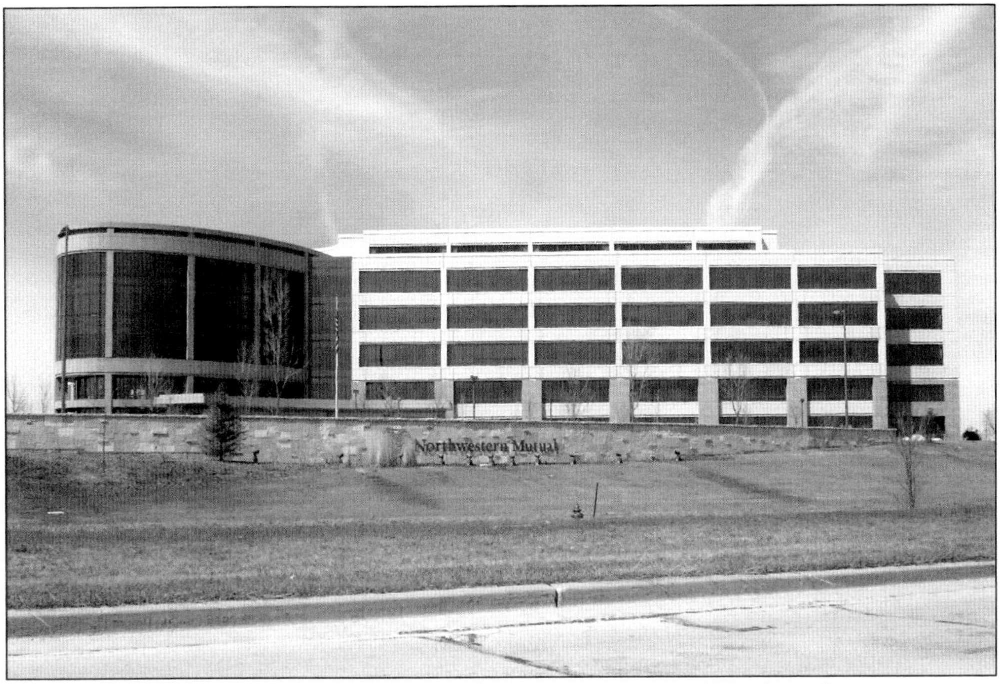

The 41 Twin Outdoor Theater became a distant memory in 2001 when the property was purchased by Northwestern Mutual Insurance. Northwestern tore down the theater and built its new corporate headquarters on the site along Twenty-seventh Street north of Drexel Avenue.

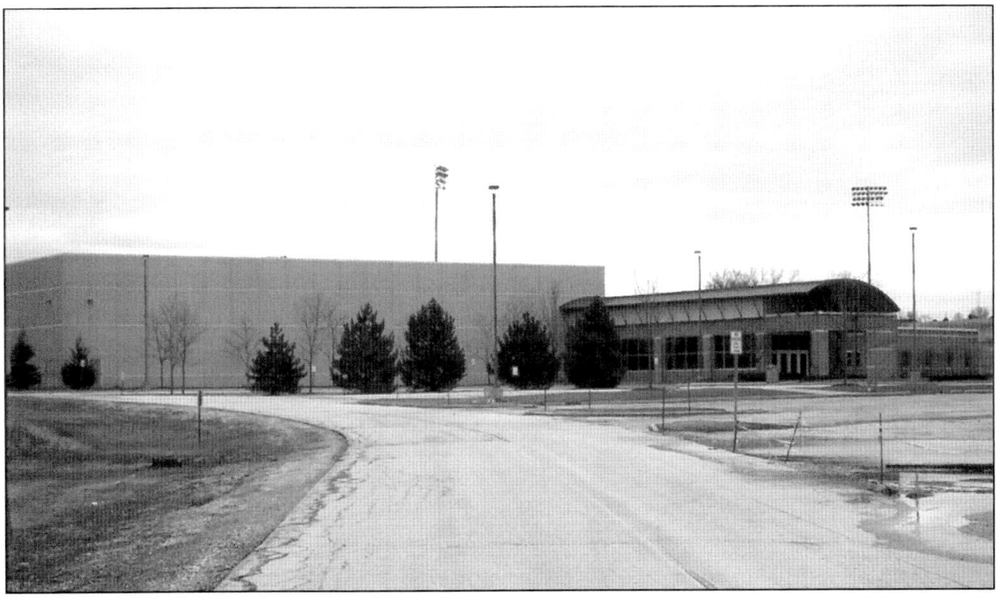
In 1994, Milwaukee County erected this 55,000-square-foot sports complex on parkland north of Ryan Road and east of the Root River in Franklin. Along with sports, the building is used for trade shows, senior activities, and election polls. The grounds surrounding the building also feature football, soccer, and rugby fields.

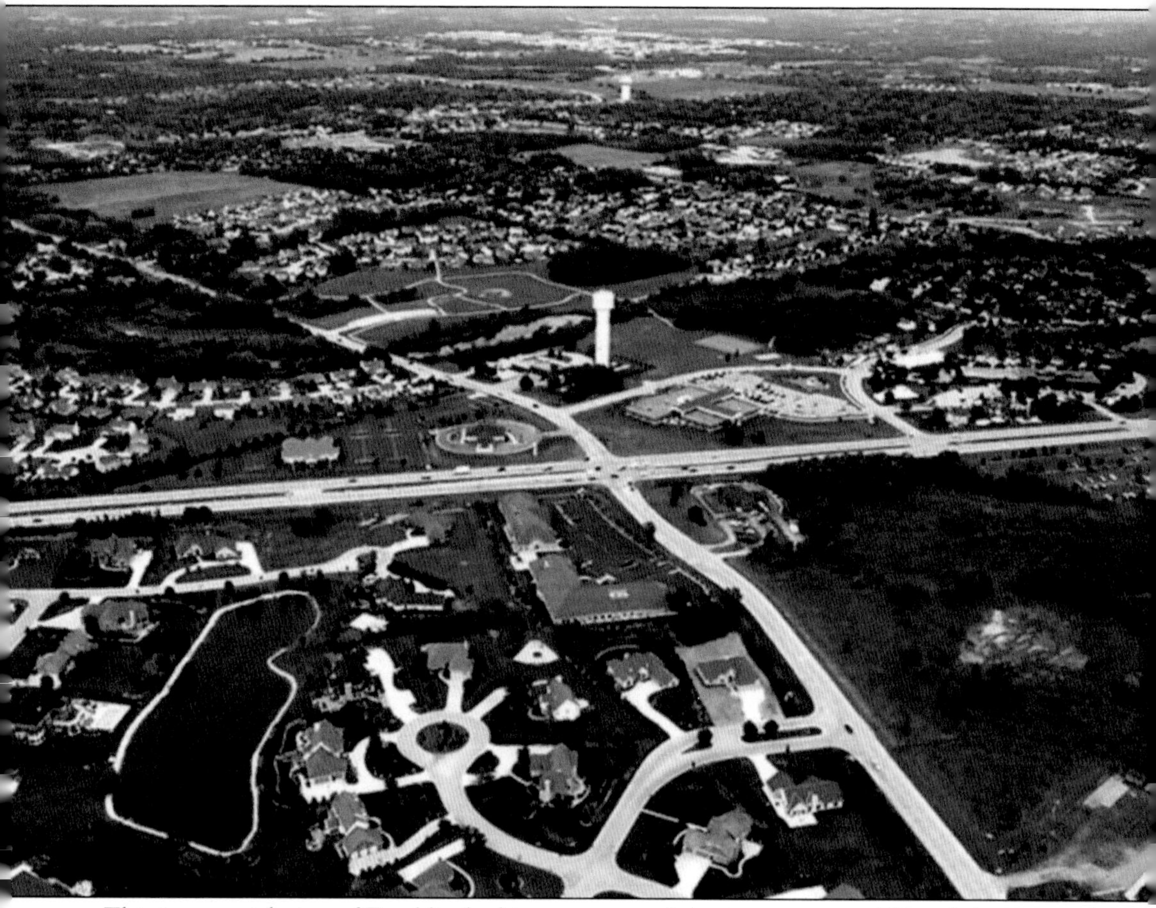

This is an aerial view of Franklin looking east toward the intersection of Drexel Avenue and Loomis Road (Highway 36). Located along Drexel Avenue east of Loomis Road (upper right) are the Franklin Public Library and Franklin Fire Station No. 1, which fronts a water tower and Lions Legend Park. Located in the lower left sector is Franklin's luxury home development called Wyndham Ridge, built on the former Walter Barbian farm.

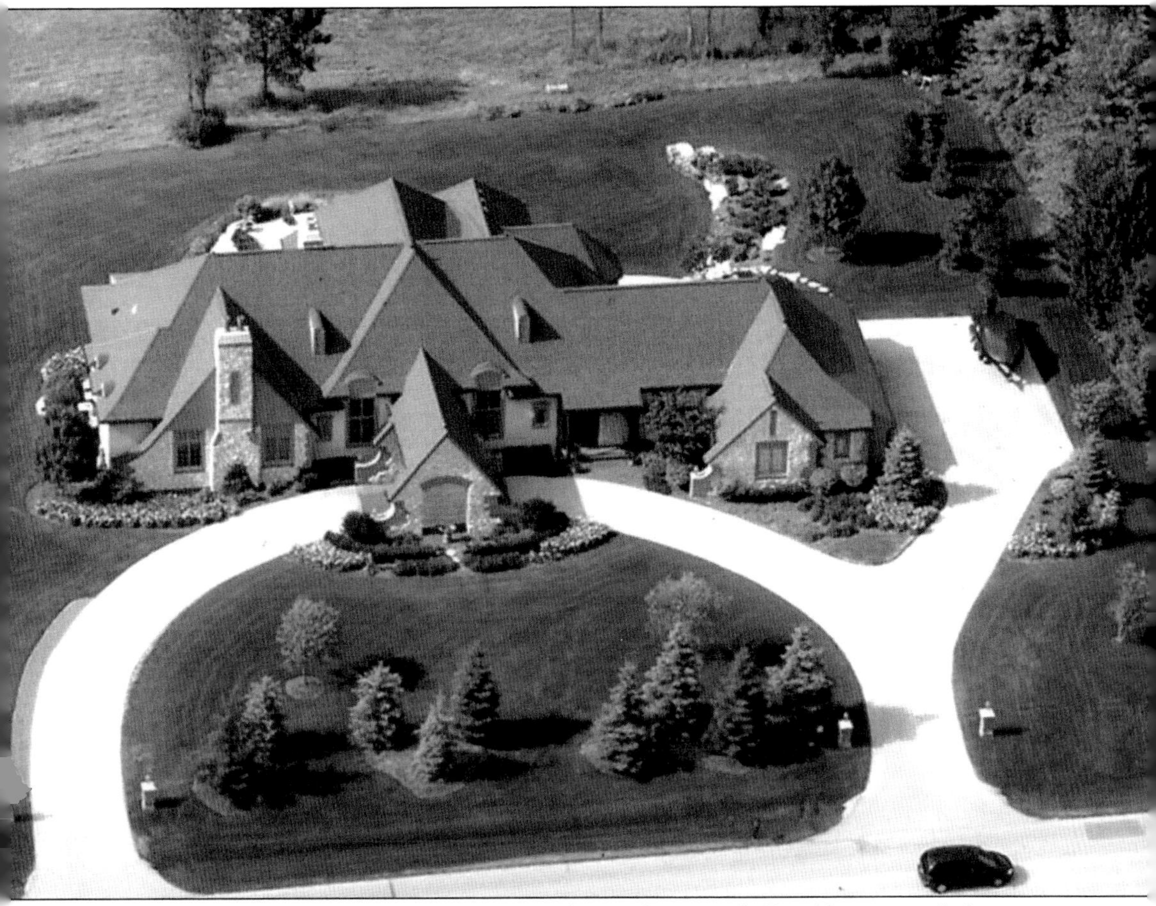

Shown here is a Wyndham Ridge estate. Pricey homes have made Franklin appear light-years removed from its rural origins during the 1800s.